Page

Preface (v)

Unit 1 Introduction to Bookkeeping

Unit 2 Accounting adjustments

Unit 3 Practical Bookkeeping and final accounts

AAT Bookkeeping Certificate

(AAT Level 2 Certificate in Bookkeeping)

Workbook

Denise Gallagher

First edition February 2001
Third edition August 2005

ISBN 0 7517 2485 8 (previous ISBN 0 7517 1418 6)

British Library Cataloguing-in-Publication Data
A catalogue record for this book
is available from the British Library

Published by BPP Professional Education (formerly known as EQL International Ltd)
3 Michaelson Square
Kirkton Campus
Livingston
EH54 7DP
Scotland

Printed in England

Preface

This workbook is designed to reinforce the learning provided in the BPP's AAT Bookkeeping Certificate computer based training package. It does so by providing a series of questions based on information contained in the package. The level to which that learning has been effective is further tested by additional questions and a number of other general questions.

The chapters in this workbook follow the same sequence as the modules in the computer based package.

- As you go through the modules on the disk, answer the **Note form** questions in the workbook. These use a form of structured note taking for self testing.

- Read the **summaries**

- There are other integrated questions, with answers, at the end of each unit of this workbook.

The AAT's Bookkeeping Certificate is a major step forward for many who work as bookkeepers. It is a recognised qualification from a major professional body to the many people who work as or aspire to become a bookkeeper.

BPP Professional Education is proud to support the qualification with training and assessment materials.

How to use the package: Student version

Insert the CD-ROM into your computer and follow the on-screen instructions.

You will be able to launch the program from the Start menu under *AAT Bookkeeping Certificate* and click on *Course*. There is also an icon on the desktop with the same name; you can also launch the program from there. You will then be asked to license the copy of the software. This can be done on the Internet at:

www.eql.co.uk/licensing/

This only has to be done once.

Once the package has been licensed the following screen will appear.

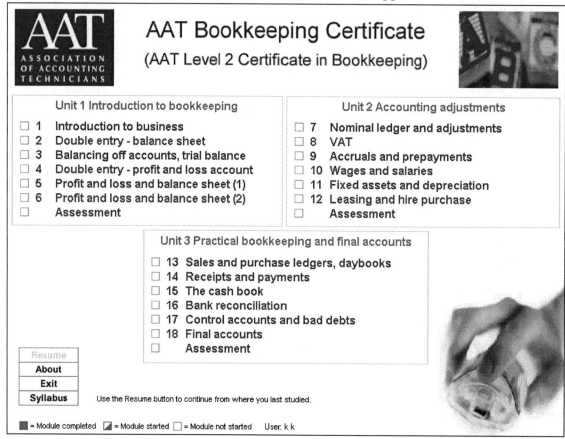

To proceed click on Module 1 : Introduction to business, after which the following screen will appear.

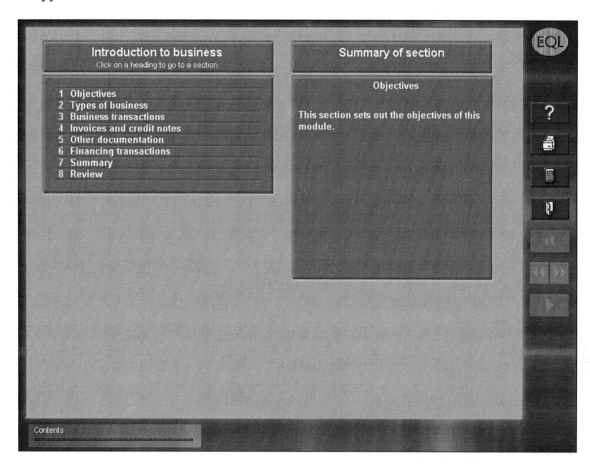

To start the module, click on Section 1 – Objectives.

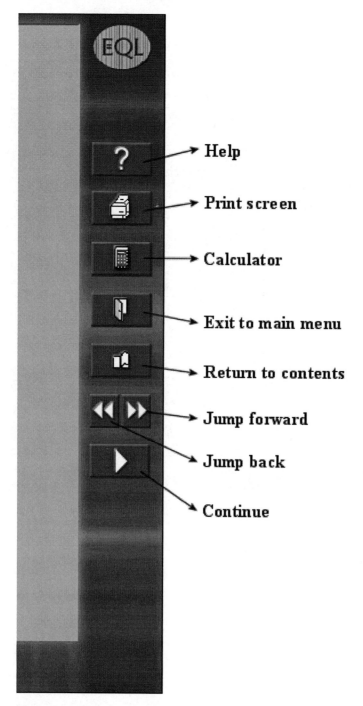

Help

Print screen

Calculator

Exit to main menu

Return to contents

Jump forward

Jump back

Continue

To proceed, point your mouse over the Continue button and click once.

How to use the Package : College Version

Log onto the "AAT Bookkeeping Certificate" according to your network (or PC) instructions.

From the start menu you will have two options: Course and Reporter. Select Course.

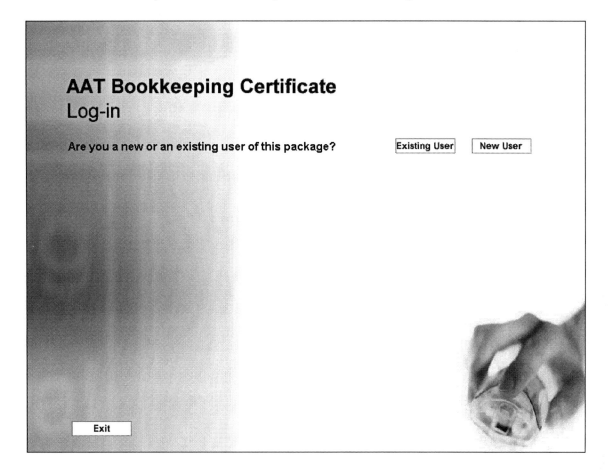

The AAT Bookkeeping Certificate will ask if you are a new or existing user. Click on the new user then enter your details, taking particular care with the password which will be required when the software is reused. On future entry to the package you should select the "Existing User" option. You will then be requested to log in your surname, first name and password.

This information can be used to set up a unique progress record for each user of the system which can be accessed by the college lecturer or training supervisor.

Once the package has been accessed the following screen will appear.

AAT Bookkeeping Certificate
(AAT Level 2 Certificate in Bookkeeping)

Unit 1 Introduction to bookkeeping

- ☐ 1 Introduction to business
- ☐ 2 Double entry - balance sheet
- ☐ 3 Balancing off accounts, trial balance
- ☐ 4 Double entry - profit and loss account
- ☐ 5 Profit and loss and balance sheet (1)
- ☐ 6 Profit and loss and balance sheet (2)
- ☐ Assessment

Unit 2 Accounting adjustments

- ☐ 7 Nominal ledger and adjustments
- ☐ 8 VAT
- ☐ 9 Accruals and prepayments
- ☐ 10 Wages and salaries
- ☐ 11 Fixed assets and depreciation
- ☐ 12 Leasing and hire purchase
- ☐ Assessment

Unit 3 Practical bookkeeping and final accounts

- ☐ 13 Sales and purchase ledgers, daybooks
- ☐ 14 Receipts and payments
- ☐ 15 The cash book
- ☐ 16 Bank reconciliation
- ☐ 17 Control accounts and bad debts
- ☐ 18 Final accounts
- ☐ Assessment

Resume
About
Exit
Syllabus

Use the Resume button to continue from where you last studied.

■ = Module completed ◪ = Module started ☐ = Module not started   User: k k

To proceed click on Module 1 : Introduction to business, after which the following screen will appear.

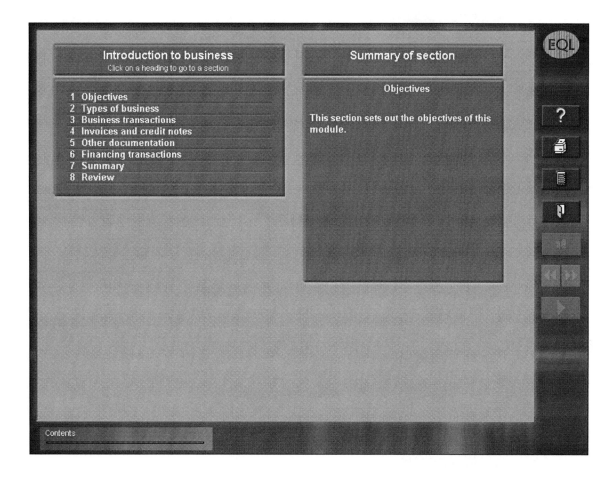

To start the module, click on Section 1 – Objectives.

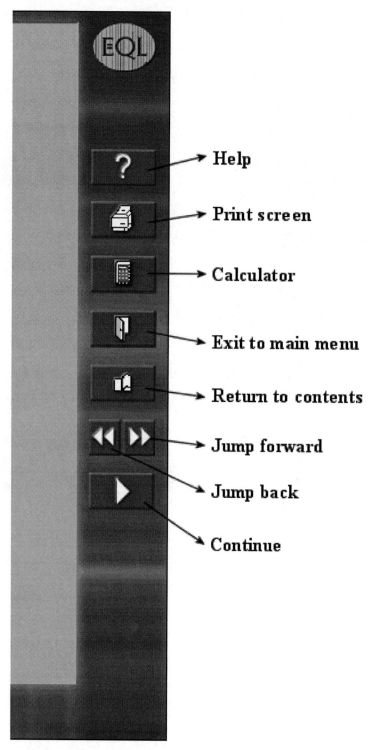

To proceed, point your mouse over the continue button and click once.

Using the package : Student and College versions

Main menu

From the main menu screen users may work through the modules in any order. However, new users to this subject are advised to cover the modules in the order shown.

Users may go through each module as often as they wish and can leave a module at any time.

The main menu screen shows which modules have been partially or totally completed by showing a clear box = not started, half coloured box = started and complete grey box = completed.

To exit from the Main menu click on the exit button in the bottom right hand corner.

Assessments : Student and College Versions

The AAT Bookkeeping Certificate provides a large amount of question practice to prepare you for your final assessment. To access the questions you should select the Assessments option from the main menu. These tests contain questions similar to those you will meet in your final assessment. You should also make sure you are comfortable with the operation of the software, especially the submission of answers, before attempting the final assessments.

The 3 mock assessments are based on the following modules:-

• Introduction to bookkeeping (Modules 1-6)

• Accounting adjustments (Modules 7-12)

• Practical bookkeeping (Modules 13-17) and Final accounts (Module 18)

Assessments: Student version

The student version provides *revision* mode access to the assessments. This includes advice and feedback. You can attempt the assessments as many times as you like.

Assessments: Network version

The network version has two assessment modes which are set using Reporter, these are *revision* mode and *exam* mode. Revision mode gives advice and feedback with answers and can be accessed as many times as you like. In exam mode, the assessment can only be accessed once, and will not provide advice and feedback.

You are recommended to attempt all questions. Remember to click the 'Submit' button (to submit your answer for marking) which is placed at the end of the question.

If you are unable to answer any question you can proceed with the assessment and return to unanswered questions later. You may return to any question at a later stage during the assessment to change your answer.

When you have finished the test click 'Finish' at the top right-hand corner of the screen.

Before you attempt the on-line assessment at one of the AAT Approved Assessment Centres, you will be required to provide some personal details about yourself. This information will be recorded by BPP Professional Education. BPP will provide this information to the Association of Accounting Technicians (AAT) as part of the assessment process. Information about you will not be used by or passed to any person or organisation not connected with the administration of the AAT Bookkeeping Certificate.

Assessments: the real thing

The AAT may also contact you with relevant information about other AAT accounting qualifications. If you do not wish to receive such material, please write to Student Support, Association of Accounting Technicians, 154 Clerkenwell Road, London EC1R 4AD.

Students studying alone will need to attend an AAT Approved Assessment Centre or Recognised Centre for on-line assessment. You will be required to pay the Assessment Centre a fee of £40 (plus VAT).

For details of Approved or Recognised Centres, contact AAT.

Unit 1

Introduction to Bookkeeping

Module 1

Introduction to business

Introduction

Businesses vary greatly, ranging from small one-man businesses, such as a window cleaner who is providing a service in a small locality, to large multi-national companies who may be manufacturing or processing goods to be sold internationally. To give some context to the bookkeeping that you will soon be studying, this module starts by looking at the different ways in which we might classify businesses. Bookkeeping and accounting principles will apply to them all, no matter how large or small.

As a representative business, we have chosen the jewellery business of Mr Allen. In terms of complexity, his business lies somewhere between the window cleaner and the multi-national manufacturer! In future modules we look at the recording of Mr Allen's transactions. To help you understand this, we firstly consider here what those transactions might be and see what documentation is involved; for example, we follow through the process of ordering and receiving goods for resale – this may involve stock lists, purchase orders, goods received notes and purchase invoices.

This look at the transactions in a business introduces you to some of the jargon of the accounting world. Some other words with special accounting meanings are also explained; for example the word 'drawings' means money taken out of a business by its owner, and as you will see that the term 'cash sale' really means 'non-credit sale' – it could be paid by cheque! Make sure you get these various terms clear at this stage – it will avoid confusion later on.

We will use Mr Allen as a basis of our study for much of the package. In Module 18 we look at the specific variations that apply to clubs and societies, partnerships and limited companies.

Learning objectives

The objectives of this module are to ensure you:

- Become aware of different types of business.

- Understand various categories of business transactions, in particular the difference between cash and credit transactions.

- Know what information may be found on invoices and credit notes.

- Become familiar with other financial documentation in a business.

- Become aware of transactions relating to the financing of a business.

BPP
PROFESSIONAL EDUCATION

Note form questions

Types of business

The following questions relate to Module 1 of Section 2 of AAT Bookkeeping Certificate.

1. In the table below, write explanations of the different ways businesses can be classified.

Business	Explanation
Sole trader	
Partnership	
Limited company	

2. In what situation may the shareholders and the directors of a company be the same people?

3. In the table below, write a description of the different types of business listed.

Type of business	Description
Manufacturer	
Retailer	
Service provider	

4. Identify two methods that can be used to classify businesses in relation to size.

5. What is the level of turnover that is 'small' according to the Companies Act?

6. What are cash sales?

---

7. What are credit sales?

---

8. Are cash sales always paid for in cash?

---

9. What does the word 'credit' mean in the term 'credit sale'?

If you are having difficulties go back to Module 1 Section 2 of the disc.

Business transactions

The following questions relate to Module 1 Section 3 of AAT Bookkeeping Certificate.

10. A customer that buys goods for cash is known as a ....

11. A credit customer becomes a .... when a sale is made.

12. A debtor owes money to...

13. Why is a sales invoice from Gem Supplies a purchase invoice for Mr Allen?

---

14. What might happen when a customer purchases goods from a new supplier?

---

15. What is a cash purchase?

---

16. What is a credit note?

_____

_____

17. What is a return inwards (or sales return)?

_____

18. What happens if a customer has already paid for goods when a credit note is issued?

_____

19. What is a return outwards (or a purchase return)?

_____

_____

20. What does the term 'purchases' usually mean in business terms?

_____

21. Other than payment for goods bought on credit, what other bank payments might there be?

_____

22. What does the term 'drawings' mean?

_____

23. What are petty cash payments?

_____

24. What is a settlement by a debtor?

_____

If you are having difficulties go back to Module 1 Section 3 of the disc.

Invoices and credit notes

The following questions relate to Module 1 Section 4 of AAT Bookkeeping Certificate.

25. Complete the table below, explaining the contents of a sales invoice.

Term	Explanation
Credit terms	
Amount due	
Invoice number	

26. How are invoices usually numbered?

----

27. What is a credit note?

----

28. If the same numbering system is used for credit notes as for invoices, how might the credit note be distinguished?

----

29. What other visible differences might there be between invoices and credit notes?

----

30. What is a till receipt?

----

31. Why are till receipts an important part of cash control?

BPP
PROFESSIONAL EDUCATION

32. Why does a business enter its own purchase invoice number onto a purchase invoice?

....

....

If you are having difficulties go back to Module 1 Section 4 of the disc.

Other documentation

The following questions relate to Module 1 Section 5 of AAT Bookkeeping Certificate.

33. What information is normally included on a stock list?

....

34. What additional information might be contained on a stock list produced by a computer system?

....

....

....

....

35. In the table below, complete the description of the documents listed.

Document	Description
Purchase order	
Delivery or advice note	
Invoice	

36. What are price lists?

....

37. What is a quotation?

38. What is a pro-forma invoice?

39. What is a remittance advice?

40. What is a sales order?

41. Why are two copies of sales invoices required?

42. What is a statement?

43. What are goods received notes?

44. What are expense claims?

45. What are time sheets/job cards?

....

If you are having difficulties go back to Module 1 Section 5 of the disc.

Financing transactions

The following questions relate to Module 1 Section 6 of AAT Bookkeeping Certificate.

46. Suggest three ways a sole trader might obtain capital.

....

....

....

47. What bookkeeping transactions would be generated as a result of your answer to question 44?

....

....

48. From what two sources does a limited company obtain finance?

....

If you are having difficulties go back to Module 1 Section 6 of the disc.

SUMMARY

A **business** may be:

- A sole trader
- A partnership
- A limited company
- A manufacturer
- A retailer
- A service provider
- Some combination of the above

Sales may be:

- Cash sales (non-credit sales)
- Credit sales (payment at some later date)

A **debtor** is someone who owes money **to** the business
A **creditor** is someone to whom the business owes money
Purchases are goods bought for resale
Returns outwards are goods returned by the business
Returns inwards are goods returned to the business

The main business transactions and documents are:

Credit sales (sales invoice to customer)
Returns inwards (credit note to customer)
Bank receipts:

- Capital introduced by proprietor
- Loan received
- Payment by debtors (possibly remittance advice received)
- Cash sales, money banked (till receipts issued)

Credit purchases (purchase invoice from supplier):

- Goods for resale
- Other items eg insurance, telephone

Returns outwards (credit note from supplier)
Bank payments:

- Payment of creditors (possibly with remittance advice issued)
- Payment of certain expenses such as rent
- Drawings
- Cash purchases
- Payment of wages
- Repayment of loans
- Petty cash payments

BPP
PROFESSIONAL EDUCATION

Other business documents include:

- Purchase orders
- Delivery notes
- Advice notes
- Price lists
- Quotations
- Pro-forma invoices
- Statements
- Expense claims
- Goods received notes
- Time sheets
- Job cards

Review

In this module you have learnt that:

- Businesses can be classified in various different ways, according to the different methods of ownership, type of business, size or type of sales.

- There are several different types of business transactions which will, in due course, be recorded in business records. It is important to distinguish between cash and credit transactions.

- There is a wide range of business documentation relating to the various different business transactions.

- Finance will usually be provided for a business both by the owner(s) and others in the form of some type of loan.

Answers

Types of business

1.

Business	Explanation
Sole trader	Person owning the business on his own
Partnership	Persons sharing the ownership and managing the business with others
Limited company	Business owned by the shareholders and run by the directors.

2. Small companies often have the same directors and shareholders.

3.

Type of business	Description
Manufacturer	Manufacturer makes goods for resale
Retailer	Retailer buys goods and sells them on to the public at higher prices
Service provider	Service provider provides a service

4. Size may be judged according to the number of employees or value of turnover.

5. 'Small' includes companies with sales of up to nearly £3 million.

6. Cash sales are sales paid for by the customer at the time when the sale was made.

7. Credit sales are sales made to customers who have a certain length of time to pay.

8. Cash sales might be paid for by cheque, debit or credit card, as well as actual cash.

9. Credit means delayed payment.

Business transactions

10. A customer that buys goods for cash is a **cash customer.**

11. A credit customer becomes a **debtor** when a sale is made.

12. A debtor owes money to **a business.**

13. Mr Allen is purchasing goods from Gem Supplies who are selling the goods to him (one of their customers).

14. The new supplier might ask for references, and ask the customer to pay for goods at the time of purchase.

15. A cash purchase is one that has to be paid for when the goods are bought.

16. A credit note effectively cancels an invoice (or part) as the goods may have been damaged, not suitable or incorrectly priced when invoiced.

17. Returns inwards are goods that have been returned to the business – effectively negative sales.

18. Either a refund will be given or a reduction will be made against future sales.

19. Returns outwards (or purchase returns) are purchases that have been returned to the supplier – effectively negative purchases.

20. Purchases are usually goods bought for resale.

21. Other bank payments could be rent and wages.

22. Drawings are amounts of money the proprietor has taken out of the business for his own use.

23. Petty cash payments are small amounts paid out of a cash float – usually small items such as stamps, tea and coffee.

24. Settlement by a debtor is when a credit customer pays the amount owed to the business.

Invoices and credit notes

25. Contents of a sales invoice

Term	Explanation
Credit terms	Length of time a customer has to pay
Amount due	Amount owing for the goods including VAT
Invoice number	Used for control and reference purposes

26. Invoices are usually numbered sequentially.

27. A credit note is effectively a negative invoice.

28. The number on a credit note may have C/N added to it.

29. Credit notes could be headed Credit Note or might be printed in a different colour or may have brackets round the figures.

30. A till receipt is a document generated by a cash till and given to a customer who buys goods for cash.

31. The total of the till receipts should equal the cash in the till.

32. The business produces its own sequential purchase invoice number to provide its own sequence for invoices from all of its suppliers.

Other documentation

33. A stock list normally contains details of stock item and number in stock.

34. The additional information may be:

   - Stock code identifying each item
   - Supplier
   - Description of item
   - Number in stock
   - Number ordered, but not yet received
   - Cost

35.

Document	Description
Purchase order	Completed with details of goods required when it is decided to order goods from supplier.
Delivery or advice note	Accompanies goods which have been ordered and contains details of goods despatched by the supplier; usually contains no price information; if delivery matches the order then it is complete.
Invoice	Details the amount due to be paid, usually received separately from the goods; should be matched with the delivery note and purchase order.

36. Price lists show the full price and trade discounts for goods a supplier is selling.

37. A quotation is information regarding the offered price of an item that is to be specially made.

38. A pro-forma invoice is often sent out by a supplier who will not allow credit to a new business customer. The invoice must be paid before the goods are despatched.

39. A remittance advice is a document sent with a cheque detailing which invoices and credit notes make up the payment.

40. A sales order is an order received from a customer.

41. One copy is sent to the customer and the other is kept in the business usually filed in numerical order.

42. A document detailing the amounts outstanding from the customer.

43. Goods received notes are forms detailing goods that have been received by the warehouse.

44. Expense claims set out details of expenses incurred by the employee when seeking repayment from the employer.

45. Time sheets/job cards are filled in by employees allocating their time to different products or jobs.

Financing transactions

46. Ways for a sole trader to raise capital include:

    - His own initial capital contribution
    - Subsequent capital introduced
    - Loan from bank or others

47. The following transactions could be generated.

    - Bank receipts from the proprietor and loans
    - Bank payments to repay loans, drawings by proprietor

48. The two sources from which a limited company obtains finance are the issue of shares or loans.

Module 2

Double entry – Balance sheet

Introduction

The whole process of bookkeeping and accounting is based on the double entry system. This, in turn, is based on the accounting equation – for any business we can say that:

Capital = Assets – Liabilities

This module introduces the terms **capital**, **assets** and **liabilities** and explains this accounting equation. We will see that, to keep the equation in balance, every business transaction must have a dual effect. For example, a transaction may cause an asset to increase while a liability increases by the same amount, or one asset increases while another decreases.

We will look at a simple balance sheet which lists the assets, liabilities and capital of a business and see how the balance sheet changes (and remains in balance) for a series of business transactions. We will then introduce double entry and you will see how we record the same transactions in double entry terms.

There are a lot of examples for you to complete yourself to give you practice in double entry. It is important that you understand the principle at this stage, as it is developed further in the module 4 and provides the basis for most of the rest of the package. Do not worry if it all seems slightly strange when you do the module for the first time. Once you have tried a few examples, go back and complete the module again if you need to – it should make more sense when you read it for the second time.

Accountancy is based on many underlying concepts and conventions. This module introduces you to two of these – the **dual aspect** concept (as outlined above, every transaction has two aspects which must be equal to keep the accounting equation in balance) and the **business entity** concept (the owner and his business are two distinct entities). Further concepts and conventions will be brought in later as appropriate.

WARNING

Forget your bank statement!

You may be familiar with the idea that it is not a good thing to have a debit balance on your bank statement (a debit balance is an overdrawn balance). In this module, we will see that a debit balance in the *bank* account means that you have money in the bank, while a credit balance means that the account is overdrawn. These statements may seem to conflict, but they are in fact in agreement. The bank produces statements from their own point of view – if you have money in the bank, it is as asset to you (debit balance), but, from the bank's point of view, they owe you that money, so you are a liability to the bank (credit balance). This is explained in more detail in Module 16 where we look at the process of reconciling our own records with the bank statement.

Learning objectives

The objectives of this module are to:

- Help you understand the classification of balance sheet items into assets, liabilities, capital and realise how these items are linked by the accounting equation.

- Show you that every transaction has a dual effect.

- Explain how you can record double entry transactions in balance sheet accounts.

- Give you an awareness of the business entity and dual aspect concepts.

Note form questions

The accounting equation

The following questions relate to Module 2 Section 2 of AAT Bookkeeping Certificate.

1. Give six reasons why a business keeps accounting records.

2. Give five reasons why financial accounts are prepared.

3. What are the three steps involved in the preparation for financial accounts?

4. What are the two main statements making up a set of financial accounts?

5. What is the name given to the profit and loss account of a non-profit seeking organisation?

    ....

6. What is a balance sheet?

    ....

    ....

7. Assets are ....

8. Give four examples of assets.

    ....

    ....

9. Liabilities are ....

10. Give two examples of liabilities.

    ....

    ....

11. Describe the term 'net assets'.

    ....

12. Net assets = ... − ....

13. On whose behalf are the assets and liabilities of the business acquired?

    ....

14. What is capital?

    ....

15. How does the accounting equation remain in balance?

If you are having difficulties go back to Module 2 Section 2 of the disc.

Balance sheet worked examples: Mr Allen

The following questions relate to Module 2 Sections 3, 4 and 5 of AAT Bookkeeping Certificate.

16. What is the accounting equation?

----

17. Insert the following headings in their correct position on the balance sheet in the space below.

- Assets
- Total liabilities
- Loans
- Total assets
- Creditors
- Liabilities

- Net assets
- Stock
- Capital
- Fittings
- Bank
- Debtors

Balance sheet

BPP
PROFESSIONAL EDUCATION

The following question relates to a jewellery business started by Mr Allen.

18. Using example 5 from Section 4.2 of the disc. Mr Allen sells a ring at cost price of £50. This money is lodged in the business bank account. Complete the *Transaction* and *After* column for this transaction, including your reasons in the bubble and connect the bubble to the appropriate balance sheet line.

Mr Allen's balance sheet

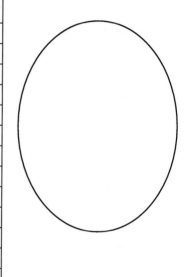

ASSETS		Before	Transaction	After
Fittings		1,000		
Stock		1,500		
Debtors		0		
Bank		3,000		
Total assets	A	5,500		
LIABILITIES				
Loans		0		
Creditors		500		
Total liabilities	L	500		
Net assets	A – L	5,000		
Capital		5,000		

19. In the balance sheet below fill in the changes required for examples 6-9 and calculate the balance sheet after transaction 9.

Example 6   Mr Allen sells a necklace, which cost him £75 to Mr Hansen on credit. This sale is made at cost price.

Example 7   Mr Allen writes a cheque for £40 for his own personal use from the business bank account.

Example 8   Mr Allen banks a cheque for £2,000 as a business loan from Diamond Investment Co

Example 9   Mr Allen buys further stock of £1,000 by writing a cheque from his personal bank account.

ASSETS	Balance sheet after example 5	Example 6	Example 7	Example 8	Example 9	Final balance sheet
Fittings	1,000					
Stock	1,450					
Debtors	0					
Bank	3,050					
Total assets A	5,500					
LIABILITIES						
Loans	0					
Creditors	500					
Total liabilities L	500					
Net assets A-L	5,000					
Capital	5,000					

SUMMARY

To keep the accounting equation in balance:

Capital = Assets – Liabilities

every transaction affects two items in the Balance Sheet.

---

20. Describe the effect of example 8 above on Mr Allen's balance sheet.

If you are having difficulties go back to Module 2 Sections 3, 4 and 5 of the disc.

Double entry – Introduction

The following questions relate to Module 2 Section 6 of AAT Bookkeeping Certificate.

21. What is double entry bookkeeping?

---

22. What is a ledger account?

....

23. What would be recorded in a ledger account?

....

....

24. What is a T account?

....

25. What do the two sides of the T represent?

....

26. On the T account below show the details contained in Section 6.1 of the software.

27. The debit side is ....

28. The credit side is...

29. What entry is made if an asset increases?

....

30. What entry is made if an asset decreases?

....

31. What entry is made to increase a liability?

....

32. What entry is made to decrease a liability?

---

33. How is a capital account increased?

---

34. How is a capital account decreased?

---

35. Explain why it is necessary to make an entry in two T accounts.

If you are having difficulties go back to Module 2 Section 6 of the disc.

Multi-part entries/overdrawn bank

The following questions relate to Module 2 Section 9 of AAT Bookkeeping Certificate.

36. Mr Allen wrote a business cheque for £2,000 to the Jewellery Supply Co to cover the purchase of stock of £500 and the purchase of fittings of £1,500. Describe how this transaction will be recorded in the accounting records of Mr Allen.

---

37. If a business operates with a bank overdraft would there be changes to the normal accounting rules?

If you are having difficulties go back to Module 2 Section 9 of the disc.

Accounting concepts and conventions

The following questions relate to Module 2 Section 10 of AAT Bookkeeping Certificate.

38. What are accounting concepts and conventions?

39. What is the business entity concept?

40. Give an example that shows the use of this concept.

41. Explain why a payment by the business is treated differently to a payment made personally by the proprietor on behalf of the business.

42. Explain whether this concept is reinforced in legal terms.

43. Who is responsible for the debts of a sole trader's business?

44. What is the dual aspect (or duality) concept?

45. Give two examples where the dual aspect concept is demonstrated.

If you are having difficulties go back to Module 2 Section 10 of the disc.

Example questions

The following questions relate to Module 2 Sections 11 and 12 of AAT Bookkeeping Certificate.

46. Using the examples in Section 11 of the software, complete the table below by entering the account to be debited, and the account to be credited.

Example number	Transaction details	Debit	Credit
7	Part of loan repaid by business cheque		
8	Goods for resale bought on credit		
9	Faulty goods taken from stock and returned to supplier		
10	Business car bought on credit		
11	New shop is purchased. Deposit paid by investor on behalf of business.		
12	Proprietor repays part of investor's loan by personal cheque		

47. Using the example set 2, Miss Hassan, from Section 12 of the software complete the T accounts below, as you work through the transactions.

A1 Property

A2 Motor van

A3 Stock

A4 Bank

L1 Loan from Pole

L2 Creditors

C1 Capital

If you are having difficulties go back to Module 2 Sections 11 and 12 of the disc.

SUMMARY

The Balance Sheet of a business demonstrates the accounting equation:

Capital = Assets – Liabilities

- **Assets** are items that the business **owns**
- **Liabilities** are amounts that the business **owes**
- **Capital** is the owner's investment in the business
  ie what the business **owes to the owner**

Business transactions are recorded by DEBITS and CREDITS in ledger accounts (often shown as T accounts).

DEBIT	T account	CREDIT
ASSETS		LIABILITIES CAPITAL

ASSETS are represented by DEBIT balances.

LIABILITIES and CAPITAL are represented by CREDIT balances

To INCREASE an ASSET a Debit entry is made

To DECREASE an ASSET a Credit entry is made

ASSET

+	–

To INCREASE a LIABILITY a Credit entry is made

To DECREASE a LIABILITY a Debit entry is made

LIABILITY

–	+

To INCREASE CAPITAL a Credit entry is made

To DECREASE CAPITAL a Debit entry is made

CAPITAL

−	+

Many accounting concepts and conventions underlie bookkeeping and accounting.

Business entity concept

In accounting terms, the business is a separate entity from its owner(s).

Dual aspect for quality concept

Every transaction has two aspects which must be equal.

Review

In this module you have learnt that:

- Balance sheet items can be classified as assets, liabilities or capital.

- The accounting equation (C = A − L) is kept in balance by recording transactions in terms of double entry. Each transaction has a dual effect – debit and credit.

- Many accounting concepts and conventions underlie double entry bookkeeping and accounting.

Answers

Accounting equation

1. A business keeps accounting records to provide:

    a. A permanent record of financial transactions
    b. Information from which financial accounts can be prepared
    c. Information from which management reports can be prepared
    d. A means of controlling assets
    e. Information for decision making
    f. Compliance with statutory regulations

2. Financial accounts are prepared to:

    a. Provide owners who are not directly involved in the business with information
    b. Provide a basis for calculation of tax liabilities
    c. Give information to government to be used in economic planning
    d. Give information to suppliers and loan creditors including applications for assistance
    e. Comply with statutory requirements

3. The three steps involved in the preparation of financial accounts are:

    a. Each transaction is classified into the appropriate category
    b. The totals for these categories are accumulated in the accounting records
    c. Financial accounts are prepared from the accounting records

4. The two main statements making up a set of Financial Statements are:

    - balance sheet
    - profit and loss account

5. The profit and loss account of a non-profit seeking organisation is an income and expenditure account

6. The balance sheet of an entity shows the state of affairs of a business at a point in time.

7. Assets are **things owned by the business.**

8. Examples of assets are property, vehicles, debtors and cash at bank.

9. Liabilities are **amounts owed by the business.**

10. Examples of liabilities are creditors and bank overdraft.

11. The term 'net assets' is what the business is worth to the owners.

12. Net assets = **assets – liabilities.**

13. Assets and liabilities are acquired on behalf of the owners.

14. Capital is the amount owed to the owners.

15. The accounting equation remains in balance as every transaction must alter both sides of the equation by the same amount (often zero).

Balance sheet worked examples: Mr Allen

16. The accounting equation is Capital = Assets – Liabilities

17. Balance sheet

ASSETS	
Fittings	
Stock	
Debtors	
Bank	
Total assets	A
LIABILITIES	
Loans	
Creditors	
Total liabilities	L
Net assets	A–L
Capital	C

18. Increase assets (*Bank* account) by £50, and reduces assets (*Stock*) by £50.

   Reasons: *Bank* account has received £50, which has therefore increased; Stock has been sold, and therefore reduced.

19.

ASSETS	Balance sheet after example 5	Example 6	Example 7	Example 8	Example 9	Final balance sheet
Fittings	1,000					1,000
Stock	1,450	(75)			1,000	2,375
Debtors	0	75				75
Bank	3,050		(40)	2,000		5,010
Total Assets A	5,500					8,460
LIABILITIES						
Loan	0			2,000		2,000
Creditors	500					500
Total Liabilities L	500					2,500
Net assets A-L	5,000					5,960
Capital	5,000		(40)		1,000	5,960

20. The effect of example 8 is assets and liabilities are both increased.

Double entry – Introduction

21. Double entry bookkeeping is the system used to record the two sides of an individual transaction.

22. An account for each item that is being affected by transactions.

23. The page is divided in two, one half to show increases in the account, the other to show decreases.

24. A T account represents an account page.

25. The two sides of the T represent C = A – L or A = C + L

26.

DEBIT	CREDIT
ASSETS	CAPITAL
	LIABILITIES

27. The debit sides is the left hand side.

28. The credit side is the right hand side.

29. To increase an asset a debit entry is made.

30. To decrease an asset a credit entry is made.

31. To increase a liability a credit entry is made.

32. To decrease a liability a debit entry is made.

33. To increase a capital account a credit entry is made.

34. To decrease a capital account a debit entry is made.

35. Entries are made in two T accounts in order to keep the accounting equation in balance.

Multi-part entries/overdrawn bank

36. *Stock* and *Fittings* will be debited with £500 and £1,500 respectively, whilst the *Bank* account will be credited with £2,000.

37. The normal rules still apply:

   • Debit increases (or deposits in) the bank
   • Credit decreases (or payments from) the bank

Accounting concepts and conventions

38. Accounting concepts and conventions are assumptions upon which the whole accounting process is based.

39. The business entity concept is that a business is a separate entity from its owners(s).

40. An example is setting up a proprietor's capital account to record the amount due to him from the business.

41. The business entity concept assumes that a business is a separate entity from its owners, so a payment by the owner is different to a payment by the business.

42. In legal terms there is no separation of the owner and his business.

43. The proprietor is responsible for the debts of the business.

44. The dual aspect concept is that every transaction has two aspects which must be equal.

45. The dual aspect concept is seen in:

- Double entry where debits must equal credits
- The accounting equation where C = A-L

Example questions

46.

Example number	Transaction details	Debit	Credit
7	Part of loan repaid by business cheque	*Loan*	*Bank*
8	Goods for resale bought on credit	*Stock*	*Creditors*
9	Faulty goods taken from stock and returned to supplier	*Creditor*	*Stock*
10	Business car bought on credit	*Motor vehicle*	*Creditor*
11	New shop is purchased. Deposit paid by investor on behalf of business.	*Shop*	*Loan*
12	Proprietor pays part of investor's loan by personal cheque	*Loan*	*Capital*

47.

A1 Property

Bank	12,000	Bank	400
Loan	1,500		

A2 Motor van

Creditors	2,500		

A3 Stock

Creditors	300		

A4 Bank

Capital	10,000	Property	12,000
Loan	10,000	Capital	1,000
Property	400	Creditors	1,000

C1 Capital

Bank	1,000	Bank	10,000
		Loan	10,000

L1 Loan from Pole

Capital	10,000	Bank	10,000
		Property	1,500

L2 Creditors

Bank	1,000	Van	2,500
		Stock	300

Module 3

Balancing off accounts, trial balance

Introduction

In the last module we recorded a lot of transactions in T accounts. What we now need to consider is the net effect of these transactions or, in other words, the balance in each account. The balance in each of the asset, liability and capital accounts tells us the current value of that item. For example, the balance in the *Bank* account shows how much money there is in the bank, and the balance in the *Creditors* account tells us how much the business owes to its suppliers.

The balance in any account is the difference between the sum of the debit entries and the sum of the credit entries. An excess of debits over credits gives a debit balance, and excess of credits over debits gives a credit balance. Assets should finish up with debit balances, while liabilities and capital should have credit balances.

While the calculation of the balance in an account is a straightforward matter (totals debits – total credits), there is a particular means of showing this in the T accounts. You should be familiar with the process of 'balancing off' a T account, although, as keeping records in this actual format is not now common, you are unlikely to have to do this in practice.

The trial balance is a means of summarising the balances calculated. This is simply a listing of all the balances in a set of records. At this stage we have only asset, liability and capital accounts, so in the **debit** column we will have the **asset** balances while in the **credit** column we will see the balances in the **liability and capital** accounts. Because of the accounting equation and the principles of double entry, the total of the debit balances should equal the total of the credit balances. We will see in a later module how the profit & loss account and balance sheet are prepared from the figures listed in the trial balance.

Learning objectives

The objectives of this module are to show you how to:

- Calculate the balance in an account.

- Draw up a trial balance.

Note form questions

The following questions relate to Module 3 Section 2 of AAT Bookkeeping Certificate.

Introduction

1. How is the balance on an account calculated?

    ....

2. The balance on an asset account is a .... balance, and is calculated as the

    excess..

3. The balance on a liability account is a .... balance, and is calculated as the

    excess ....

4. The balance on the capital account is a .... balance, and is calculated as

    the excess ....

If you are having difficulties go back to Module 3 Section 2 of the disc.

Mr Allen – worked examples

The following questions relate to Module 3 Section 3 of AAT Bookkeeping Certificate.

5. Enter the balance on the stock account below.

A2 Stock

Creditors	1,500	Bank	50
Capital	1,000	Debtors	75

6. Explain why a debit entry of £2,375 was made in the above stock account.

    ....

    ....

7. What does the term *Bal c/f* mean and when is it used?

    ....

    ....

8.   Why would you expect a stock account to have a debit balance?

----

9.   Balance off the following *Bank* account.

A4 Bank

Capital	5,000	Fittings	1,000
Stock	50	Creditors	1,000
Loan	2,000	Capital	40

If you are having difficulties go back to Module 3 Section 3 of the disc.

Trial balance and Mr Allen – examples

The following questions relate to Module 3 Sections 5 and 6 of AAT Bookkeeping Certificate.

10.   What is a trial balance?

----

11.   Produce the trial balance for Mr Allen using the information given in section 5 of the software.

Mr Allen

Trial balance

Account	Debit	Credit

12. What is the essential feature of all trial balances?

---

13. What do the debit balances on the trial balance represent?

---

14. What do the credit balances on the trial balance represent?

---

15. The following example is Miss Hassan from Section 6 of the software. Balance off the accounts and produce a trial balance for Miss Hassan.

A1 Property

Bank	12,000	Bank	400
Loan	1,500		

A2 Motor van

Creditors	2,500	

A3 Stock

Creditors	300	

A4 Bank

Capital	10,000	Property	12,000
Loan	10,000	Capital	1,00
Property	400	Creditors	1,000

L1 Loan from Pole

Capital	10,000	Bank	10,000
		Property	1,500

L2 Creditors

Bank	1,000	Van	2,500
		Stock	300

C1 Miss Hassan's Capital

Bank	1,000	Bank	10,000
		Loan	10,000

If you are having difficulties go back to Module 3 Sections 4, 5 and 6 of the disc.

SUMMARY

To calculate the balance in an account we calculate:

the excess of DEBITS over CREDITS for a **Debit** balance

the excess of CREDITS over DEBITS for a **Credit** balance

We carry the balance down in the account after balancing it off

……….	XX	………….	X
……….	X		
……….	<u>X</u>	Bal c/d	<u>X</u>
	<u>XX</u>		<u>XX</u>
Bal b/d	X		

The **trial balance** is a listing of the balance in each of the accounts. The DEBIT total should equal the CREDIT total

ASSETS will show as DEBIT balances

LIABILITIES and CAPITAL will show as CREDIT balances

Review

In this module you have learnt:

- How to calculate the balance is an account, and what the balance means.

- How to draw up a trial balance.

Answers

Introduction

1. The balance is the difference in the totals on the two sides of the T account.

2. The balance on an asset account is a **debit** balance and is calculated as the excess of debits over credits.

3. The balance on a liability account is a **credit** balance, and is calculated as the excess of credits over debits.

4. The balance on the capital account is a **credit** balance, and is calculated as the excess of credits over debits.

Mr Allen – worked examples

5. You were asked to enter the balance on the stock account below.

A2 Stock

Creditors	1,500	Bank	50
Capital	1,000	Debtors	75
	____	Bal c/d	2,375
	2,500		2,500
Bal b/d	2,375		

6. The debit entry was made to complete the double entry (the credit entry having been made to make the two totals agree).

7. *Bal c/f* is short for Balance to be carried forward and is used when the balance is carried forward from one page to another.

8. A stock account would be expected to have a debit balance as it is an asset account.

9. You were asked to balance off the following *Bank* account.

A4 Bank

Capital	5,000	Fittings	1,000
Stock	50	Creditors	1,000
Loan	2,000	Capital	40
	____	Balance c/d	5,010
	7,050		7,050
Balance b/d	5,010		

Trial balance and Mr Allen – examples

10. A trial balance is a list of an organisation's accounts and their balances.

11. **Mr Allen**

     Trial balance

Account	Debit	Credit
A1 Fittings	1,000	
A2 Stock	2,375	
A3 Debtors	75	
A4 Bank	5,010	
L1 Loan		2,000
L2 Creditors		500
C1 Capital	_____	5,960
	8,460	8,460

12. The totals of the debit and credit sides should always agree.

13. The debit balances on the trial balance are assets.

14. The credit balances are either liabilities or capital.

15. You were required to balance off the accounts and produce a trial balance for Miss Hassan.

A1 Property

Bank	12,000	Bank	400
Loan	1,500	Bal c/d	13,100
	13,500		13,500
Bal b/d	13,100		

A2 Motor van

Creditors	2,500		
	_____	Bal c/d	2,500
	2,500		2,500
Bal b/d	2,500		

A3 Stock

Creditors	300		
	____	Bal c/d	300
	300		300
Bal b/d	300		

A4 Bank

Capital	10,000	Property	12,000
Loan	10,000	Capital	1,000
Property	400	Creditors	1,000
	____	Bal c/d	6,400
	20,400		20,400
Bal b/d	6,400		

L1 Loan from Pole

Capital	10,000	Bank	10,000
Bal c/d	1,500	Property	1,500
	11,500		11,500
		Bal b/d	1,500

L2 Creditors

Bank	1,000	Van	2,500
Bal c/d	1,800	Stock	300
	2,800		2,800
		Bal b/d	1,800

C1 Miss Hassan's capital

Bank	1,000	Bank	10,000
Bal c/d	19,000	Loan	10,000
	20,000		20,000
		Bal b/d	19,000

Miss Hassan

Trial balance

Account	Debit	Credit
A1 Property	13,100	
A2 Motor van	2,500	
A3 Stock	300	
A4 Bank	6,400	
L1 Loan from Pole		1,500
L2 Creditors		1,800
C1 Miss Hassan's Capital	____	19,000
	22,300	22,300

Module 4

Double entry – Profit and loss account

Introduction

In Module 2, when we recorded transactions for Mr Allen, very conveniently for us, he made any sales at cost price. A business, however, is generally in existence to make profits for its owner – or, in other words, to increase the owner's capital. So that we can record the sales and the various on-going costs of a business, we now introduce two more categories of accounts – **income** (usually sales) and **expenses** (wages, rent, telephone, motor expenses and all the other costs necessary to keep the business running and make it thrive).

WARNING – TRICKY AREA AHEAD

One of the notoriously tricky areas in bookkeeping is how to deal with the cost of goods purchased for resale. The problem is that these goods are an asset until they are sold, at which point the cost becomes an expense (the *cost of sales* expense). Some computerised stock control and accounting systems can mirror this by transferring the cost to the expense account when items are sold but, in many situations, this is not possible.

There are several different methods used for the recording of stock/cost of sales. We have selected one particular, commonly used, method and used it throughout the package. This method is explained in 5.2. The rest of Section 5 explains other methods of dealing with stock/cost of sales. If this is all new to you, do not read the alternative method in 5.4 at this stage. However if you have used a different method before, you might like to read it now to see how the method in use here compares with the one you are used to. Once you are completely happy with the method in use here, you may wish to read the alternative method later (there will not, however, be any questions in the exam on any other method).

Again, in this module, there are many examples for you to complete – get plenty of practice and make sure that you understand the double entry principles involved before proceeding to apply them to different situations in future modules.

As you are entering figures in expense accounts, remember that you are building up a total cost for that particular item (eg wages) for the year to date. Similarly, the sales account balance at any point shows the total sales for the year to date. At the end of the year, the figures for the income and expense accounts in the trial balance show the totals for the year. We will see in the next module that deducting these expense account balances from the sales account balance will give the profit for the year, as calculated in the profit & loss account.

Learning objectives

The objectives of this module are to:

- Ensure you understand the classification of profit and loss account items into income and expenses.

- Show that the net figure of income less expenses (ie profit) goes to increase capital.

- Show you how to record double entry transactions in profit and loss accounts as well as balance sheet accounts.

Note form questions

Sales

The following questions relate to Module 4 Section 2 of AAT Bookkeeping Certificate.

1.   Suggest why Mr Allen will not continue in business for long if he sells goods at cost.

....

2.   Explain the effect on the individual accounts of Mr Allen of selling goods for more than cost price.

....

....

3.   What is the effect of making a profit on Mr Allen's *Capital* account?

....

If you are having difficulties go back to Module 4 Section 2 of the disc.

Expenses

The following question relate to Module 4 Section 3 of AAT Bookkeeping Certificate.

4.   Which accounts are effected when Mr Allen pays wages of £50 by a business cheque?

....

If you are having difficulties go back to Module 4 Section 3 of the disc.

Income and expense accounts

The following questions relate to Module 4 Section 4 of AAT Bookkeeping Certificate.

5.   In the table below give four examples of expenses and two examples of income.

Expenses	Income

6.   Where will information on expenses and income be kept?

....

7.   What is the effect on the *Capital* account of opening income and expense accounts?

....

....

8.   How is the figure to be transferred to *Capital* calculated?

....

9.   How often is this figure usually transferred to *Capital?*

....

10. How is the accounting equation changed as a result of recording items of income and expenditure in their own accounts?

....

....

If you are having difficulties go back to Module 4 Section 4 of the disc.

Cost of sales

The following questions relate to Module 4 Section 5 of AAT Bookkeeping Certificate.

11. What is shown in the first part of the profit and loss account?

....

....

12. How is cost of sales calculated and where is the figure shown?

....

....

13. What does the *Stock* figure shown in the balance sheet represent?

....

....

14. Summarise the steps necessary to calculate the *Cost of sales/Stock* (using the method in use in the package).

....

....

....

....

15. Why is it necessary to transfer the values of unsold goods from the *Cost of sales* account?

....

....

16. What are the accounting entries necessary to remove the unsold goods from the *Cost of sales* account?

....

17. Why might a *Purchases* account be considered a better name than *Cost of sales*?

....

....

18. Why is the terminology of the method being used not strictly correct?

....

....

19. What alternative method can be used to record *Cost of sales/Stock*?

....

....

....

If you are having difficulties go back to Module 4 Section 5 of the disc.

> ## SUMMARY
>
> Method of recording the purchase of goods for resale in use in the package:
>
> - Purchases are debited to an **expense account** (*Purchases/Cost of sales*).
> - Cost of unsold stock is transferred to the **balance sheet** *Stock* account at the year end.

Mr Allen

The following questions relate to Module 4 Sections 6 and 7 of AAT Bookkeeping Certificate.

20. In the table below fill in the changes required for examples 1–3 and calculate the balances after transaction 3.

   Transaction 1 Stock of goods £2,375 for resale transferred from *Stock* account to *Cost of sales* account.

   Transaction 2 Mr Allen sells an item for £250 in cash, which is banked.

   Transaction 3 Mr Allen pays wages of £50 by business cheque.

ASSETS	Balances	Transaction 1	Transaction 2	Transaction 3	Final balance sheet
INCOME					
Sales	0				
EXPENSES					
Cost of sales	0				
Wages	0				
Rent	0				
Heat & light	0				
Post, tel, stat	0				
Total expenses	0				
Capital	5,960				
C + (I –E)	5,960				
ASSETS					
Fittings	1,000				
Stock	2,375				
Debtors	75				
Bank	5,010				
Total assets A	8,460				
LIABILITIES					
Loans	2,000				
Creditors	500				
Total liabilities L	2,500				
Net assets A-L	5,960				

If you are having difficulties go back to Module 4 Sections 6 and 7 of the disc.

Double entry

The following questions relate to Module 4 Section 8 of AAT Bookkeeping Certificate.

21. What is the extended version of the accounting equation?

....

22. Using the T account below fill in what is represented by the debit and credit sides.

DEBIT	CREDIT

23. What entry is made to increase an income account?

....

24. What entry is made to decrease an income account?

....

25. What entry is made to increase an expense account?

....

26. What entry is made to decrease an expense account?

....

27. From the list below indicate whether the balance is normally debit or credit.

	Debit	**Credit**
Assets		
Expenses		
Liabilities		
Capital		
Income		

If you are having difficulties go back to Module 4 Section 8 of the disc.

Double entry – Mr Allen

The following questions relate to Module 4 Sections 9 and 10 of AAT Bookkeeping Certificate.

28. In the T accounts below fill in the entries required for questions 3–6 from Section 10.3-10.6 and extract the trial balance after question 6.

Question 3	Mr Allen pays rent of £400 by personal cheque.
Question 4	Mr Allen receives an electricity bill for £340. He intends to pay this in two weeks' time.
Question 5	Mr Allen receives and banks £500 of the amount owing to him by his customers.
Question 6	Mr Allen gives the local stationer a business cheque for £25 for books and stationery, which he now needs.

A1 Fittings

Bal b/f	1,000		

A2 Stock

Bal b/f	2,375	Cost of sales	2,375

A3 Debtors

Bal b/f	75		
Sales	2,475		

A4 Bank

Bal b/f	5,010	Wages	50
Sales	250	Cost of sales	2,500

L1 Loan

		Bal b/f	2,000

L2 Creditors

		Bal b/f	500

C1 Capital

		Bal b/d	5,960

I1 Sales

		Bank	250
		Debtors	2,475

E1 Cost of sales

Stock	2,375		
Bank	2,500		

E2 Wages

Bank	50		

E3 Rent

E4 Heat and light

E5 Post, tel, stat

Trial balance

		Debit	Credit
I1	Sales		
E1	Cost of sales		
E2	Wages		
E3	Rent		
E4	Heat and light		
E5	Post, tel, stat		
A1	Fittings		
A2	Stock		
A3	Debtors		
A4	Bank		
L1	Loan		
L2	Creditors		
C1	Capital		

If you are having difficulties go back to Module 4 Sections 9 and 10 of the disc.

SUMMARY

The accounting equation can be expanded to:

- Capital + (Income – Expenses) = Assets – Liabilities

Periodically the figure of (income – expenses) ie profit is calculated and added to capital.

DEBIT   CREDIT

ASSETS EXPENSES	CAPITAL LIABILITIES INCOME

Double Entry

ASSET

+	–

CAPITAL

–	+

EXPENSE

+	–

LIABILITY

–	+

INCOME

–	+

Assets and expenses are represented by **DEBIT** balances

Capital, liabilities and income are represented by **CREDIT** balances

Review

In this module you have learnt:

- Which items belong in the balance sheet and which belong in the profit and loss account.

- That the accounting equation can be extended to include income (I) and expenses (E) and that, periodically the profit (I–E) is added to the capital.

- How to record transactions in double entry terms in all the usual classes of accounts.

Answers

Sales

1. Mr Allen is making no profit on his sales, but he will still have to cover expenses.

2. *Bank* or *Debtors* will increase, whilst *Stock* will reduce. The difference (profit) will increase *Capital*.

3. The effect has been to increase Mr Allen's investment by the profit.

Expenses

4. *Bank* is reduced by £50 and *Capital* reduced by £50.

Income and expense accounts

5.

Expenses	Income
Purchase cost of goods sold	Sales
Rent	Interest received
Electricity	
Postages	

6. Information will be kept in a ledger.

7. The effect of opening income and expenses accounts is that it is not necessary to alter *Capital* for each transaction.

8. The figure transferred is the net figure of total income less total expenses.

9. The figure is usually transferred to *Capital* once a year.

10. The accounting equation becomes:

    Capital + (Income less Expenditure) = Assets less Liabilities

Cost of sales

11. The first part of the profit and loss account shows *Sales* less *Cost of goods* sold to give the *Gross profit*.

12. Cost of sales is the cost of items actually sold. It is shown in the profit and loss account.

13. The *Stock* figure shown in the balance sheet is the cost of items purchased for resale, but not as yet sold.

14. Steps necessary to calculate *Cost of sales/Stock* are:

   - Goods purchased for resale are recorded in the *Cost of sales* account at cost price

   - Sales both for cash and on credit are recorded in the *Sales* account at selling price

   - Prior to the preparation of the profit and loss account the value of unsold stock must be removed from the *Cost of sales* account

   - The balance in the *Cost of sales* account represents the cost of items sold

15. The *Cost of sales* account includes all goods that have been purchased, and must be reduced to the cost of goods that have actually been sold.

16. The accounting entry is to debit *Stock* and credit *Cost of sales*.

17. For most of the year *Purchases* is probably a better name as it represents all purchases of goods for resale, rather than the cost of goods actually sold.

18. The account represents purchases during the year and only becomes the cost of sales once the closing stock has been transferred out.

19. Purchases are recorded in the balance sheet *Stock* account and at the time of sale the cost of items sold is transferred from the *Stock* account to the *Cost of sales* account.

Mr Allen

20.

ASSETS	Balances	Transaction 1	Transaction 2	Transaction 3	Final balances
INCOME					
Sales	0		250		250
EXPENSES					
Cost of sales	0	2,375			2,375
Wages	0			50	50
Rent	0				0
Heat & light	0				0
Post, tel, stat	0				0
Total expenses	0				2,425
Capital	5,960				5,960
C + (I –E)	5,960				3,785
ASSETS					
Fittings	1,000				1,000
Stock	2,375	(2,375)			0
Debtors	75				75
Bank	5,010		250	(50)	5,210
Total assets A	8,460				6,285
LIABILITIES					
Loans	2000				2,000
Creditors	500				500
Total liabilities L	2500				2,500
Net assets A-L	5,960				3,785

Double entry

21. $C + (I - E) = A - L$ or $A + E = C + L + I$

22.

DEBIT	CREDIT
ASSETS	CAPITAL
EXPENSES	LIABILITIES
	INCOME

23. A credit entry is made to increase an income account.

24. A debit entry is made to decrease an income account.

25. A debit entry is made to increase an expense account.

26. A credit entry is made to decrease an expense account.

27.

	Debit	Credit
Assets	✓	
Expenses	✓	
Liabilities		✓
Capital		✓
Income		✓

Double entry – Mr Allen

28.

A1 Fittings

Bal b/f	1,000	Bal c/d		1,000
	1,000			1,000
Bal b/d	1,000			

A2 Stock

Bal b/f	2,375	Cost of sales		2,375

A3 Debtors

Bal b/f	75	Bank	500
Sales	2,475	Bal c/d	2,050
	2,550		2,550
Bal b/d	2,050		

A4 Bank

Bal b/f	5,010	Wages	50
Sales	250	Cost of sales	2,500
Debtor	500	Stationery	25
		Bal c/d	3,185
	5,760		5,760
Bal b/d	3,185		

L1 Loan

Bal c/d	2,000	Bal b/f	2,000
	2,000		2,000
		Bal b/d	2,000

L2 Creditors

		Bal b/f	500
Bal c/d	840	Electricity	340
	840		840
		Bal b/d	840

C1 Capital

		Bal b/f	5,960
Bal c/d	6,360	Rent	400
	6,360		6,360
		Bal b/d	6,360

I1 Sales

		Bank	250
Bal c/d	2,725	Debtors	2,475
	2,725		2,725
		Bal b/d	2,725

E1 Cost of sales

Stock	2,375		
Bank	2,500		4,875
	4,875	Bal c/d	4,875
Bal b/d	4,875		

E2 Wages

Bank	50	Bal c/d	50
	50		50
Bal b/d	50		

E3 Rent

Bank	400	Bal c/d	400
	400		400
Bal b/d	400		

E4 Heat and light

Creditors	340	Bal c/d	340
	340		340
Bal b/d	340		

E5 Post, tel, stat

Bank	25	Bal c/d	25
	25		25
Bal b/d	25		

Trial balance

		Debit	Credit
I1	Sales		2,725
E1	Cost of sales	4,875	
E2	Wages	50	
E3	Rent	400	
E4	Heat and light	340	
E5	Post, tel, stat	25	
A1	Fittings	1,000	
A2	Stock	0	
A3	Debtors	2,050	
A4	Bank	3,185	
L1	Loan		2,000
L2	Creditors		840
C1	Capital		6,360
		11925	11925

Module 5

Profit and loss account and balance sheet (1)

Introduction

In the previous modules you have spent a lot of time learning how to record transactions correctly in accounts. This has been done with the purpose of providing information to the business and others, for example the tax authorities. We have seen that the balances in asset, liability and capital accounts represent the value of those items at that point – for example, the amount owed to creditors or the amount of money in the bank. Similarly, at the end of the year, the balances in the income and expense accounts show the amount of income earned or the amounts of different costs incurred during the year.

To summarise the two different aspects of the business, its profitability and its financial position, we produce the two statements – the **profit and loss account** and **balance sheet** (often termed the **accounts**) of the business. These statements differ in several ways.

In the profit and loss account, **expense** account balances are deducted from **income** to give the net profit (or loss). The balance sheet lists the final balances of **assets**, **liabilities** and **capital**. Because the profit and loss account is for one year only, all income and expense accounts must start again from zero in the next year. This is different for balance sheet items – the balances here carry forward from one year to the next. For example, the balance in the bank at the end of this year become the balance at the start of next year. Thus, what actually happens, in general 'behind the scenes', is that the profit and loss account is in fact part of the double entry system. The balances in the income and expense accounts are transferred, at the end of the year, to the profit and loss account. The resulting balance is transferred from there to the *Capital* account (any profit made by the business belongs to the owner). This process is explained in Section 7, although you can actually prepare a profit and loss account and balance sheet without being aware of what is really happening.

Remembering that we are entering the cost of all goods purchased for resale in the *Cost of sales* expense account, the first thing that we need to do before drawing up the Profit and loss account and Balance sheet is to remove, from *Cost of sales*, the cost of any goods not yet sold – the closing stock. This is explained in Section 3.

The profit and loss account and balance sheet that we have produced here are in a basic form. Traditionally, these statements are drawn up in a particular format. The next module takes these basic statements into the traditional format.

Learning objectives

The objectives of this module are to ensure you:

- Understand the calculation of gross profit.

- Are able to make the adjustment for closing stock.

- Are able to draw up a profit and loss account and a simple balance sheet.

Note form questions

Profit

The following questions relate to Module 5 Section 2 of AAT Bookkeeping Certificate.

> ### Summary of steps taken so far:
> 1.   Record the dual effect of all transactions (using double entry and T accounts)
> 2.   Extract the balances from the T accounts to give a trial balance

1.   In which account have goods for resale been recorded?

2.   What is the result of deducting *Cost of sales* from *Sales*?

3.   What is the trading account?

If you are having difficulties go back to Module 5 Section 2 of the disc.

Stock

The following questions relate to Module 5 Section 3 of AAT Bookkeeping Certificate.

4.   How should items for resale bought, but not yet sold, be described and shown?

5.   What accounting entry should be made for the cost of items not yet sold?

6. Describe how the cost of goods purchased for resale is dealt with in the accounting records of a business (using the method in use in the package).

....

....

....

....

7. The information below relates to items bought and sold over a period.

Item	Cost price	Selling price
1	20	40
2	25	
3	15	
4	40	60
5	25	35
6	50	

Using the method employed in the package, calculate from the above information:

a. The amount originally recorded in *Cost of sales*

....

b. The value of unsold stock

....

c. The actual cost of sales

....

d. The gross profit

....

If you are having difficulties go back to Module 5 Section 3 of the disc.

Mr Allen Profit and loss account and balance sheet

The following questions relate to Module 5 Section 4 of AAT Bookkeeping Certificate.

8. Describe why it was necessary for Mr Allen to transfer £3,375 from *Cost of sales* to the *Stock* account.

    ....

    ....

9. How is net profit calculated?

    ....

10. How is net balance of the income and expense (profit and loss) accounts dealt with at the end of an accounting period?

    ....

11. What accounts are left containing balances after income and expense accounts have been cleared to the *Capital* account?

    ....

12. What financial statement do all these remaining accounts relate to?

    ....

13. From the following trial balance prepare the profit and loss account and balance sheet for Mr Allen.

Account number	Description	Debit	Credit
I 1	Sales		2,725
E1	Cost of sales	4,875	
E2	Wages	50	
E3	Rent	400	
E4	Heat and light	340	
E5	Post, tel, stat	25	
A1	Fittings	1,000	
A2	Stock	0	
A3	Debtors	2,050	
A4	Bank	3,185	
L1	Loan		2,000
L2	Creditors		840
C1	Capital		6,360
		11,925	11,925

The cost of goods remaining unsold is £3,375.

Profit and loss account

Sales		
Less Cost of sales		
Gross profit		
Less: Expenses		
Wages		
Rent		
Heat & light		
Post, tel, stat		
Net profit		

Balance sheet

Assets		
Fitting		
Stock		
Debtors		
Bank		
Liabilities		
Loan		
Creditors		
Capital		
Mr Allen		
Net profit		

If you are having difficulties go back to Module 5 Section 4 of the disc.

Example set – Miss Clark

The following questions relate to Module 5 Section 6 of AAT Bookkeeping Certificate.

14. Using the following information for Miss Clark produce in the space below her profit and loss account and balance sheet.

Sales		6,420
Cost of sales	7,100	
Wages	450	
Rent	315	
Heat and light	300	
Loan interest	320	
Property	30,500	
Stock		
Debtors	6,020	
Bank		2,185
Bank loan	0	
Creditors		750
Capital		35,650
	45,005	45,005

The cost of goods remaining unsold is £2,285.

BPP
PROFESSIONAL EDUCATION

Miss Clark – Profit and loss account

Miss Clark – Balance sheet

If you are having difficulties go back to Module 5 Section 6 of the disc.

Profit and loss account – double entry

The following questions relate to Module 5 Section 7 of AAT Bookkeeping Certificate.

15. What happens to all income and expense accounts at the end of an accounting period?

....

....

16. What is the name of the account that is used as a clearing account when transferring the resultant net figure of all income and expenditure accounts to the *Capital* account?

....

17. Is the profit and loss account is part of the double entry accounting system and why?

....

18. Complete the following table of steps to be taken when transferring the balances from the income and expense accounts.

1	
2	
3	
4	
5	

19. As a result of the above which accounts now have a zero balance?

....

If you are having difficulties go back to Module 5 Section 7 of the disc.

SUMMARY

> Gross profit = Sales *less* Cost of sales

Note. Before this can be calculated, the value of closing stock must be transferred out of *Cost of sales*:

	Dr	Cr
Stock	xx	
Cost of sales		xx

> Net profit = Gross profit *less* all other expenses

Both gross and net profits are shown in the profit and loss account.

All income and expense figures are taken to the profit and loss account.

Mr Allen's trial balance

Account	Debit	Credit
I1 Sales		2,725
E1 Cost of sales	1,500	
E2 Wages	50	
E3 Rent	40	
E4 Heat and light	340	
E5 Post, tel, stat	25	
A1 Fittings	1,000	
A2 Stock	3,375	
A3 Debtors	2,050	
A4 Bank	3,185	
L1 Creditors		2,000
L2 Creditors		840
C1 Capital		6,360
	11,926	11,926

Mr Allen's profit and loss account

Sales		2,725
Less: Cost of sales		1,500
Gross profit		1,225
Less expenses:		
Wages	60	
Rent	400	
Heat and light	340	
Post, tel, stat	25	
		815
Net profit/(loss)		410

The remaining accounts – assets, liabilities and capital are listed in the balance sheet.

Remember that the profit (or loss) figure must be transferred to *Capital* from the profit and loss account. The balance sheet will not balance until this is done.

Mr Allen's trial balance

Account	Debit	Credit
I1 Sales		2,725
E1 Cost of sales	1,500	
E2 Wages	50	
E3 Rent	40	
E4 Heat and light	340	
E5 Post, tel, stat	25	
A1 Fittings	1,000	
A2 Stock	3,375	
A3 Debtors	2,050	
A4 Bank	3,185	
L1 Creditors		2,000
L2 Creditors		840
C1 Capital		6,360
	11,926	11,926

Mr Allen's balance sheet

Assets		
Fittings		1,000
Stock		3,375
Debtors		2,050
Bank		3,185
		9,610
Liabilities		
Loan	2,000	
Creditors	840	
		2,840
Net assets		6,770
Capital		
Mr Allen		6,360
Net profit		410
		6,770

Review

In this module you have learnt:

- Why a closing stock adjustment is necessary, and how to make such an adjustment.

- How to draw up a profit and loss account and simple balance sheet showing gross and net profits and net assets.

Answers

Profit

1. Goods for resale have been recorded in the *Cost of sales* account.

2. The result of deducting *cost of sales* from *sales* is the *gross profit*.

3. The trading account is the part of the profit and loss account that shows *sales* less *cost of sales* thus computing the *gross profit*.

Stock

4. These items should be described as *Stock* and shown as an asset of the business.

5. The cost of items not yet sold should be transferred out of the *Cost of sales* account to the *Stock* (asset) account.

6. The procedure for recording goods purchased for resale is as follows:

    *   Good for resale are firstly recorded in the *Cost of sales* account.

    *   Goods unsold at the end of accounting period are transferred from *Cost of sales* to *Stock*.

    *   The balances on the *Sales* account and *Cost of sales* account are used to calculate the gross profit, and the unsold stock is recorded as an asset.

7. a.   20 + 25 + 15 + 40 + 25 + 50 = 175

    b.   25 + 15 + 50 = 90

    c.   20 + 40 + 25 = 85

    d.   Sales (40 + 60 + 35) − cost of sales (85) = 50 (gross profit)

Mr Allen Profit and loss account and balance sheet

8. £3,375 was the cost price of goods that have not yet been sold; they are an asset and should be shown on the balance sheet.

9. Gross profit less expenses = net profit.

10. At the end of an accounting period the net balance is transferred to the *Capital* account.

11. The accounts remaining are assets, liabilities and capital.

12. The remaining accounts represent the balance sheet accounts.

13. Profit and loss account

Sales		2,725
Less Cost of sales (4,875 – 3,375)		1,500
Gross profit		1,225
Less: Expenses		
Wages	50	
Rent	400	
Heat and light	340	
Post, tel, stat	25	
		815
Net profit		410

Balance sheet

Assets		
Fitting		1,000
Stock		3,375
Debtors		2,050
Bank		3,185
		9,610
Liabilities		
Loan	2,000	
Creditors	840	
		2,840
		6,770
Capital		
Mr Allen		6,360
Net profit		410
		6,770

14. Miss Clark: Profit and loss account

Sales		6,420
Less Cost of sales (7,100 – 2,285)		4,815
Gross profit		1,605
Less: Expenses		
Wages	450	
Rent	315	
Heat and light	300	
Loan interest	320	
		1,385
Net profit		220

Miss Clark: Balance sheet

Assets		
Property		30,500
Stock		2,285
Debtors		6,020
		38,805
Liabilities		
Creditors	750	
Bank	2,185	
		2,935
		35,870
Capital		
Miss Clark's capital		35,650
Net profit		220
		35,870

Profit and loss account – Double entry

15. All income and expense accounts at the end of an accounting period are taken back to zero to start accumulating the figures for the next period.

16. The clearing account is the *Profit and loss* account.

17. The *Profit and loss* account is part of the double entry system in the same way as *Sales*.

18.

1	A new double entry account is opened – the *Profit and loss* account.
2	Income balances are transferred – debit income accounts, credit *Profit and loss* account.
3	Expenses accounts are transferred – credit expense accounts, debit *Profit and loss* account.
4	The balance in the *Profit and loss* account is calculated – the net profit/loss.
5	The profit or loss resulting from step 4 is transferred to the *Capital* account; debit *Profit and loss* account, credit *Capital* or visa versa if a loss.

19. All income and expense accounts as well as the *Profit and loss* account.

Module 6

Profit and loss account and balance sheet (2)

Introduction

Having seen in the last module that expenses are deducted from income in the profit and loss account to give the profit or loss, and that assets less liabilities are balanced with capital in the balance sheet, we now look at refining the way that we produced these statements. The aim is to produce statements that are useful to the owner of the business. The financial statements are often used by others as well, but they are produced principally with the owners in mind.

Assets employed in a business can be of two distinct types – either they are acquired by the business for long-term use (eg property, machinery, vehicles) or they are of a short-term nature, held with a view of conversion into cash (eg stock, debtors). To make the balance sheet more useful, assets will be split into these two categories – fixed and current. Similarly, liabilities will be split into those of a short-term nature that will require settlement fairly soon (eg creditors) and those that are there in the long-term, generally as a means of financing the business (eg bank loans).

When companies produce their accounts for the shareholders, they are required, by law, to produce them in a specified format (you will see more of this in Module 18). Otherwise, accounts are produced in a fairly standard way, but certain variations are possible. These standard formats, and variations, are explained in this module.

A full example set towards the end of the module takes you through several double entry questions, the trial balance and production of the profit and loss account and balance sheet.

Once you have completed this module, you have learnt all the basics of bookkeeping. You can record all the basic transactions, produce a trial balance and draw up a profit and loss account and balance sheet. You should also have some understanding of the use and meaning of these statements. In the next series of modules we will look at various accounting adjustments necessary to produce a more realistic and meaningful profit figure. In the following series of modules we look at the recording of information in the books of the business, bearing in mind that we want to have various checks and controls in the system to try to catch any errors made in the recording.

Learning objectives

The objectives of this module are to ensure you:

- Are able to classify assets into fixed and current, and liabilities into current and long-term.

- Are able to draw up a profit and loss account and balance sheet in a commonly used format.

- Understand the significance of various totals on the balance sheet.

Note form questions

Accounts, dates and gross profit

The following questions relate to Module 6 Section 2 of AAT Bookkeeping Certificate.

1.   What term is often used for the profit and loss account and balance sheet together?

....

2.   What might the term 'accounts' **also** mean?

....

3.   What information should be shown at the top of the profit and loss account?

....

....

4.   What information should be shown at the top of the balance sheet?

....

....

5.   What type of organisation will prepare a profit and loss account that does not contain any cost of sales?

....

....

6.   What would be included in the cost of sales figure for a business that charges for work that has been done?

....

....

If you are having difficulties go back to Module 6 Section 2 of the disc.

Format of capital accounts

The following questions relate to Module 6 Section 3 of AAT Bookkeeping Certificate.

7.   Describe the detail that is normally shown in the capital account.

8.   What are drawings?

----

9.   How is a net loss dealt with in a proprietor's *Capital* account?

----

10. Prepare the capital section of Miss Clark's balance sheet from the information in Section 3.5 of the software.

If you are having difficulties go back to Module 6 Section 3 of the disc.

PROFESSIONAL EDUCATION

Classification of balance sheet items – assets

The following questions relate to Module 6 Section 4 of AAT Bookkeeping Certificate.

11. What two categories of assets are usually shown?

12. What are fixed assets?

13. In what order are fixed assets shown?

14. List four fixed assets that are often found on a balance sheet.

15. What are current assets?

16. In what order are current assets shown?

17. What happens in the 'chain of conversion'?

18. List, in order of appearance, the four items that are normally shown under the current assets heading?

19. Into what two categories are liabilities split?

20. What does the term 'current liabilities' mean?

21. Give two examples of current liabilities.

22. What does the term 'long-term liabilities' mean?

23. Give two examples of long-term liabilities.

If you are having difficulties go back to Module 6 Section 4 of the disc.

Balance sheet format

The following questions relate to Module 6 Section 5 of AAT Bookkeeping Certificate.

24. How has the original accounting equation been amended?

25. Give explanations of the following sub totals that appear on a balance sheet.

Total fixed assets	
Total current assets	
Total current liabilities	
Net current assets or working capital	
Total long-term liabilities	
Net assets	
Proprietor's capital	

26. Why is the net current assets figure important?

....

....

27. If current liabilities exceed current assets, how is the difference described?

....

28. How is the term 'working capital' calculated?

....

29. How are the net assets calculated?

....

30. What does the proprietor's capital represent?

....

....

31. Describe an alternative balance sheet format shown in the software.

....

32. Who might use this alternative balance sheet format?

---

33. What information is highlighted by using this alternative presentation?

---

34. Who requires companies to produce their balance sheet in the specific format?

---

35. What is highlighted by the original presentation of the balance sheet?

---

36. In the table below show the major headings in a double-sided balance sheet.

Balance sheet

If you are having difficulties go back to Module 6 Section 5 of the disc.

Trading account

The following questions relate to Module 6 Section 6 of AAT Bookkeeping Certificate.

37. What adjustment is required to the *Cost of sales* balance to arrive at the correct cost of sales figure in a business's first year of trading?

---

38. What adjustments are required to be made to the *Cost of sales* figure to arrive at the correct cost of sales figure in business's second year of trading?

---

39. Describe the alternative method used for adjusting stock described in Module 6, Section 6.6 of the software.

------

40. What method do computer systems usually use to record the stock figures?

If you are having difficulties go back to Module 6 Section 6 of the disc.

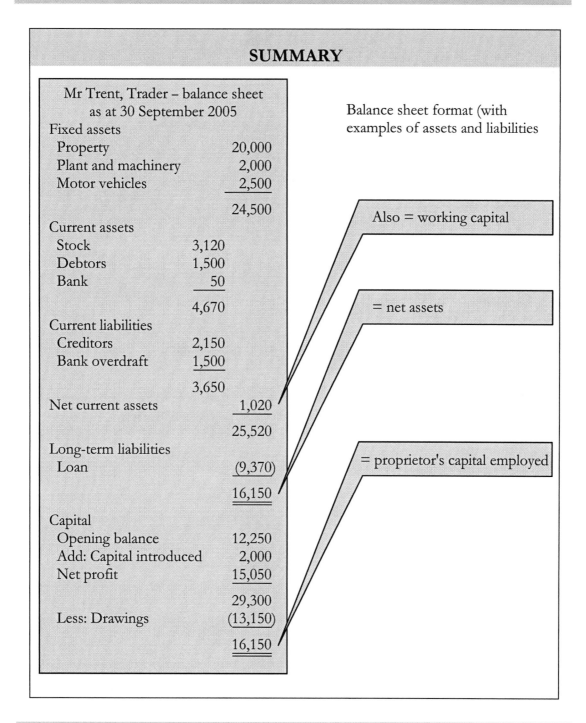

SUMMARY

Mr Trent, Trader – balance sheet
as at 30 September 2005

Fixed assets		
Property		20,000
Plant and machinery		2,000
Motor vehicles		2,500
		24,500
Current assets		
Stock	3,120	
Debtors	1,500	
Bank	50	
	4,670	
Current liabilities		
Creditors	2,150	
Bank overdraft	1,500	
	3,650	
Net current assets		1,020
		25,520
Long-term liabilities		
Loan		(9,370)
		16,150
Capital		
Opening balance		12,250
Add: Capital introduced		2,000
Net profit		15,050
		29,300
Less: Drawings		(13,150)
		16,150

Balance sheet format (with examples of assets and liabilities

Also = working capital

= net assets

= proprietor's capital employed

Review

On completion of this module you should be able to:

- Draw up a profit and loss account and balance sheet, with all items properly classified.

- Understand the meaning of various totals appearing in the profit and loss account and balance sheet.

Answers

Accounts, dates and gross profit

1. The profit and loss account and balance sheet together are often termed the **final accounts**, or just **accounts** of the business. They are sometimes referred to as financial statements.

2. An account is where transactions are classified and posted eg *Telephone expenses* account.

3. The name of the individual or organisation whose profit and loss account it is, and the accounting period covered by it.

4. The name of the individual or organisation whose balance sheet it is and the date at which it is prepared.

5. The profit and loss account of a service organisation such as an insurance company would not contain a cost of sales figure.

6. The following would be included within the cost of sales figure – wages to employees doing the work, materials, other costs (all costs that directly relate to producing the sales figure).

Format of capital accounts

7. Capital

Opening balance		X
Add:	Capital introduced	X
	Net profit	X
		X
Less:	Drawings	(X)
Closing balance		X

8. Drawings are usually cash withdrawn from the business by the proprietor; it can also include private payments made by the business for him and the value of any goods taken by him from the business.

9. A net loss is deducted from capital along with the drawings.

10. Capital

Opening balance		24,850
Add:	Capital introduced	12,000
	Net profit	220
		37,070
Less:	Drawings	(1,200)
Closing balance		35,870

Classification of balance sheet items

11. Assets are usually shown as fixed assets or current assets.

12. Fixed assets are those purchased by a business for long-term use.

13. Fixed assets are listed in order of permanence.

14. Fixed assets often found on a balance sheet:

    - Property
    - Plant and equipment
    - Fixtures and fittings
    - Motor vehicles

15. Current assets are those that are turning over frequently during the year. They can be thought of as being held with a view to converting them into cash.

16. The further up the 'change of conversion' they are, the further up the list they appear.

17. On making credit sales, *stock* is converted into *debtors*. When the *debtors* pay, *debtors* are converted in *bank* or *cash*.

18. The following items are normally shown under current assets:

    - Stock
    - Debtors
    - Bank
    - Cash

19. Liabilities are split into current liabilities and long-term liabilities.

20. Current liabilities are those that are due in the short-term, usually within one year.

21. Trade creditors and bank overdraft are current liabilities.

22. Long-term liabilities are those that are due at a date later than one year from the balance sheet date.

23. Bank loan due after 12 months and other long-term loans are long-term liabilities.

Balance sheet format

24. The amended accounting equation is FA + CA – CL – L/TL = C

25.

Total fixed assets	Total of the assets in long-term use by the business.
Total current assets	Total of assets in liquid form (cash and bank) and those held with a view to conversion into cash (stock and debtors).
Total current liabilities	Total of liabilities due in less than 1 year. This will normally consist creditors and bank overdraft.
Net current assets or working capital	Net current assets = current assets – current liabilities.
Total long-term liabilities	The amount of finance for the business provided by third parties. The providers will usually be paid interest to reward them for their investment.
Net assets	Total of top section of the balance sheet = Fixed assets + net current assets – long-term liabilities.
Proprietor's capital	The proprietor's investment in his business.

26. Net current assets is an important figure as it gives an indication of the liquidity of the business.

27. Current liabilities – current assets = net current liabilities.

28. Working capital = current assets – current liabilities.

29. Net assets = total assets – total liabilities (= net current assets).

30. The proprietor's capital is the amount of finance for the business provided by the proprietor.

31. $FA + (CA - CL) = C + L/T\,L$

32. Sole traders and partnerships might use the alternative balance sheet presentation.

33. The funding provided from all sources is highlighted.

34. The Companies Act requires companies to use the specific format.

35. The original presentation highlights the capital provided by the owners of the business.

36. Balance sheet

Capital	Fixed assets
Long-term liabilities	Current assets
	Less Current liabilities

Trading account

37. The closing stock needs to be deducted from the original balance in the cost of sales account.

38. The opening stock needs to be added and the closing stock needs to be deducted from the original balance in the cost of sales account.

39. The *Cost of sales* account is renamed *Purchases* and two adjustments are made:

    - The opening stock for the period is credited to the *Stock* account on the balance sheet and debited to the account *Opening stock (P&L)*.

    - There will also be an entry to debit the balance sheet *Stock* account and credit the account *Closing stock (P&L)* with the closing stock figure.

40. The opening stock, purchases and closing stock are generally shown as separate figures.

Unit 1

Additional questions

Additional questions

Questions based on Module 1 of this Workbook

You are required to list in the space below information that should be shown on the following documents:

Purchase order

Goods received note

Purchase invoice

Remittance advice to supplier

Cheque with remittance advice

Sales order

Delivery notes

Sales invoice

Questions based on Modules 2 and 3 of this Workbook

Mr Clock has been selling clocks and watches for many years. His assets and liabilities at 31 December 2005 are as follows:

	£
Shop premises	56,000
Bank balance	3,765
Creditors	12,890
Debtors	9,990
Bank loan	10,000
Stock	23,500

1. Prepare Mr Clock's Balance Sheet at 31 December 2005 using the format in Module 2.

2. Complete the table below by entering the account to be debited and the account to be credited. (Note that, at this stage, we have no expense accounts, so stock purchased will be debited to the stock account as in Module 2.)

No	Transaction	Debit	Credit
1	Mr Clock buys stock on credit of £2,459.		
2	A debtor pays Mr Clock £2,000 which is paid into the business bank account.		
3	Mr Clock uses a clock from the business that cost £100 as a present for his great aunt.		
4	Mr Clock sells a clock, which cost him £150 on credit at cost price.		
5	Mr Clock pays a business cheque of £5,000 as a deposit on a new extension to the existing premises.		
6	Mr Clock returns faulty goods originally invoiced at £450 to a supplier		
7	Following negotiation with the bank Mr Clock receives a £25,000, which is paid to the vendor for the extension.		
8	Mr Clock uses his own chequebook in error to pay a creditor £850.		
9	Mr Clock withdraws £700 for his own use from the business bank account.		
10	Mr Clock decides to pay £1,000 off the bank loan.		

3. Open T accounts and record the above opening balances and transactions and balance off the accounts.

Shop premises

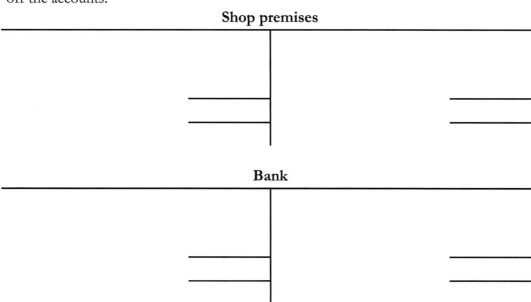

Bank

Creditors

Debtors

Bank loan

Stock

Capital

4. Produce a trial balance from the above T accounts.

   Trial balance for Mr Clock

	Debit	**Credit**

Questions based on Modules 4 and 5 of this Workbook

1. Open Mr Clock's T accounts with the following balances:

	Debit	Credit
Premises	86,000	
Bank		935
Creditors		14,049
Debtors	8,140	
Bank loan		34,000
Stock	25,259	
Capital		70,415
	119,399	119,399

Shop premises

Bank

Creditors

Debtors

Bank loan

Stock

Capital

Drawings

Cost of sales

Wages

Heating and light

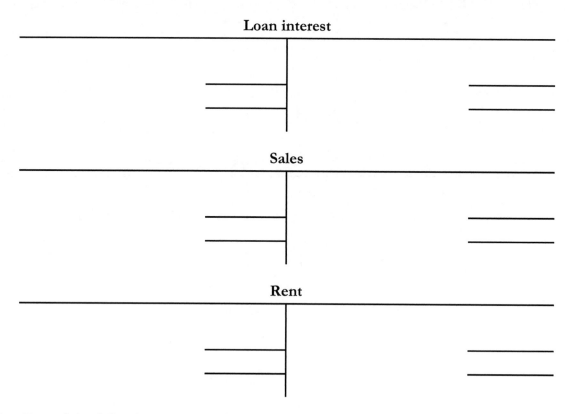

Loan interest

Sales

Rent

2. Record the following transactions in the above T accounts. (Note that we now have a *Cost of sales* account which will be used to record the purchase of goods for resale as in Module 4.)

1. Transfer the opening stock to the *Cost of sales* account.

2. Mr Clock pays creditors of £1,500 by a business cheque.

3. Mr Clock buys goods on credit for £3,670.

4. Faulty goods returned to the supplier; a credit note is received for £90.

5. Wages of £670 paid by cheque.

6. Mr Clock buys goods on credit costing £9,980.

7. An electricity bill of £150 was paid by cheque

8. Interest of £450 is added to the bank loan

9. Mr Clock makes credit sales of £19,800

10. Rent of £750 is paid by cheque

11. Mr Clock withdraws £700 for his own use from the business bank account.

12. Mr Clock decides to transfers £5,000 from his own bank account to pay off part of the loan.

13. Mr Clock receives £6,440 from debtors, which is paid into the business bank account.

14. Closing stock has been valued at £23,469.

3. Prepare the trial balance for Mr Clock at the end of the above transactions.

4. Prepare in the space below Mr Clock's profit and loss account and balance sheet.

    Balance sheet

    Profit and loss account

5. Close off the income and expense accounts above, and then prepare another trial balance.

Answers to questions based on Module 1

Purchase order

> Organisation's name and address
> Name of supplier
> Date
> VAT registration number
> Product reference
> Description
> Quantity
> Price
> Any discounts
> Delivery details

Goods received note

> Name of organisation
> Name and address of supplier
> Reference number
> Date
> Quantity of items received
> Description
> Purchase Order number
> Details of state of goods on receipt

Purchase invoice

> Organisation's name
> Supplier's name and address
> Supplier's invoice number
> Date
> VAT number
> Order number
> Number of items
> Description
> Price
> Total price
> VAT
> Discount

Remittance advice to supplier

> Organisation's name and address
> Supplier's name and address
> Date
> Details of invoices and credit notes making up the payment
> Total amount of cheque

Cheque with remittance advice

> Name or organisation
> Payee
> Date
> Amount in words and numbers
> Sort code
> Signature

BPP PROFESSIONAL EDUCATION

Sales order

> Organisation's name
> Customer's name and address
> Supplier's invoice number
> Date
> VAT number
> Order number
> Number of items
> Description
> Price
> Total price
> VAT
> discount

Delivery notes

> Organisation's name
> Supplier's name
> Details of delivery method
> Date
> Details of goods being delivered

Sales invoice

> Organisation's name
> Customer's name and address
> Organisation's invoice number
> Date
> VAT number
> Order number
> Number of items
> Description
> Price
> Total

Answers to questions based on Modules 2 and 3

1.

Mr Clock

Balance sheet at 31 December 2005

Assets	£
Shop premises	56,000
Stock	23,500
Debtors	9,990
Bank	3,765
Total assets	93,255
Liabilities	
Creditors	12,890
Bank loan	10,000
Total liabilities	22,890
Net assets	70,365
Capital	70,365

2.

No	Transaction	Debit	Credit
1	Mr Clock buys stock on credit of £2,459.	Stock	Supplier
2	A debtor pays Mr Clock £2,000 which is paid into the business bank account.	Bank	Debtor
3	Mr Clock uses a clock from the business that cost £100 as a present for his great aunt.	Capital	Stock
4	Mr Clock sells a clock, which cost him £150 on credit at cost price.	Debtor	Stock
5	Mr Clock pays a business cheque of £5,000 as a deposit on a new extension to the existing premises.	Premises	Bank
6	Mr Clock returns faulty goods originally invoiced at £450 to a supplier.	Supplier	Stock
7	Following negotiation with the bank Mr Clock receives a £25,000, which is paid to the vendor for the extension.	Premises	Bank Loan
8	Mr Clock uses his own chequebook in error to pay a supplier £850.	Supplier	Capital
9	Mr Clock withdraws £700 for his own use from the business bank account.	Drawings	Bank
10	Mr Clock decides to pay £1,000 off the bank loan using a business cheque.	Bank Loan	Bank

3.

Shop premises

Bal b/d	56,000	Bal c/d	86,000
Bank (1)	5,000		
Loan (7)	25,000		
	86,000		86,000
Bal b/d	86,000		

Bank

Bal b/d	3,765	Premises (5)	5,000
Debtors (2)	2,000	Capital (9)	700
Bal c/d	935	Loan (10)	1,000
	6,700		6,700
		Bal b/d	935

Creditors

Stock (6)	450	Bal b/d	12,890
Capital (8)	850	Stock (1)	2,459
Bal c/d	14,049		
	15,349		15,349
		Bal b/d	14,049

Debtors

Bal b/d	9,990	Bank (2)	2,000
Stock (4)	150	Bal c/d	8,140
	10,140		10,140
Bal c/d	8,140		

Bank loan

Bank (10)	1,000	Bal b/d	10,000
Bal c/d	34,000	Premises	25,000
	35,000		35,000
		Bal c/d	34,000

Stock

Bal b/d	23,500	Capital (3)	100
Creditors (1)	2,459	Debtors (4)	150
		Creditors (6)	450
		Bal c/d	25,259
	25,959		25,959
Bal b/d	25,259		

Capital

Stock (3)	100	Bal b/d	70,365
Bank (9)	700	Creditors (8)	850
Bal c/d	70,415		71,215
	71,215	Bal b/d	70,415

4. Trial balance for Mr Clock

	Debit	Credit
Premises	86,000	
Bank		935
Creditors		14,049
Debtors	8,140	
Bank loan		34,000
Stock	25,259	
Capital		70,415
	119,399	119,399

Answers to questions based on Modules 4 and 5

1. & 2.

Shop premises

Bal b/d	86,000	Bal c/d	86,000
	86,000		86,000
Bal c/d	86,000		

Bank

Debtors (13)	6,440	Bal b/d	935
		Creditors (2)	1,500
		Wages (5)	670
		Electricity (7)	150
		Rent (10)	750
		Drawings (11)	700
		Bal c/d	1,735
	6,440		6,440
Bal b/d	1,735		

Creditors

Bank (2)	1,500	Bal b/d	14,049
Purchases (4)	90	Purchases (3)	3,670
Bal c/d	26,109	Purchases (6)	9,980
	27,699		27,699
		Bal b/d	26,109

Debtors

Bal b/d	8,140	Bank (13)	6,440
Sales (9)	19,800	Bal c/d	21,500
	27,940		27,940
Bal b/d	21,500		

Bank loan

Capital (12)	5,000	Bal b/d	34,000
Bal c/d	29,450	Interest (8)	450
	34,450		34,450
		Bal b/d	29,450

Stock

Bal b/d	25,259	Cost of sales (1)	25,259
Cost of sales (14)	23,469		

Capital

Drawings	700	Bal b/d	70,415
Bal c/d	77,145	Loan (12)	5,000
		P & L a/c	2,430
	77,845		77,845
		Bal b/d	77,145

Drawings

Bank (11)	700	Capital	700
	700		700

Cost of sales

Stock (1)	25,259	Creditors (4)	90
Creditors (3)	3,670	Stock (14)	23,469
Creditors (6)	9,980	P&L a/c	15,350
	38,909		38,909

Wages

Bank (5)	670	P & L a/c	670
	670		670

Heating and light

Bank (7)	150	P & L a/c	150
	150		150

Loan interest

Loan (8)	450	P & L a/c	450
	450		450

Sales

P & L a/c	19,800	Debtors (9)	19,800
	19,800		19,800

Rent

Bank (10)	750	P & L a/c	750
	750		750

3. Mr Clock's trial balance before accounts are closed off.

Premises	86,000	
Bank	1,735	
Creditors		26,109
Debtors	21,500	
Bank loan		29,450
Stock	23,469	
Capital		75,415
Drawings	700	
Wages	670	
Heat and light	150	
Loan interest	450	
Sales		19,800
Rent	750	
Cost of sales	15,350	
	150,774	150,774

4. Mr Clock's Profit and loss account

	£	£
Sales		19,800
Less Cost of sales		15,350
Gross profit		4,450
Less: Expenses		
Wages	670	
Rent	750	
Heat & light	150	
Loan interest	450	
		2,020
Net profit		2,430

Balance sheet

Assets		
Property		86,000
Stock	23,469	
Debtors	21,500	
Bank	1,735	46,704
		132,704
Liabilities		
Creditors	26,109	
Bank loan	29,450	55,559
		77,145
Capital – opening balance		70,415
Capital introduced		5,000
Net profit		2,430
Drawings		(700)
		77,145

5. Mr Clock's trial balance after accounts have been closed off.

	£	£
Premises	86,000	
Bank	1,735	
Creditors		26,109
Debtors	21,500	
Bank loan		29,450
Stock	23,469	
Capital		77,145
	132,704	132,704

Unit 2

Accounting Adjustments

Module 7

Nominal ledger and adjustments

Introduction

You have, so far, made a lot of entries in T accounts. These T accounts are a representation of practical ledger accounts – so far we have used **nominal ledger** accounts. This module explains the nominal ledger, and also the sales and purchase ledgers that we will see a lot more of in the *Practical bookkeeping* section. In practice, a ledger may well look very different to the T accounts that we have been using and, indeed, it is more likely to be a computerised ledger than a book. These various different forms of ledger are explained here. For the purposes of learning double entry however, we will still continue to use T accounts as they demonstrate very clearly the double-sided aspect of bookkeeping.

Adjustments are made to the figures in the nominal ledger by **journal entries**. One type of adjustment, that will frequently be encountered, is the correction of errors. An example set in the module gives several examples of this.

Errors are then looked at in more detail. You will see that certain errors affect the balancing of the trial balance, while others do not. (Errors affecting the balancing of the trial balance should not be possible in a computerised system.)

Of particular importance to the accuracy of the accounts produced is the correct classification of expenditure as either **capital** (to purchase an asset to appear in the balance sheet) or **revenue** (on an expense to appear in the profit and loss account).

You will see that the classification is not necessarily as straightforward as you might think.

Having seen how to make adjustments by means of journal entries, the next few modules cover particular adjustments such as depreciation and accruals and prepayments. You will first, however, be introduced to VAT.

Learning objectives

The objectives of this module are to ensure that you:

- Become familiar with the contents of the nominal, sales and purchases ledgers.

- Understand some of the different types of ledgers kept in practice.

- Realise that several accounting adjustments are required before a set of accounts can be prepared.

- Know how various errors affect the trial balance and which types of error will not be possible in a computerised system.

- Appreciate the importance of the distinction between capital and revenue expenditure.

Note form questions

The nominal ledger and adjustments

The following questions relate to Module 7 Section 2 of AAT Bookkeeping Certificate.

1. In the bubbles below write the names of the three ledgers, and at the bottom of the arrows what is contained within that ledger.

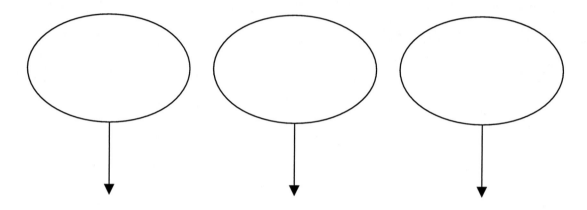

2. What is another name for the nominal ledger?

    ----

3. Where is the double entry for the sales and purchase ledger accounts?

    ----

4. If a business only has a small number of customers or suppliers, where might the individual accounts be kept?

    ----

5. How would the trial balance be affected if the individual sales and purchase ledger accounts were included in the nominal ledger?

----

6. Using the bank account example in Section 2.3 of the software why was the balance not readily available at 22 April 2005?

If you are having difficulties go back to Module 7 Section 2 of the disc.

Three-column format

The following questions relate to Module 7 Section 3 of AAT Bookkeeping Certificate.

7. Why is the three-column format used to record transactions?

----

8. In a three-column format below fill the descriptions for A to F.

A =					
B =	C =		D =	E =	F =

9. What do the abbreviations Dr. and Cr. mean in the balance column?

----

10. Suggest two alternative means of indicating a credit balance?

If you are having difficulties go back to Module 7 Section 3 of the disc.

Types of ledger

The following questions relate to Module 7 Section 4 of AAT Bookkeeping Certificate.

11. In what two formats can ledgers be found?

12. Describe how a book would be used to record ledger accounts.

13. What is an advantage of using a loose-leaf binder?

14. How does a computerised ledger record ledger accounts?

15. What needs to be taken into account when designing a coding system for a computerised ledger?

16. Include on the table below the suggested fixed asset account numbers from the package.

Account number	Name
	Factory – cost
	Factory – acc dep
	Offices – cost
	Offices – acc dep
	Motor lorries – cost
	Motor lorries – acc dep
	Motor vans – cost
	Motor vans – acc dep
	Motor cars – cost
	Motor cars – acc dep

17. What is the meaning of each digit of the fixed asset number?

Digit	Meaning
First digit	
Second digit	
Third digit	
Fourth digit	

18. Using the code system described in question 16 what number may be given to the cost of new shop premises and explain why?

19. Why should gaps be left in a coding system?

If you are having difficulties go back to Module 7 Section 4 of the disc.

Balancing off accounts – year end

The following questions relate to Module 7 Section 5 of AAT Bookkeeping Certificate.

20. How are income and expenditure accounts balanced off at the year-end?

----

21. How are accounts balance off in a computerised accounting system?

----

22. What happens to the balances on asset, liability and capital accounts?

----

23. What happens to the net profit or loss for the year?

If you are having difficulties go back to Module 7 Section 5 of the disc.

Journal entries/Adjustments

The following questions relate to Module 7 Section 6 of AAT Bookkeeping Certificate.

24. What is a journal entry?

----

25. How many debits and credits should there be in a journal entry?

----

26. What four adjustments are often required to produce meaningful accounts?

----

27. How often are the above adjustments made?

----

28. Draft a journal entry that contains more than one line in the space below.

If you are having difficulties go back to Module 7 Section 6 of the disc.

Example set – Mr Wilson

The following question relates to Module 7 Section 7 of AAT Bookkeeping Certificate.

29. For the adjustments below enter on the table below the account to be debit and the one to be credited.

Error	Debit	Credit
Mr Wilson finds extra unrecorded stock amounting to £230		
Sales for March were under added by £30		
New desk costing £250 is to be transferred from Office expenses to fixtures and fittings		
Mr Wilson paid his employee a bonus of £100 in personal cash. This has not yet been recorded.		

If you are having difficulties go back to Module 7 Section 7 of the disc.

Trial balance – errors

The following questions relate to Module 7 Section 8 of AAT Bookkeeping Certificate.

30. Complete the following table explaining what each error is, and give an example of the error.

Error	What error is	Example
Transposition		
Omission		
Principle		
Commission		
Compensating		

31. In the table below list four possible errors that could result in a trial balance being out of balance, and suggest how the errors should be corrected.

Description of error	Adjustment required to correct

32. In table below list five possible errors that could occur, but the trial balance would still balance.

Description of error	Adjustment required to correct

33. What is a suspense account?

----

34. Explain how a debit suspense account balance will be treated in a set of financial statements.

----

35. Explain how a credit suspense account balance will be treated in a set of financial statements.

----

36. List four possible errors that it is possible to make when using a computer system.

----

37. Explain why a computer system does not let the other mistakes be made.

If you are having difficulties go back to Module 7 Section 8 of the disc.

Capital/Revenue expenditure

The following questions relate to Module 7 Section 9 of AAT Bookkeeping Certificate.

38. What would be the result of the following errors on the profit and loss account and the balance sheet?

Error	Profit and loss account	Balance sheet
Item entered in *Cost of Sales* instead of *Rent*		
Item entered in *Rent* rather than *Motor vehicles*		

39. What is capital expenditure?

....

....

40. What is revenue expenditure?

....

....

41. Capital expenditure is shown in ....

42. Revenue expenditure is shown in..

43. Tick in appropriate box as to whether the following expenditure is capital or revenue.

	Capital expenditure	Revenue expenditure
Delivery costs for new machine		
Repairs to buildings		
Additional computer		
Insurance for new machine		
Replacement central heating		

If you are having difficulties go back to Module 7 Section 9 of the disc.

SUMMARY

Ledgers

The nominal (or general) ledger contains accounts for all the income, expense, asset, liability and capital accounts required in a business.

The sales ledger contains accounts for each credit customer. (This is a breakdown of the *Debtors* account in the nominal ledger.)

The purchase ledger contains accounts for each credit supplier – suppliers of both goods and services. (This is a breakdown of the *Creditors* account in the nominal ledger.)

Ledgers will take many different forms in practice. They may be manual books or may be computerised.

Adjustments

Before preparation of the profit and loss account and balance sheet, several adjustments will be required:

These include:

- Stock adjustment
- Accruals & prepayments
- Depreciation
- Correction of errors

These are entered in the books as journal entries.

Types of errors

Errors of transposition – where two adjacent figures in an amount are reversed.

Errors of omission – where an entry or part of an entry has been left out.

Errors of principle – where some fundamental accounting principle has been contravened, often the wrong class of account has been used.

Errors of commission – where the correct amount is entered in the wrong account, but it is the right class of account.

Errors can result in:

A trial balance still balancing
- Reversal of debits and credits
- Entry in the wrong account (mistake or error in principle)
- Omission of entry
- Incorrect figure used for both debit and credit
- Compensating errors

BPP
PROFESSIONAL EDUCATION

A trial balance out of balance
- Omission of one part of an entry
- Error in the entry of one figure in an account
- Account balance incorrect
- Incorrect addition of column(s)

Capital/Revenue expenditure

Capital expenditure
- Expenditure to purchase or improve fixed assets (includes such things as delivery and installation costs)
- Belongs in the balance sheet

Revenue expenditure
- Expenditure for running the business on a day-to-day basis (this will include the cost for repairing and maintaining fixed assets)
- Belongs in the profit and loss account

Review

In this module you have learnt:

- An accounting system will often contain three ledgers – the sales, purchase and nominal ledgers.

- In practice, ledgers will often be kept in a three column format.

- In a computerised nominal ledger, the allocation of account codes is very important.

- Several adjustments, in the form of journal entries, will usually be required before a set of accounts can be prepared.

- There are several different types of errors that can be made in the processing of transactions. Some errors will affect the profit and/or the balancing of the trial balance.

- It is important to classify expenditure correctly as either capital or revenue.

Answers

The nominal ledger and adjustments

1.

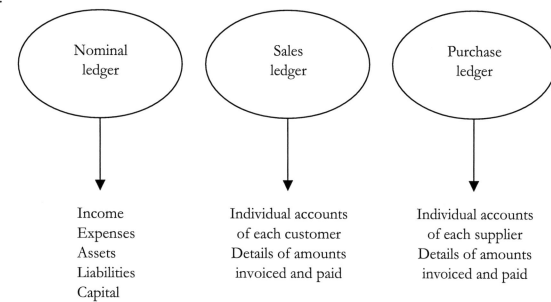

2. The nominal ledger can also be called the general ledger.

3. The double entry for the sales and purchase ledger accounts is in the nominal ledger.

4. If there are only a small number of accounts they could be kept in the nominal ledger.

5. In these circumstances the individual sales and purchases ledger balances would be included in the trial balance.

6. The balance at 22 April 2005 was not readily available as it is usual only to balance off an account at the end of each month.

Three column format

7. It is used so that it is possible to extract balances at any required date.

8.

A = Name of account					
B = Date	C = Description		D = Debit	E =Credit	F = Balance

9. Dr. means debit and Cr. means credit.

10. Credit balances can be indicated by either a minus sign or by brackets.

Types of ledger

11. Ledger accounts can be recorded in paper-based books or in computer files.

12. The book can be either hard-backed or loose-leaf in a binder. Each page of the book will be either divided in two in the traditional double entry (Dr/Cr) format, or ruled off in three columns.

13. The advantage of loose-leaf binders is that new pages can be added, and out of date ones removed.

14. Either two or three columns can be used for recording. Each account will usually be given a code. The accounts can be displayed on the screen or printed out.

15. The following need to be taken into account:

   - Length of code 4-16 characters
   - Like items to be grouped together
   - Contain alphanumeric characters
   - Group items as they appear on profit and loss account or balance sheet

16.

Account number	Name
1110	Factory – cost
1111	Factory – acc dep
1120	Offices – cost
1121	Offices – acc dep
1410	Motor lorries – cost
1411	Motor lorries – acc dep
1420	Motor vans – cost
1421	Motor vans – acc dep
1430	Motor cars – cost
1431	Motor cars – acc dep

17.

Digit	Meaning
First digit	Fixed asset
Second digit	Fixed asset category eg property
Third digit	Sub group of fixed assets eg warehouse
Fourth digit	Cost or accumulated depreciation

18. 1140 – 1 for fixed assets, 1 for property, 4 for next sub group and 0 for cost

19. Gaps will be left so that additional accounts can be fitted into their correct position.

Balancing off accounts – year end

20. They may just be ruled off and started again from zero at the start of the next accounting period. In other cases the balance on the account might be transferred to the profit and loss account.

21. After all transactions have been posted and the accounts prepared, the year-end procedures are run and income and expense accounts are zeroed.

22. These balances on these accounts are carried forward.

23. The net profit or loss is added or deducted respectively to the designated capital account.

Journal entries/Adjustments

24. A journal entry is an adjustment that debits one or more account(s) and credits one or more.

25. There can be many debits and credits, but the total debits must always equal the total credits.

26. The following adjustments may be required:

    - Accruals
    - Prepayments
    - Depreciation
    - Correction of errors

27. The adjustments are made whenever accounts are prepared.

28.

		Dr	*Cr*
Date	Account name 1	X	
	Account name 2	X	
	Account name 3		XX
	Account name 4	X	—
		XX	XX
	Narrative		

Example set – Mr Wilson

29.

Error	Debit	Credit
Mr Wilson finds extra unrecorded stock amounting to £230.	A3 Stock	E1 Cost of sales
Credit sales for March were under added by £30.	A4 Debtors	I1 Sales
New desk costing £250 is to be transferred from *Office expenses* to *Fixtures and fittings*.	A1 Fixtures and fittings	E5 Office expenses
Mr Wilson paid his employee a bonus of £100 in personal cash. This has not yet been recorded.	E2 Wages	C1 Capital (or C2 Drawings)

30.

Error	What error is	Example
Transposition	Two adjacent figures in an amount are reversed.	£243 recorded as £423.
Omission	An entry or part of an entry has been left out.	Invoice posted to *Creditors*, but the expense omitted or invoice left out altogether.
Principle	Some fundamental accounting principle has been contravened; often wrong class of account has been used.	Purchase invoice recorded in *Debtors* instead of *Creditors*.
Commission	Correct amount is entered in the wrong account, but it is the right class.	Invoice for petrol posted to *Heat and light*.
Compensating	Where by coincidence, errors are equal and opposite and the effect of one cancels out the effect of the other.	Invoice for £230 included as £320 and invoice for £870 included as £780.

31.

Description of error	Adjustment required to correct
Omission of part of an entry.	Missing entry needs to be included.
Error in the entry of one figure is an account.	Incorrect figure is amended.
Account balance incorrect.	The account should be correctly balanced.
Incorrect addition of column(s).	Amend addition

32.

Description of error	Adjustment required to correct
Reversal of debits and credits.	The original entry is eliminated and correct entry included.
Entry in wrong account (mistake or error in principle).	The original entry is eliminated and the correct entry included.
Omission of entry.	Enter transaction.
Incorrect figure used for both debit and credit.	Elimination of original entry and inclusion of correct entry.
Compensating error.	Correction of both errors.

33. Account used to temporarily balance a trial balance.

34. A debit balance goes to profit and loss account as an expense.

35. A credit balance goes to the balance sheet as a liability.

36. The following are possible errors in a computer system:

    - Reversal of debits and credits
    - Entry in wrong account
    - Omission of entry
    - Incorrect figure used for both debit and credit

37. A computer system does not let the other mistakes be made because it is good at additions and keeping a check on entries.

If you are having difficulties go back to Module 7 Section 8 of the disc.

Capital/revenue expenditure

38.

Error	Profit and loss account	Balance sheet
Item entered in *Cost of sales* instead of *Rent*	*Cost of sales* will be incorrect resulting in an incorrect gross profit; also the figure for *Rent* will be incorrect; the net profit will be correct	No effect
Item entered in *Rent* rather than *Motor vehicles*	Expenses would be too high, and net profit incorrect	Assets understated

39. Capital expenditure is expenditure to purchase or improve fixed assets (including such things as the delivery and installation costs).

40. Revenue expenditure is expenditure for running the business on a day-to-day basis (this will include the cost of repairing and maintaining fixed assets).

41. Capital expenditure is shown in the **balance sheet**

42. Revenue expenditure is shown in the **profit and loss account**

43.

	Capital expenditure	Revenue expenditure
Delivery costs for new machine	yes	
Repairs to buildings		yes
Additional computer	yes	
Insurance for new machine		yes
Replacement central heating		yes

Module 8

VAT

Introduction

This module deals with the subject of Value Added Tax (VAT). For the sake of simplicity, we have, so far, ignored VAT. From now on, however, we deal with things in a more realistic way and bring in VAT as appropriate. VAT is a very complex subject – we cover here only the basic rules of the tax, and how to account for it. Most countries have some similar tax, with a different name, and at a different rate. For this reason, and also so that you can see clearly how the VAT figure relates to the original, net of VAT, charge, we will use a 10% rate of VAT for most of this tutorial. The principles involved are exactly the same, it is only the VAT figure itself that will be different, depending on the actual rate of tax in use at the time in your particular country.

Learning objectives

The objectives of this module are to ensure that you:

* Know the basic rules of VAT.

* Understand the accounting entries required to record VAT.

Note form questions

General rules

The following questions relate to Module 8 Section 2 of AAT Bookkeeping Certificate.

These questions are in respect of a VAT registered trader unless otherwise stated.

1. What is output tax?

---

2. What is input tax?

---

3. What happens when output tax exceeds input tax?

---

4. What happens when input tax exceeds output tax?

---

5. What are the current rates of VAT?

---

6. If the cost of standard rated goods is £400, what is the gross price including VAT (at the current rate)?

---

7. Who does the VAT in question 6 belong to?

---

8. When is the above VAT accountable to the Customs and Excise?

---

9. What happens to the above VAT when the invoice is received by another business?

---

10. What is a zero-rated sale?

---

11. What happens to input tax when a business is zero-rated?

---

12. List five categories of goods that are zero-rated.

---

13. Give three examples of standard-rated goods.

---

14. How often are VAT returns prepared?

---

15. What is included on a VAT return?

---

16. If the VAT inclusive figure is given, how will the VAT be calculated?

If you are having difficulties go back to Module 8 Section 2 of the disc

Exceptions to general rules

The following questions relate to Module 8 Section 3 of AAT Bookkeeping Certificate

17. What are four exceptions to the general rules included in the previous section?

18. How does the calculation of VAT differ for a business that supplies exempt goods and services?

----

19. Into what two categories do goods and services supplied by businesses fall?

----

20. Give three examples of goods and services that are exempt.

----

21. Give an example when a business need not register for VAT.

----

22. What is the effect on a business of not being registered for VAT?

----

23. What is cash accounting?

----

24. Give two categories of input tax that are non-deductible.

----

25. What is the effect on the business of incurring non-deductible VAT on expenses?

----

26. How is VAT accounted for in other countries within the European Union?

If you are having difficulties go back to Module 8 Section 3 of the disc.

Accounting treatment

The following questions relate to Module 8 Section 5 of AAT Bookkeeping Certificate.

27. Fill in the T account below:

VAT account

28. When goods are sold the net amount is ....

29. The VAT on the sale is credited to ....

30. What is the effect of crediting output tax to the *VAT* account?

----

31. What is the accounting treatment when an invoice is received from a supplier?

----

32. What is the effect of charging the VAT on the expense to the *VAT* account?

----

33. What happens to the balance on the *VAT* account at the end of a quarter?

---

34. Fill in the following table.

Balance on VAT account	Due to/from Customs and Excise
Credit balance	
Debit balance	

If you are having difficulties go back to Module 8 Section 5 of the disc.

Three VAT Accounts

The following questions relate to Module 8 Section 7 of AAT Bookkeeping Certificate.

35. What would accounting procedures be if three VAT accounts were used?

---

36. Why can it be advantageous to keep three VAT accounts?

If you are having difficulties go back to Module 8 Section 7 of the disc.

SUMMARY

Adjustments

VAT is charged by many businesses on the goods and services they provide.

Output VAT is charged by a business on its sales. This is credited to the *VAT* account.

Input VAT is suffered by a business on goods and services it buys. This is debited to the *VAT* account.

VAT

Input VAT	Output VAT

If output VAT exceeds input VAT, the balance is due to be **paid** to HMRC.

If input VAT exceeds output VAT, the balance is due to be **recovered** from HMRC.

For a VAT rate of 17.5%:

	%
Net	100.0
VAT	17.5
Gross	117.5

In practice, it may be best to keep three VAT accounts:

* Input VAT

* Output VAT

* VAT liability

Review

In this module you have learnt that:

* VAT will be charged on the supply of most goods and services. This VAT is collected by a business on behalf of HMRC, to whom it must be paid over (after deduction of input VAT).

* A VAT account must be kept to record the liability to HMRC. VAT collected must be kept separate from the income of the business.

Answers

General rules

1. Output tax is the VAT charged on the selling price when a business provides goods and services.

2. When a business buys goods or services, input tax is the VAT charged by the supplier.

3. The excess of the output tax over the input tax is paid over periodically (usually every three months) to HMRC.

4. The difference is recovered periodically from HMRC.

5. The current rates are 17.5%, 0% and 5%.

6. The gross price = £400 × 1.175 = £470; VAT = £70

7. The £70 is due to be paid over to the HMRC.

8. VAT is accountable at the time the goods are invoiced.

9. The purchasing business is entitled to recover the VAT from the HMRC.

10. A sale when the applicable rate of VAT is zero.

11. The input tax will be recoverable in full.

12. Basic food, books and newspapers, public transport, children's clothes, exports outside EU.

13. Alcohol, sweets and chocolates, private hire and adult clothes.

14. The normal period of a VAT return is three months.

15. Total output VAT, total input VAT and the net amount due are entered, together with other statistical data.

16. VAT will be gross invoice value × 17.5/117.5 (or 7/47).

Exceptions to general rules

17. The exceptions are:

    *   Exempt goods and services
    *   Businesses not registered for VAT
    *   Accounting for VAT on a cash basis
    *   Non-deductible input tax

18. The business is exempt from VAT registration, and therefore is not allowed to charge output tax. These businesses cannot recover any input tax on their purchases.

19. The two categories are:

    - Taxable supplies (includes standard and zero rated)
    - Exempt supplies

20. Exempt goods include:

    - Betting
    - Finance
    - Postage

21. A businesses does not need to register for VAT until its turnover reaches a certain level – the VAT threshold.

22. If a business is not registered for VAT it does not charge VAT on outputs and it cannot recover VAT on inputs.

23. Cash accounting may be used by small businesses. The output tax is accounted for when the cash is received from the customer, and the input tax recovered when payment is made to the supplier.

24. Two examples are:

    - Entertaining expenses
    - Purchase of motor car, which will not be used totally for business use

25. The total amount of the expense including the VAT is recorded as a business expense.

26. VAT applies at different rates to all countries within the European Union.

Accounting treatment

27.

VAT account

Include VAT on expenses – Input tax	Include VAT on sales – Output tax

28. When goods are sold the net amount is **credited to** *Sales*.

29. The VAT on the sale is credited to the *VAT* account.

30. The effect of this credit is to record a liability that is due to HMRC.

31. The net amount will be debited to the appropriate expense account, and the VAT will be posted to the debit of the *VAT* account.

32. The effect is to reduce the liability due to HMRC.

33. At the end of a quarter the balance will be due to or from HMRC.

34.

Balance on VAT account	Due to/from HMRC
Credit balance	To HMRC
Debit balance	From HMRC

Three VAT accounts

35. The procedures are:

- Input tax is debited to the *Input tax* account

- Output tax is credited to the *Output tax* account

- Balances on *Input* and *Output tax* are transferred periodically to the *VAT liability* account (monthly or quarterly)

- The input tax will be figure of input tax included on the VAT return, and the output will be the figure of output tax to be included. The balance on the *VAT liability* account will be paid over to the HMRC, as shown by the amount due on the VAT return.

36. The use of three VAT accounts can be advantageous as the input and output tax figures are cleared periodically, and the amounts to be entered on the return are easy to identify. The amount due to HMRC is clearly shown on the *VAT liability* account.

Module 9

Accruals and prepayments

Introduction

You have now been introduced to the idea that various accounting adjustments may be necessary so that a realistic profit figure can be produced – you have already dealt with the adjustment for stock. We now deal with another, very commonly required, set of adjustments – accruals and prepayments. If an expense has been incurred, but not yet billed, it will not appear in the expense account. For example, electricity will have been used since the last bill was issued. This is an expense of the period, even though it has not yet been billed, and must therefore be included in the electricity expense figure – it is an accrued expense, and will be brought in by adjustment. Similarly, if an amount has been paid, but the figure relates to a future period, the amount must be excluded – it is a prepaid expense, for example, rent paid for the first month of the next accounting year.

There are two aspects of accruals and prepayments adjustments – firstly, arriving at the right figure to be adjusted, and, secondly, recording the adjustment correctly. There are many examples in the module for you to get plenty of practice in both aspects.

Accruals and prepayments adjustments are made so that the final figures in expense accounts are all the amounts that relate to the expenses incurred in that year, and only that year. This is an application of one of the basic concepts of accounting – the matching or accruals concept. The profit and loss account is a means of matching against the income for the year, all the expenses incurred in generating that income. We will see further applications of this concept in the next few modules.

Learning objectives

The objectives of this module are to ensure you:

- Understand the accruals concept.

- Are able to calculate the amount of an accrual and prepayment.

- Are able to record accruals and prepayments in the books by means of journal entries.

- Understand the subsequent reversal of prepayments and accruals.

Note form questions

Accruals concept

The following questions relate to Module 9 Section 2 of AAT Bookkeeping Certificate.

1. What does the matching or accruals concept require?

    ----

2. How does accruing or matching differ from the actual receipt of payment of expenses?

    ----

3. What does the term 'matched' mean?

    ----

4. As a result of the matching concept, how is profit calculated?

    ----

5. What anomalies can surround expenses at the year-end?

    ----

6. Why do adjustments have to be made for accruals and prepayments in the year-end accounts?

If you are having difficulties go back to Module 9 Section 2 of the disc.

Prepayments – First year

The following question relates to Module 9 Section 3 of AAT Bookkeeping Certificate.

7. Use the example from the software. A trader prepares accounts to June each year. On 1 March 2004 the trader moves to a new property and pays rent of £1,200 for a year in advance. How will this expense be shown in the trader's accounts at 30 June 2004?

8. What double entry is required to account for the payment and prepayment in question 7 above?

9. What happens to the *Rent* account when the profit and loss account is prepared for the above question?

10. Where is the *Prepayments* account shown in the year-end accounts?

If you are having difficulties go back to Module 9 Section 3 of the disc.

Prepayments – Second year

The following question relates to Module 9 Section 4 of AAT Bookkeeping Certificate.

11. Describe the accounting entries required in the year ended 30 June 2005, assuming a payment of £1,260 for a year has been made on 28 February 2005.

If you are having difficulties go back to Module 9 Section 4 of the disc.

Accruals – First year

The following questions relate to Module 9 Section 6 of AAT Bookkeeping Certificate.

12. Use the example from section 6.1 of the software. A trader makes up his accounts to 30 June. On 1 March 2004 he moves into a new property, but pays no rent until 15 July 2004, when he pays £1,200 for the year 1 March 2004 to 28 February 2005. Explain what figure will be shown for rent in the Accounts for the period ended 30 June 2004.

13. What double entry is required to account for the accrual in question 12 above?

14. What happens to the *Rent* account when the profit and loss account is prepared?

15. Explain where the accrual is shown on the balance sheet of the trader.

If you are having difficulties go back to Module 9 Section 6 of the disc.

Accruals – Second year

The following questions relate to Module 9 Section 7 of AAT Bookkeeping Certificate.

16. Describe the accounting entries required in the year ended 30 June 2005, assuming a rental payment of £1,260 for a year was made on 10 August 2005.

17. What is the value of the accrual and where is it shown?

If you are having difficulties go back to Module 9 Section 7 of the disc.

Miscellaneous points

The following questions relate to Module 9 Sections 8 and 9 of AAT Bookkeeping Certificate.

18. Suggest an alternative method to making individual journal entries for each accrual or prepayment when monthly accounts are being prepared.

----

19. Why would an organisation prepare monthly accounts?

----

20. What procedure is used to record accruals and prepayments at each month end?

21. How are the accruals and prepayments accounted for at the start of the next month?

22. Why is it essential that accruals and prepayments are included each month?

23. Describe two methods a computer system could use to process accruals and prepayments

24. How is the accounting fee usually accounted for in the year-end accounts?

25. What happens to VAT on accruals and prepayments?

26. What is accrued income?

27. What types of income are often accrued?

----

28. What accounting entries are necessary to account for accrued income?

----

29. How should sales made, but not yet invoiced be accounted for at the year-end?

If you are having difficulties go back to Module 9 Section 9 of the disc.

SUMMARY

The **accruals or matching concept** tells us that revenues and expenses are to be brought in to the profit & loss account in the period in which they are incurred.

ACCRUALS

Expenses are accrued when they have been incurred but not yet billed.

The expense accounts must be debited to increase the expense.

Expense 1			Expense 2		
Bal	XX		Bal	XX	
Accrual	XX		Accrual	XX	

The *accruals* account is credited to record the liability.

Accruals		
	Accruals	XX

PREPAYMENTS

Where expenses recorded in part relate to the following year, they must be reduced by a prepayment adjustment.

The expense accounts must be credited to reduce the expense.

Expense 1				Expense 2		
Bal	XX	Prepayment	XX	Bal	XX	Prepayment	XX

The *Prepayments* account is debited to record the asset of prepayments.

Prepayments	
Prepayments XX	

ACCRUED INCOME

Income can also be accrued: credit *Income* to increase the balance, debit *Sundry debtors* to record the asset.

Income			Sundry debtors	
	Balance	XX	Accrued income XX	
	Accrual	XX		

Review

In this module you have learnt that:

- The accruals or matching concept is fundamental to the drawing up of the profit and loss account.

- Expense figures in the profit and loss account should reflect the costs incurred for the year. To arrive at this position, accruals and prepayments adjustments are often necessary.

- Accruals and prepayments adjustments made in one year will affect the figures for the following year.

Answers

Accruals concept

1. The matching or accruals concept requires that revenue and costs are to be recognised when they are earned or incurred.

2. The matching concept means that income is included when it is earned, not when received, and that expenses are recognised as soon as they are incurred, not when paid.

3. 'Matched' means that revenues and costs are both included in the period to which they relate, and matched against each other in the profit and loss account for that period.

4. Profit is revenue for a period less all costs incurred in generating those revenues.

5. At the year-end there are usually expenses incurred that have not been billed, and other expenses that have been paid in advance.

6. These adjustments have to be made so that all the income and expenses of the year are included, and only of that year.

Prepayments – First year

7. £1,200 payment made in trader's accounts. The amount paid in advance 8/12 × £1200 = £800 will be shown as a prepayment, leaving £400 remaining as a rent expense in the year ended 30 June 2004.

8. The accounting entries are:

    *   Payment is debit *Rent*, credit *Bank* of £1,200
    *   Prepayment is credit *Rent*, debit *Prepayments* of £800

9. The *Rent* account has a balance of £400, which is transferred to the profit and loss account.

10. The *Prepayments* account is shown as an asset under *Current assets*, usually entered after *Debtors*, on the balance sheet.

Prepayments – Second year

11. The prepayment from year-end 30 June 2004 of £800 is reversed (debit *Rent*, credit *Prepayments*).

    The payment of £1,260 is made (debit *Rent*, credit *Bank*).

    The amount of the Prepayment £1,260 × 8/12 = £840 is transferred to *Prepayments* account (credit *Rent*, debit *Prepayments*).

    This leaves a balance on the *Rent* account to be transferred to profit and loss account of £1,220.

    The prepayment of £840 is shown under *Current assets* on the balance sheet at 30 June 2005.

Accruals – First year

12. The rent figure will be £1,200 × 4/12 = £400 (rent for period 1 March 2004 to 30 June 2004.

13. The entries are debit *Rent* with £400, and credit *Accruals* with the same amount.

14. The *Rent* account has a balance of £400, which is transferred to the profit and loss account.

15. The accrual is shown as a *Current liability* usually after *Trade creditors*.

Accruals – Second year

16. The accrual from 2004 is first reversed – debit *Accruals*, credit *Rent*.

    The payment of rent is then made – debit *Rent*, credit *Bank*.

    At 30 June 2005 the accrual at the end of the period is calculated £1,260 × 8/12 = £420 - this amount will be debited to *Rent*, credited to *Accruals*.

    The balance on the *Rent* account – £1220 is transferred to profit and loss account.

17. The accrual is £420 and it is shown as an *Accrual* under *Current liabilities* on the balance sheet.

Miscellaneous points

18. Several accruals or prepayments can be entered as one journal entry instead of making several entries.

19. Monthly accounts are prepared so that the business can be monitored on a regular basis.

20. Accruals and prepayments are calculated at the end of each month and entered in the nominal ledger before the monthly accounts are prepared.

21. The accruals and prepayment are reversed at the start of the next month.

22. If accruals and prepayments are not included then the accounts will not reflect the true income and expenditure and might not be meaningful.

23. a. Accruals and prepayments in some computerised systems are entered by means of special month end journal routines, the reversing being carried out automatically.

    b. Prepayments may be set up when the payment is made, and each month a defined portion is transferred to the appropriate expense account.

24. An accrual is set up for the estimated costs of the accounting fee.

25. Accruals and prepayments deal with the actual expense recording. VAT on prepayments has already been dealt with when the original payment was made, and for accruals there is no liability yet as no invoice has been received.

26. Accrued income arises when an income account does not include all the income earned for the year.

27. Rent and interest receivable are often accrued.

28. Credit to the *Income* account and a debit to *Sundry debtors*.

29. Credit to the *Sales* account and a debit to *Sundry debtors*.

Module 10

Wages and salaries

Introduction

Often, one of the largest expense figures in the profit and loss account is the *Wages and salaries* figure. The recording of wages and salaries is not usually as simple as debiting the expense account with the amounts paid. In most countries, wages and salaries are paid after deducting tax, and perhaps some other statutory amount, such as UK national insurance contributions. Our main concern is how to account for these various deductions and payments, so that the full expense of employing individuals appears in the profit and loss account. To give some understanding of the accounting required, we firstly outline the UK deduction system. We then see how best to record the full wages and salaries cost as an expense, and any deductions made, not yet paid over, as a liability.

Businesses with any number of employees will now usually calculate wages and salaries using computerised payroll systems. Special aspects of this, in particular, the use of a *Wages control* account, are covered in the last part of the module.

We will see the recording of payments relating to wages and salaries when we deal with the cash book, in the *Practical bookkeeping* unit.

Learning objectives

The objectives of this module are to ensure you:

- Understand the basis of the UK deduction system for tax and national insurance.

- Are able to record the various elements of pay in the appropriate ledger accounts.

- Become familiar with the use of a *Wages control* account in a computerised system.

Note form questions

Deductions systems – Tax and NI

The system described in this module refers to the UK system for tax and national insurance

The following questions relate to Module 10 Section 2 of AAT Bookkeeping Certificate.

1. When will there be no deductions for either tax or national insurance?

....

....

2. If the amount an employee is paid is below the tax and national insurance limits, what accounting entries are required?

....

3. Fill in the bubbles below, describing key facts about each item.

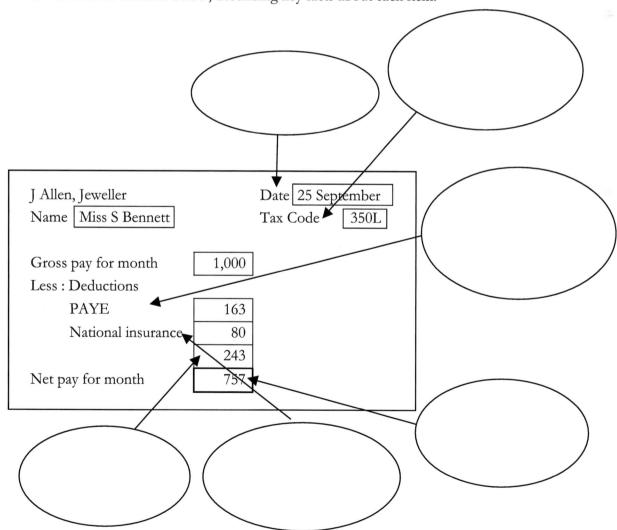

J Allen, Jeweller

Name | Miss S Bennett

Date | 25 September

Tax Code | 350L

Gross pay for month	1,000
Less : Deductions	
PAYE	163
National insurance	80
	243
Net pay for month	757

4.   Who is responsible for the calculation of PAYE?

----

5.   How is employee's and employer's national insurance calculated?

----

6.   How is the national insurance figure calculated?

----

7.   Who remits the total deductions and to whom?

----

8.   When are the deductions paid to the Inland Revenue?

----

9.   What is a tax code?

----

10. What is meant by the term 'tax-free' pay?

----

11. What is the employer's national insurance contribution?

----

12. How does employer's national insurance differ from employee's national insurance?

----

13. How is the amount payable to the Revenue made up in Section 2.4 of the software?

14. What two elements make up the salary cost?

----

15. What is the date by which the payment to the Revenue must be made?

If you are having difficulties go back to Module 10 Section 2 of the disc.

Double entry

The following questions relate to Module 10 Section 3 of AAT Bookkeeping Certificate.

16. What amounts need to be paid out for salaries and to whom?

----

17. What accounting entries are necessary to record an employee's salary?

If you are having difficulties go back to Module 10 Section 3 of the disc.

General points

The following questions relate to Module 10 Section 5 of AAT Bookkeeping Certificate.

18. What three stages should be followed when recording salaries transactions?

----

19. Apart from monthly, what other intervals are often used to pay wages?

----

20. How are wages of employees summarised?

----

21. What method is often used to operate a pension scheme?

----

22. Describe the accounting treatment that will record pension payments.

23. What happens to the *employer's national insurance* account at the year-end?

24. Where can employer's national insurance be shown in the profit and loss account?

25. How are salaries and wages affected by VAT?

If you are having difficulties go back to Module 10 Section 5 of the disc.

Ledger accounts variations

The following questions relate to Module 10 Section 6 of AAT Bookkeeping Certificate.

26. In which two accounts can the *Revenue creditor* be split?

27. Why can it be advantageous to split the *Revenue creditor* into two accounts?

28. How does the use of two *Revenue Creditor* accounts change the accounting entries required?

29. If no *Revenue creditor* account is kept, explain the entries required.

    ----

30. Explain the possible problem at the end of the month if no creditor account is kept.

    ----

31. Why may this not affect small businesses?

    ----

32. When is it essential that an adjustment is required for any outstanding PAYE and national insurance?

    ----

33. How is the year-end adjustment made?

If you are having difficulties go back to Module 10 Section 6 of the disc.

Computerised payrolls

The following questions relate to Module 10 Section 10 of AAT Bookkeeping Certificate.

34. How do the accounting entries change when a wages system is an integrated computerised system?

    ----

35. Why is a *Wages control* account used with a computerised wages system?

    ----

36. What entries will be included in the *Wages control* account?

If you are having difficulties go back to Module 10 Section 10 of the disc.

SUMMARY

Employees receive their pay after the deduction of income tax (PAYE) and national insurance (unless they are below the tax and NI thresholds).

In addition the employer must pay employer's NI

Deductions and employer's NI contributions are due to be paid to the Revenue during the following month

Accounting for wages and salaries

There are several different ways of accounting for wages.

It is clearest to make three entries:

1.	Payment of net wages	Debit	*Wages and salaries* (expense)
		Credit	*Bank*
2.	Record employee's Deductions	Debit	*Wages and salaries* (expense)
		Credit	*Revenue* (liability)
3.	Record employer's NI	Debit	*Employer's NI* (expense)
		Credit	*Revenue* (liability)

Wages control account

Wages control account

Net pay paid	XX	Net pay from payroll	XX

Review

In this module you have learnt that:

- Employees will be paid their wages/salaries net of tax and NI deducted. In addition, the employer is due to pay employer's NI.

- The profit and loss expense figures must include the full cost of employing personnel.

- The balance sheet must show the full liability to the Revenue for tax and NI and the pension creditor, if any.

- A wages control account will give a check within the accounting system that the net pay actually paid equals the pay due, as calculated by the payroll system.

Answers

Deductions systems – Tax and NI

1. If an employee's pay falls below the limits for both tax and national insurance there will be no deductions.

2. The accounting records are debit to *Wages*, credit to *Bank*.

3.

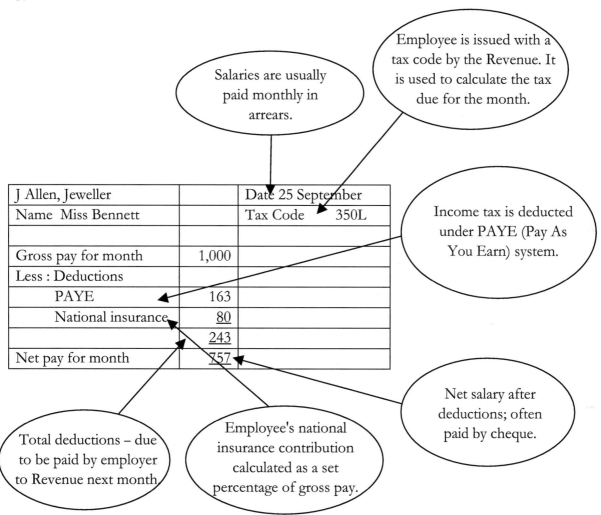

4. The employer calculates the amount of tax due and pays it over to the Revenue.

5. The employee's national insurance contribution is calculated as a percentage of gross pay. Employer's NI is also a percentage of gross profit.

6. It is calculated either from tables issued by the Government or by a computerised payroll system containing the same information as the tables.

7. The total deductions should be paid over by the employer on behalf of all employees to the Revenue.

8. The deductions should be paid over during the month following the salary payment.

9. The tax code is an alpha numeric code which takes account of a person's annual allowances. It is used to calculate the tax-free pay for the month (or pay period).

10. Tax-free pay is the amount a person can earn before any tax need be deducted.

11. Employer's national insurance is an additional amount, over and above the employee's gross pay, that has to be paid to the government by the employer.

12. Employee's national insurance is deducted from an employee's salary and paid over to the Revenue on their behalf. Employer's national insurance is an extra amount the employer must pay to the Inland Revenue.

13.

PAYE	163
National insurance	
Employee's	80
Employer's	<u>102</u>
	<u>345</u>

14. Gross salary + employer's national insurance.

15. The payment must be made by 19th of the month following.

Double entry

16. To the employee – net pay.
    To the Revenue – the tax deducted, and all the national insurance (employees' and employer's).

17. Debit *Wages and salaries*, credit *Bank* with net pay.
    Debit *Wages and salaries*, credit *Revenue* with deductions from salaries.
    Debit *Wages and salaries*, credit *Revenue* with employer's national insurance.
    Debit *Revenue*,   credit *Bank* with amount due to Revenue.

General points

18. The payment of salary.
    Recording the deductions from the employee's salary.
    Recording the employer's NI.

19. Wages can be paid on a weekly, two weekly or four weekly basis.

20. Wages are summarised in a wages book or on a wages sheet.

21. Often operated similar to national insurance with the employee making a contribution (maybe a fixed percentage of pay) and employer making a further contribution (again this may be a fixed percentage of pay).

22   Recording pension payments

- Deduction from employee's pay is debited to *Wages* credited to *Pension company* account as a creditor.

- The employer's pension contribution is debited to *Pensions expense* credited to *Pension creditor.*

- When the payment is made, the amount is debited to *Pension company* account and credited to the *Bank.*

23.   The employer's national insurance account is cleared to the profit and loss account.

24.   The amount can be either be shown as a separate item or included within the *Wages and salaries* figure.

25.   Salaries and wages are unaffected by VAT, being outside the scope.

Ledger accounts variations

26.   The *Revenue creditor* can be split into accounts for *PAYE* and *NI* creditors.

27.   These accounts show separately the amount due to the Inland Revenue for tax and NI.

28.   Instead of crediting *Revenue creditor* account the following entries will be made:

PAYE deductions: credit to *R – PAYE*
NI deductions: credit to *R – NI*
Employer's NI: credit to *R – NI*

29.   All payments for wages and salaries will be debited to the *Wages and salaries* account – the net pay followed by the amount paid to the Revenue.

30.   The creditor may be overlooked within the accounting records at the month end.

31.   Small businesses might not be affected, as they may not prepare monthly accounts.

32.   An adjustment for the creditor is necessary at the year-end.

33.   The accounting entries are debit to *Wages and salaries* with the unpaid PAYE and national insurance, and credit to *Sundry creditors*. This entry will be reversed at the start of the following year.

Computerised payrolls

34   In an integrated system the postings to the nominal ledger are made automatically from the payroll program.

35.   The *Wages control* account provides a check that the right amount of wages have been paid, and that the wages payments are being properly included in the deduction system.

36.   The net pay actually paid will be debited, and the net pay calculated from the payroll will be credited.

Module 11

Fixed assets and depreciation

Introduction

In Module 9, you met the accruals or matching concept – in the profit and loss account, we match, against the income for the year, all the costs incurred in generating that income. One of the costs involved will be the provision of the fixed assets in use in the business. We have, so far, simply recorded the cost, of for example a piece of machinery, as an asset in the balance sheet. The machinery does not, however, last forever and cannot remain indefinitely in the balance sheet at its original cost. The asset will be wearing out, or **depreciating**. It is this cost that must be charged against profits.

We do not try to value the assets at the end of each year, charging any reduction in value as an expense. What we do is rather simpler – we decide, at the outset, on some means of apportioning the original cost of the asset as a charge against profits over the number of years that we expect to be using the asset. This will be our selected method and rate of depreciation. The simplest of these methods is straight-line depreciation. For example, if we purchase an asset for £1,000 and expect it to be in use for 10 years, we would charge £1000/10 = £100 depreciation each year (assuming we expect it to have no value at the end of the 10 years – zero residual value).

The other commonly used method of depreciation, also covered in the module, is the reducing balance method. Using this method, the depreciation charge is higher in earlier years, and the asset's value never reduces to zero. There are several other methods of depreciation that are not covered in the tutorial – these, however, are not commonly used, straight-line and reducing balance being the most commonly used methods.

It often happens that an asset is not kept in use for the full expected life estimated when it was acquired, or even if it is, it may be sold at that point for an amount quite different to the residual value estimated at the outset. When an asset is disposed of, there will usually be some gain or loss on disposal – the difference between the value in the books (the original amount less all depreciation charged to date) and the proceeds of the sale. At this point any figures relating to the asset sold must be removed from the asset accounts, with any gain or loss on disposal appearing in the profit and loss account.

In showing assets in this way in the balance sheet, at cost less depreciation charged to date, we are applying several accounting concepts and principles. These are covered in the final section of this module. You should remember, however, that these principles apply throughout everything that you are learning about bookkeeping and accounts.

Learning objectives

The objectives of this module are to ensure you:

- Understand the reason for depreciation.

- Are able to compute depreciation using straight-line and reducing balance methods.

- Know how to record depreciation in accounts.

- Are able to record the disposals of assets.

- Are aware of various underlying accounting concepts and conventions.

Note form questions

Depreciation

The following questions relate to Module 11 Section 2 of AAT Bookkeeping Certificate.

1. What are fixed assets?

    ----

2. In what order are fixed assets listed in the balance sheet?

    ----

3. What are current assets?

    ----

4. In what order are current assets listed in the balance sheet?

    ----

5. Give an example of a fixed asset that often appreciates in value.

    ----

6.   What happens to most fixed assets during their period of use in the business?

7.   What is the cost to the business during their period of use?

8.   What does the matching or accruals concept say?

9.   What is depreciation?

10.   Describe how the depreciation charge is calculated in Section 2.3 of the software.

If you are having difficulties go back to Module 11 Section 2 of the disc.

Methods of depreciation

The following questions relate to Module 11 Section 3 of AAT Bookkeeping Certificate.

11.   Which is one of the most common and simplest method of depreciation?

12.   What is a commonly used view of the residual value?

13.   What is the effect of ignoring any residual value?

14. What is the depreciation charge if an asset is used beyond its useful economic life?

----

15. What is the other commonly used method of depreciation?

----

16. On what is the reducing balance method calculated?

----

17. What is the formula that will calculate the net book value of a fixed asset?

18. What is the effect of using the reducing balance method of depreciation?

----

19. Who decides which depreciation method and rate should be used?

----

20. Why is the net book value not an estimate of the market value of the fixed asset?

----

21. What are capital allowances?

----

22. How much depreciation is it usual to charge in the year a fixed asset is bought?

----

23. How much depreciation is it usual to charge in the year a fixed asset is sold?

----

24. What procedure is normally followed for depreciation when monthly accounts are prepared?

If you are having difficulties go back to Module 11 Section 3 of the disc.

This space has been left for making notes, if required, regarding the examples included in Section 4 of the software.

Double entry – Purchase of assets

The following questions relate to Module 11 Section 5 of AAT Bookkeeping Certificate.

25. How is the purchase of a fixed asset recorded?

----

26. When is VAT included in the cost of a fixed asset as shown on the balance sheet?

----

27. What happens to VAT on most motor cars?

----

28. At what cost will a VAT registered trader record the purchase of vans or lorries?

----

29. What accounting entries are required for machinery bought on credit costing £10,000 plus VAT of £1,000?

If you are having difficulties go back to Module 11 Section 5 of the disc.

Double entry – Depreciation

The following questions relate to Module 11 Section 6 of AAT Bookkeeping Certificate.

30. What is included within the *Depreciation* (expense) account?

----

31. Using the simple approach of 6.1, what accounting entries are made in order to record the depreciation charge in the accounting records?

----

32. What happens to the balance on the *Depreciation* (expense) account?

----

33. What happens to the balance on the asset account?

----

34. What is the problem of recording the balance on the asset account at the net book value?

----

35. How can the problem in question 34 be overcome?

----

36. Describe how depreciation should be included in the accounting records using the method described in your answer to question 35.

----

37. How should the motor vehicle be included on the balance sheet?

If you are having difficulties go back to Module 11 Section 6 of the disc.

Double entry – Disposal of asset

The following questions relate to Module 11 Section 7 of AAT Bookkeeping Certificate.

38. When is VAT charged on the sale proceeds of a fixed asset disposal?

39. In what two circumstances is VAT not added to the sale proceeds?

40. What accounting entries are made when a motor car is sold?

41. What is the meaning of the final balance on the *Disposal of assets* account?

42. What do any balances left on the *Motor vehicle – cost* and *Motor vehicle – accumulated depreciation* accounts represent?

43. What happens to the gain or loss on disposal of fixed assets at the year end?

44. How does scrapping a fixed asset differ from selling a fixed asset?

If you are having difficulties go back to Module 11 Section 7 of the disc.

Accounting concepts and conventions

The following questions relate to Module 11 Section 10 of AAT Bookkeeping Certificate.

45. What is the historical cost convention?

46. Explain how the historical cost convention has been applied in depreciating assets.

47. What is the stable money concept?

48. What is the situation if the currency is not stable?

49. If the currency is not stable, what type of accounting might have to be used?

50. Which assets might be revalued?

51. Why do revalued assets need to be depreciated?

52. What other two main accounting concepts does depreciation apply?

53. Explain how the going concern concept has been applied in depreciating assets.

....

54. Explain how the accruals/matching concept has been applied in depreciating assets.

....

....

55. Explain how the comparability concept has been applied in depreciating assets?

....

....

If you are having difficulties go back to Module 11 Section 10 of the disc.

SUMMARY

Depreciation

Depreciation is a method of allocating the net cost of assets (ie cost less residual value) to the years in which they are expected to be in use.

Cost is the expenditure on a fixed asset including delivery costs etc.

Net Book Value (NBV) or Written Down Value (WDV)
= the cost – accumulated depreciation

Accumulated depreciation is the depreciation that has previously been written off the cost of a fixed asset

Straight-line depreciation

Depreciation = % × Cost

Reducing balance depreciation

Depreciation = % × Written down value

To record depreciation	Dr	Cr
Depreciation expense	xx	
Asset – accumulated depreciation		xx

Disposals

Disposals account

Asset – cost	xx	Proceeds	xx
Profit and loss account – gain	xx	Asset – accumulated depreciation	xx
	xx		xx

a)   Record proceeds

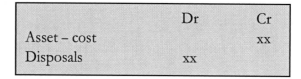

Proceeds – credit *Disposals* account

b)   Transfer cost

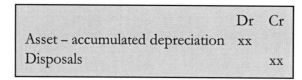

	Dr	Cr
Asset – cost		xx
Disposals	xx	

c)   Transfer accumulated depreciation

	Dr	Cr
Asset – accumulated depreciation	xx	
Disposals		xx

Balance on *Disposals* account is the gain (or loss) on sale to be transferred to the profit and loss account.

Accounting concepts and conventions

In stating fixed assets at net book value, the following concepts, conventions and desirable qualities have been applied:

a)   Historical cost convention

Transactions are recorded at their value at the time of occurrence.

b)   Going concern concept

The enterprise will continue in existence for the foreseeable future.

c)   Accruals concept

Non-cash effects of transactions and other events should be reflected in the financial statements for the accounting period in which they occur.

d)   Comparability

There is consistency of accounting treatment of like items within each accounting period and from one period to the next.

Review

In this module you have learnt that:

- The cost of providing fixed assets should be charged against profits over the useful life of the assets.

- Cost is allocated over the life of an asset by charging depreciation. This can be calculated in several ways, the most common being straight line and reducing balance methods.

- Separate ledger accounts are kept to record the accumulated depreciation on different classes of assets.

- When an asset is disposed of, any figures relating to it must be removed from the asset accounts.

- In stating fixed assets in the balance sheet at their written down value, several accounting concepts, conventions and desirable qualities are being applied.

Answers

Depreciation

1.   Fixed assets are assets purchased by a business for long-term use in the business.

2.   Listed in order of permanence, for example:

  *   Property
  *   Plant and machinery
  *   Fixtures and fittings
  *   Motor vehicles

3.   Current assets are those that turn over frequently during the year. They are thought of as being held as cash or with a view to converting into cash in the short term.

4.   Listed in order of permanence:

  *   Stock
  *   Debtors
  *   Prepayments
  *   Bank deposit account
  *   Bank current account
  *   Cash

5.   Property often appreciates in value.

6.   The value of most fixed assets is considerably reduced during their period of use in the business.

7.   The cost to the business is the original cost less any residual value at the end of the period.

8.   The matching or accruals concept says that revenues and costs should be matched to the periods to which they relate.

9.   Depreciation is mechanism of attributing, allocating, sharing the cost of the asset over the periods during which it is used.

10. Depreciation charge $= \dfrac{\text{cost of fixed asset} - \text{residual value}}{\text{number of years assets used}}$

Methods of depreciation

11. The straight-line method is one of the most common and simplest methods of depreciation.

12. The residual value is often ignored as it is thought to be too small.

13. The effect of ignoring the residual value is that the value of the asset will be reduced to nil at the end of its useful economic life.

14. There will be no depreciation charge as the asset has already been fully depreciated.

15. Reducing balance method is the other commonly used method of depreciation.

16. The depreciation rate is applied to the net book value (cost less residual value).

17. NBV = cost × $(1 - r)^n$ where n = no of years and r the depreciation rate.

18. The effect is that depreciation charged in earlier years is greater than that charged in later years.

19. The owners/managers of the business itself decide which method and rate should be used.

20. The net book value is the value of the asset to the business.

21. Capital allowances are specific rates set by Government and used to calculate depreciation for tax purposes.

22. A full year's depreciation is usually charged in year a fixed asset is bought.

23. Depreciation is not normally charged in the year a fixed asset is sold.

24. Depreciation is normally charged in the month of purchase, but not in the month of sale.

Double entry – Purchase of assets

25. It is debited to the appropriate *Fixed asset* account and credited to *Bank* or *Creditors*.

26. VAT is included in the cost of the fixed asset when the business is not registered for VAT.

27. The VAT on most motor cars is not recoverable, therefore the cost as shown on the balance sheet will be inclusive of VAT.

28. Vans and lorries are recorded net of VAT.

29. Debit *Machinery* 10,000, debit *VAT* 1,000 and credit *Creditors* with 11,000.

Double entry – Depreciation

30. The provision for the reduction in the value of the asset to the business over the trading period is included in the *Depreciation* (expense) account.

31. The entries are debit *Depreciation* (expense) account and credit *Motor car* account.

32. The balance on the *Depreciation* (expense) account is transferred to the profit and loss account, at the same time as all the other expenses.

33. The balance on the asset account is included in the balance sheet and carried forward to the next accounting period.

34. Recording the asset at the net book value makes it difficult to ascertain the original cost and depreciation of the asset.

35. The problem can be overcome by keeping separate accounts for the original cost of the asset and the accumulated depreciation.

36. Debit *Depreciation* (expense) account credit *Motor car – accumulated depreciation* account with the depreciation charge for the year.

37. The motor vehicle will be included at cost less accumulated depreciation to give the net book value.

Double entry – Disposal of asset

38. VAT is added when the asset is sold by a trader who is registered for VAT.

39. When a trader is not registered for VAT or if the asset being sold is a car.

40. • Debit *Bank* or *Debtors*, credit *Disposal of fixed assets* with the proceeds of sale.

    • Debit *Disposal of assets*, credit *Motor car – cost* with the original cost of the fixed asset sold.

    • Debit *Motor car – Accumulated depreciation*, credit *Disposal of assets* with the accumulated depreciation.

41. The balance is a gain or loss on sale of the fixed assets and can be considered to be an adjustment to the depreciation charged on them.

42. The cost and accumulated depreciation relate to any remaining vehicles.

43. The gain or loss on disposal of fixed assets is shown in the profit and loss account – it can either be shown separately from *Depreciation* or the two figures can sometimes be aggregated.

44. The entries are the same except that there are no proceeds of sale.

Accounting concepts and conventions

45. The historical cost convention requires that transactions be recorded at their value at the time of occurrence.

46. Assets are valued at their historical cost (as depreciated) rather their resale value or replacement cost.

47. Stable money concept is the presenting of figures in accounts in a reasonably stable currency.

48. If the currency is not stable, the historical cost accounts will not give a true picture.

49. In these circumstances it will be necessary to use inflation accounting.

50. Property is the asset that is most often revalued.

51. Revalued assets need to be depreciated so that the cost of providing the asset is charged against the profits of the appropriate years.

52. The going concern and accruals concepts.

53. If the enterprise was not to continue to exist for the foreseeable future then the assets would be shown at their break-up value.

54. The cost of an asset relates to many accounting periods over which it is used. Its cost is therefore spread over these periods and matched against the income it is helping to generate.

55. Once a depreciation method has been selected it should be used consistently to give comparability in accounts.

Module 12

Leasing and hire purchase

Introduction

This module continues from the previous one, in that it deals with further issues relating to fixed assets. Often, when a business comes to the point that it needs a new asset, it does not have funds in the bank to pay for it. There will then be other options open to the business. It could, for example, get a loan from the bank to buy the asset. More commonly, it could acquire the asset under a hire purchase agreement, or some kind of leasing agreement.

Hire purchase is fairly straightforward – the asset is owned by the hire purchase company, to whom the business makes regular payments to cover the capital cost plus the additional hire purchase charges. Meanwhile, however, the business treats the asset as its own, and this is in fact how it is treated in the accounting records. The asset appears on the balance sheet of the business, even though it does not legally yet own the asset.

Many leasing agreements (finance leases) are very similar to hire purchase agreements – they will be treated in the same way in the accounts. Other leases (operating leases) are more like hire charges – they will simply be charged as an expense in the profit and loss account.

One of the problems in accounting for hire purchase and finance leases is how to split the payments (often monthly payments) to the finance company, between the repayment of capital and the interest/charges being levied by the company. We use here the simplest, straight-line method, where the total charges per the agreement are divided evenly over the number of instalments.

Having covered the various accounting adjustments and methods of recording special types of transactions in this *Accounting adjustments* unit, you will be ready to think about how all of this is actually recorded in the books in a business. The next section, *Practical bookkeeping and final accounts*, covers this in detail.

Learning objectives

The objectives of this module are to ensure you:

- Are aware of the different ways in which an asset purchase may be financed.

- Understand the difference between operating leases and finance leases.

- Know how to record the acquisition of an asset on hire purchase and the subsequent repayments.

Note form questions

Introduction

The following questions relate to Module 12 Section 2 of AAT Bookkeeping Certificate.

1. List four methods of acquiring an asset when the business does not have the cash immediately available.

    ----

2. How does a company enter into a lease?

    ----

3. With a lease agreement who purchases the asset?

    ----

4. Who retains the ownership of the asset?

    ----

5. How does the business pay to use the asset?

    ----

6. How is VAT charged on the transaction?

    ----

7. What are two categories of leases?

    ----

8. What is an operating lease?

9.   What is a finance lease?

If you are having difficulties go back to Module 12 Section 2 of the disc.

Leasing

The following questions relate to Module 12 Section 3 of AAT Bookkeeping Certificate.

10. Why are asset accounts not affected by an operating lease?

----

11. How are operating leases accounted for?

----

12. What accounting entries are required to record the initial payment on an operating lease?

----

13. How are subsequent payments recorded?

----

14. At the year-end what happens to the balance on the leasing account?

----

15. How is the prepayment on the leasing account calculated at the year-end?

----

16. What is the accounting entry required to record the prepayment?

----

17. Give three pieces of information that might be contained within a lease agreement.

If you are having difficulties go back to Module 12 Section 3 of the disc.

Bank loans and overdrafts

The following questions relate to Module 12 Section 4 of AAT Bookkeeping Certificate.

18. What is a business able to do if it has a bank overdraft limit?

----

19. How is interest charged on an overdraft?

----

20. What accounting entries are required to enter bank interest?

----

21. How is bank interest paid dealt with at the year-end?

----

22. Why might it be better to obtain a loan rather than an overdraft for long-term finance?

----

23. What are the accounting entries necessary to record a bank loan and the repayments?

BPP
PROFESSIONAL EDUCATION

24. What two methods can be used to pay the interest on the loan?

----

25. When might it be necessary to include an accrual on the loan interest account?

If you are having difficulties go back to Module 12 Section 4 of the disc.

Hire purchase

The following questions relate to Module 12 Section 5 of AAT Bookkeeping Certificate.

26. What is a hire purchase contract?

----

27. When does the legal title pass on a hire purchase contract?

----

28. Explain how the substance of the transaction is used, rather than the form, in recording a hire purchase agreement.

----

29. What accounting entries are required when a hire purchase agreement is signed?

----

30. What are hire purchase charges?

----

31. Describe the meaning of these hire purchase terms.

Term	Description
Cash price	
Deposit	
Interest	
Monthly repayments	
Amount of credit	

32. Why is the true rate of interest higher than the actual interest quoted in a hire purchase agreement?

----

33. What is the easiest method of allocating interest over the period of the hire purchase agreement?

----

34. Note down the accounting entries and final accounts disclosure for a hire purchase agreement.

Event	Accounting entries
Payment of deposit	
Signing HP agreement	
Repayments	
Depreciation	
Expense entry in profit and loss account	
Balance sheet asset/liability	

35. If VAT has been charged on an asset bought under a hire purchase agreement, how will it be accounted for by a registered trader?

If you are having difficulties go back to Module 12 Section 5 of the disc.

SUMMARY

Where a new asset is required in a business that is short of funds, the business may:

- Lease the asset
- Increase/obtain a bank overdraft
- Obtain a bank or other loan
- Take out a hire purchase contract.

Leases can be either:

- **Operating leases** – where the lessee is effectively renting the asset.

- **Finance leases** – where the lessee effectively pays for the asset over the period of the lease.

Acquisition under hire purchase

		Dr	Cr
Payment of deposit	Asset – cost	x	
	VAT	x	
	Bank		x
Balance of cost on credit (not to include interest/charges)	Asset – cost	xx	
	HP creditor		xx
Subsequent repayments	HP interest	x	
	HP creditor	x	
	Bank		x

Review

In this module you have learnt that:

- There are several different ways of financing the purchase of an asset.

- Operating leases and finance leases are of a different nature, and must be accounted for differently.

- Accounting for the acquisition of an asset under a hire purchase agreement follows the substance, rather than the legal form of the transaction.

- Repayments under a hire purchase, or finance lease, agreement must be split into capital and interest elements.

Answers

Introduction

1. The four methods are:

    *   Leasing the asset
    *   Increasing/obtaining a bank overdraft to buy the asset
    *   Obtaining a bank or other loan to buy the asset
    *   Taking out a hire purchase contract.

2. The company will enter into a leasing agreement with a leasing company.

3. The leasing company purchases the asset.

4. The leasing company retains the ownership of the asset.

5. The business pays an agreed amount, usually monthly or quarterly to the leasing company.

6. The leasing company charges VAT on the full amount of the lease payments.

7. The two categories of leases are operating and finance leases.

8. An operating lease is where the lessee is really renting the asset.

9. A finance lease is where the total amount paid to the lessor over the period of the lease is equivalent to paying the full cost of the asset together with a finance charge.

Leasing

10. Asset accounts are not affected as the business does not own the asset, and has no intention of acquiring it.

11. The amounts payable under an operating lease are a business expense.

12. The accounting entries are debit *Leasing* with the payment less VAT (assuming the trader is registered for VAT), debit *VAT* account with the VAT, and credit the *Bank* with the payment.

13. In a similar manner to the initial payment.

14. At the year-end, the balance on the leasing account is transferred to the profit and loss account.

15. It is necessary to calculate the number of months the agreement has been in operation to determine the expense for the period. Any payments in excess of this will be carried forward as a prepayment.

16. The accounting entry is debit *Prepayments*, credit *Leasing.*

17. The following information would be included within a lease agreement.

    *   Period of the lease
    *   Conditions for ending lease early.
    *   Conditions about the termination of lease

Bank loans and overdrafts

18. The business is able to spend up to that overdraft limit.

19. Interest calculated by the bank on a daily basis and charged in arrears, usually monthly.

20. The accounting entries are debit *Bank interest*, credit *Bank*.

21. An accrual is usually necessary from the last charging point to the year-end. This can be either estimated or an exact figure can be obtained from the bank.

22. Long-term finance is generally better obtained in the form of a loan. Loans are more controllable as they are taken out for a set period.

23. A *Loan* account will be required. The loan will be credited to the *Loan* account and debited to the *Bank* account. The repayments will be debited to the *Loan* account and credited to the *Bank* account.

24. Interest on the loan may be either added to the balance of the loan or separately charged in the current account.

25. An accrual might be included on the loan account if interest has not be charged up to the date of the year-end.

Hire purchase

26. A hire purchase contract is one for the hire of an asset, which the hirer intends to acquire for ownership, usually by payment of a small acceptance fee with the last instalment.

27. The title passes when all the instalments have been paid.

28. The hire purchase agreement is treated as the acquisition of an asset at the beginning of the agreement, and the receipt of a loan at the same time.

29. The asset is capitalised (debit *Asset* account, credit *Hire purchase* account) and will be depreciated in the normal way. The loan is included as a hire purchase creditor.

30. These are charges by the finance company for hire purchase interest.

31.

Term	Description
Cash price	Basic price of the asset acquired
Deposit	Deposit paid at outset of agreement
Interest	HP interest/charges applied to original cash price
Monthly repayments	Partly repayment of capital and partly payment on interest/charges.
Amount of credit	Hire purchase loan

32. The rate quoted is the rate applied to the amount of credit (cash price less deposit) for the number of years of the agreement. However, throughout the period of the loan repayments are being made, so the capital amount outstanding will be constantly reducing.

33. The easiest method is to spread the interest evenly over the period of the hire purchase agreement.

34.

Event	Accounting entries
Payment of deposit	Debit *Asset* Credit *Bank* with amount of deposit
Signing HP agreement	Debit *Asset* Credit *HP creditor* with balance of cost
Repayments	Debit *HP creditor* (with capital repayment portion) Debit *HP interest* (with interest portion) Credit *Bank* with total payment
Depreciation	Depreciate asset in normal manner
Expense entry in profit and loss account	Transfer of balance in *HP interest* account - charges for the period
Balance sheet asset/liability	Asset less depreciation *HP creditor* split into current liability (amount to be paid in the next year) and the long-term liability

35. The *VAT* account will be debited with the total VAT when the deposit is paid.

Unit 2

Additional questions

Unit 2

Additional questions

Questions based on Module 7 of this Workbook

In the space below each question prepare journal entries and a narrative for the following:

a. A bank payment of £200 was posted to *Drawings* instead of *Wages*.

b. A calculation error of £1,000 was found in the stock sheets. Stock needs to be reduced by this amount.

c. Purchases for May were incorrectly added. The total purchases should have been £3,450 instead of £3,650.

d. Bank charges of £45 have been omitted from the accounting records.

e. The telephone bill should have been split as business £350 and personal £150, but had been posted the other way round.

f. Repairs to a door costing £500 had been included in *Fixtures and fittings*. Depreciation has not yet been calculated.

g. The proprietor of the business bought purchases of £90 using his own cheque book. (Ignore VAT.)

h. In the sales ledger there is an amount owing by Miss Kim of £356, and in the purchase ledger there is an amount owed to her of £245. Record the contra entry of £245, which has been agreed with Miss Kim.

The following question is based on Module 9 of this Workbook.

Enter the following information in T accounts for the year ended 31 December 2005; calculate any balances at the end of the year and show the amounts transferred to the profit and loss account.

At 1 January 2005 the prepayments were:

Rent	£140
Insurance	£180

At 1 January 2005 the accrued expenses were:

Accounting fee	£1,500
Heat and light	£200
Repairs	£550

The following bank payments were made:

Date	Description	Amount
January 10	Repairs	550
February 2	Electricity for quarter	250
March 1	Rent for quarter to 31 May	210
March 31	Insurance for year to 31 March 2006	720
April 15	Accounting fee for year to 31 December	1,800
May 8	Electricity for quarter	280
June 1	Rent for quarter to 31 August	210
August 6	Electricity for quarter	290
September 1	Rent for quarter to 30 November	210
November 7	Electricity for quarter	300

At 31 December the estimate for electricity owing was £230 and the accountancy fee was expected to be £2,000

Rent

Insurance

Heat and light

Accountancy fee

Repairs

Prepayments

Accruals

Answers to questions based on Module 7

		Debit	Credit
a.	Wages	200	
	Drawings		200
	Being correction of item incorrectly posted to *Drawings* instead of *Wages*.		
b.	Cost of sales	1,000	
	Stock		1,000
	Being correction of calculation error on stock sheets.		
c.	Creditors	200	
	Purchases		200
	Being incorrect addition of the purchases figure.		
d.	Bank charges	45	
	Bank account		45
	Being bank charges omitted from the bank account.		
e.	Telephone	200	
	Drawings		200
	Being correction of incorrect split of telephone charges.		
f.	Repairs	500	
	Fixtures and fittings		500
	Being transfer of £500 incorrectly posted to *Fixtures and fittings* instead of *Repairs*.		
g.	Purchases	90	
	Capital (or Drawings)		90
	Being payment of £90 for purchases by the proprietor.		
h.	Creditors	245	
	Debtors		245
	Being a contra entry between Miss Kim's debtor and creditor accounts.		

Answers to question based on Module 9

Rent

1 Jan	Prepayments	140	31 Dec	P and L a/c	840
1 Mar	Bank	210			
1 Jun	Bank	210			
1 Sept	Bank	210			
31 Dec	Accruals	70			
		840			840

Insurance

1 Jan	Prepayments	180	31 Dec	P and L a/c	720
31 Mar	Bank	720	31 Dec	Prepayments	180
		900			900

Heat and light

2 Feb	Bank	250	1 Jan	Accruals	200
8 May	Bank	280	31 Dec	P and L a/c	1,150
6 Aug	Bank	290			
7 Nov	Bank	300			
31 Dec	Accruals	230			
		1,350			1,350

Accountancy fee

15 April	Bank	1,800	1 Jan	Accruals	1,500
	Accruals	2,000	31 Dec	P and L a/c	2,300
		3,800			3,800

Repairs

10 Jan	Bank	550	1 Jan	Accruals	550
		550			550

Accruals

1 Jan	Accounting fee	1,500	1 Jan	Bal b/d	2,250
	Heat and light	200			
	Repairs	550			
		2,250			2,250
31 Dec	Bal c/d	2,300	31 Dec	Rent	70
				Heat and light	230
				Accountancy fee	2,000
		2,300			2,300
			1 Jan	Bal b/d	2,300

Prepayments

1 Jan	Bal b/d	320	1 Jan	Rent	140
				Insurance	180
		320			320
31 Dec	Insurance	180			

Unit 3

Practical bookkeeping and final accounts

Module 13

Sales and purchase ledgers and daybooks

Introduction

When you first met the term nominal ledger in Module 7, we also introduced the sales and purchase ledgers – the books that contain the details of transactions with credit customers and suppliers. These transactions consist of invoices sent out/received and the settlement of those invoices. At any point the balance in a customer or supplier account shows the amount owing to/by the business.

This module follows through, firstly the sales system and then the purchase system. We start with the information recorded on the invoice, see how that information is recorded in the sales or purchase daybook and then follow the figures through to the customer/supplier accounts in the sales and purchase ledgers.

In this very common method of keeping ledgers, the sales and purchase ledgers are memorandum only – they contain extra information, they do not form part of the double entry system. We will see how, at the end of the month, the totals from the daybooks are posted to the nominal ledger, updating the *Debtors* and *Creditors* accounts with the totals of invoices processed in the month (double entry being with the sales or expense accounts as analysed in the daybooks).

We saw earlier that it is easy to make mistakes in the processing of information. It is therefore an important aspect of a bookkeeping system that there are various built-in checks to catch errors. One of these checks is that the balances in the *Debtors* and *Creditors* accounts in the nominal ledger should equal the totals of the corresponding list of balances of the individual accounts in the sales or purchase ledgers. For this reason these accounts can be referred to as the *Sales ledger control* account and the *Purchase ledger control* account. We will see more of this aspect of the system in Module 17.

Most of this module is concerned with a manual accounting system. While this will not necessarily be met very often in practice, a full understanding of this system makes it much easier to follow what is happening in a computerised system. Such systems are covered later in this module and comparisons are made between the manual and computerised methods of processing.

In this module we see only one side of the transactions with customers and suppliers – the invoice side. The other aspect, the settlement of these invoices, will be covered in Module 15, where we deal with the cash book.

Learning objectives

The objectives of this module are to ensure you:

- Become familiar with the information kept in sales and purchase ledgers.

- Understand the postings from sales and purchase daybooks to sales and purchase ledgers.

- Understand the corresponding postings to the nominal ledger, in particular to the *Sales ledger control* and *Purchase ledger control* accounts.

- Appreciate the difference in operations between computerised and manual systems.

Note form questions

Introduction

The following questions relate to Module 13 Section 2 of AAT Bookkeeping Certificate.

1. For the categories in the table below, fill in two examples:

Category	Examples
Income	
Expenses	
Assets	
Liabilities	

2. What is shown in the *Debtors* account?

----

3. What information is found in the sales ledger?

----

4. What is contained in the creditors (or purchase) ledger?

----

5. Details of what type of suppliers are shown the purchase ledger?

----

6. Suggest the best system of recording the sales ledger accounts:

    a.   If there are a few accounts   ....

    b.   Many accounts   ....

If you are having difficulties go back to Module 13 Section 2 of the disc.

Sales ledger

The following questions relate to Module 13 Section 3 of AAT Bookkeeping Certificate.

7.   Which accounts are recorded in the sales ledger?

....

8.   For a sales ledger account fill in below which side of the T account increases and which side decreases the balance on a customer's account. Give an example of such increases and decreases.

A customer

9.   What is a cash sale?

....

10. What accounting entry is required to record a sales invoice for a VAT registered trader?

....

11. Why are entries in the sales ledger considered to be memorandum only?

....

....

12. Why does the entry to the sales ledger account include VAT?

....

....

....

13. What is the effect of a credit note on a sales ledger account?

....

14. Why might a credit note be issued?

---

15. What happens on a sales ledger account when a receipt is received from a customer?

---

16. What are the total outstanding sales ledger accounts equal to in the trial balance?

If you are having difficulties go back to Module 13 Section 3 of the disc.

Purchase ledger

The following questions relate to Module 13 Section 4 of AAT Bookkeeping Certificate.

17. What is contained in the purchase ledger?

---

18. What is the *Creditors* account in the nominal ledger equal to?

---

19. For a purchase ledger account fill in below which side of the T account increases and which side decreases the balances on a suppliers account, giving examples of such increases and decreases.

A supplier

20. Why do businesses normally give supplier invoices their own sequential number?

---

21. In the table below, describe how the documents listed are recorded in the purchase ledger.

Document	Accounting treatment
Supplier's invoice	
Credit note	
Cheque paid to supplier	

22. Why are items ticked off in the purchase ledger accounts?

------

23. What does the *Purchase ledger control* account represent?

If you are having difficulties go back to Module 13 Section 4 of the disc.

Sales invoices and credit notes

The following questions relate to Module 13 Section 5 of AAT Bookkeeping Certificate.

24. In the table below, fill in a description of the terms used on a sales invoice.

Term	Description
Account no	
Invoice date	
VAT No	
Details	
VAT rate	
VAT analysis	
Total VAT	
Payment terms	

25. Why are customers' accounts sometimes given an account number?

26. What are credit notes?

27. How may the numbering of credit notes compare with that of invoices?

28. What other two methods might be used to indicate that a document is a credit note?

29. Why may amounts on a sales invoice be posted to the credit of a number of different sales accounts?

If you are having difficulties go back to Module 13 Section 5 of the disc.

Sales daybook – Posting the ledger

The following questions relate to Module 13 Sections 6 and 7 of AAT Bookkeeping Certificate.

30. What is a sales daybook used for?

31. In the table below fill in a description of items entered in the sales daybook.

Term	Description
Invoice date	
Invoice number	
Customer name and account number	
Gross amount	
VAT	
Net amount	

32. Give two reasons why sequential numbers are used on sales invoices.

-----

33. What happens to the total of the gross amounts on the credit sales invoices?

-----

34. What happens to the total of the output VAT on the credit sales invoices?

-----

35. How are credit notes entered in the sales daybook?

-----

36. In the table below write in the heading used by Mr Allen for his sales daybook and indicate in the space below where the totals are posted.

37. Why is it essential that a sales daybook is cross-added?

38. Suggest an error that might not be picked up by the cross-add.

39. What is posted from the sales day book to the *Sales ledger control* account?

40. Why are items ticked off in the sales daybook?

41. List three items that should be shown in an individual sales ledger account.

42. The software mentions two methods that can be used for posting items to the nominal ledger. What is the difference between them?

43. What criteria should be used when deciding how often to post invoices to the sales ledger?

If you are having difficulties go back to Modules 13, Sections 6 and 7 of the disc.

BPP
PROFESSIONAL EDUCATION

Purchase invoices and credit notes and posting the ledgers

The following questions relate to Module 13 Sections 8, 9 and 10 of AAT Bookkeeping Certificate.

44. What procedure does Mr Allen follow when an invoice arrives?

....

45. Where are purchase invoices recorded?

....

46. In the table below fill in a description of the terms used on a purchase invoice.

Term	Description
Own invoice number	
Date	
Gross amount	
VAT	
Net amount	

47. Why is sequential numbering applied to purchase invoices?

....

....

48. Why might an invoice contain a despatch date?

....

49. How are purchase credit notes recorded?

....

50. In the table below write in the heading used by Mr Allen for his purchase daybook and indicate underneath where the totals are posted.

If you are having difficulties go back to Module 13 Sections 8, 9 and 10 of the disc.

Types of ledgers

The following questions relate to Module 13 Section 12 of AAT Bookkeeping Certificate.

51. What two methods can be used to record information in accounting records?

----

52. When using manual records, why are separate loose-leaf pages often used for each customer or supplier?

----

53. How are accounting records presented in a computerised system?

----

54. Why is it advantageous to ticked off items that are settled?

----

55. What form of sales and purchase ledgers might a small business keep?

----

56. How might a small business calculate its outstanding debtors and creditors?

If you are having difficulties go back to Module 13 Section 12 of the disc.

Computerised sales and purchase ledgers

The following questions relate to Module 13 Section 13 of AAT Bookkeeping Certificate.

57. List below the order of processing of purchase invoices in a manual system.

----

58. List below the order of processing invoices in a computerised system.

----

59. What is the procedure if the purchase and nominal ledgers are not integrated in a computer based system?

----

60. What is the procedure if the purchase and nominal ledgers are integrated in a computer based system?

-----

61. Explain the following methods of updating the nominal ledger.

Method	Description
Item-by-item	
Batch	
Monthly	

62. In a computerised accounting system, describe the first function a computer might be used to carry out in a sales transaction.

-----

63. List five errors described in the software that can occur in manual daybooks.

	Description of error
1	
2	
3	
4	
5	

64. In older systems what often happened during the period-end routine?

-----

65. How should a record of these cleared transactions be kept?

-----

66. What two methods can be used to carry sales or purchase ledger balances forward?

----

67. Explain how the open item accounts system operates.

----

68. Explain how the balance forward accounts system operates.

----

69. What is a full history account?

----

70. What is the advantage of using a full history method?

If you are having difficulties go back to Module 13 Section 13 of the disc.

Returns daybooks

The following questions relate to Module 13 Section 15 of AAT Bookkeeping Certificate.

71. What is a returns inwards daybook?

----

72. If a returns inwards daybook is kept, how is the nominal ledger posting effected?

----

73. What is a returns outwards daybook?

---

74. How are returns dealt with in a computerised system?

If you are having difficulties go back to Module 13 Section 15 of the disc.

SUMMARY

Sales system (manual)

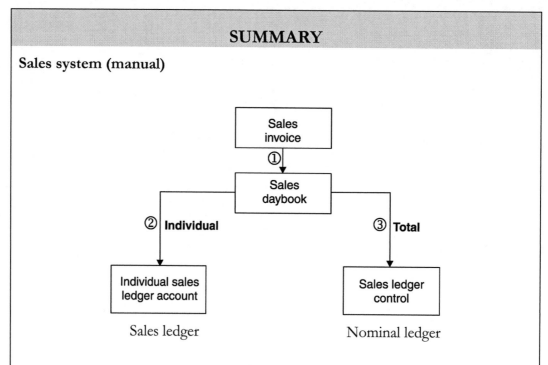

1. Sales invoice details are recorded in the sales daybook

2. Gross amounts of invoices/credit notes are posted to the sales ledger

3. Totals are posted to the nominal ledger as follows:

	Dr	Cr
Sales ledger control	xx	
VAT		x
Sales – 1		xx
Sales – 2		xx

Purchases system (manual)

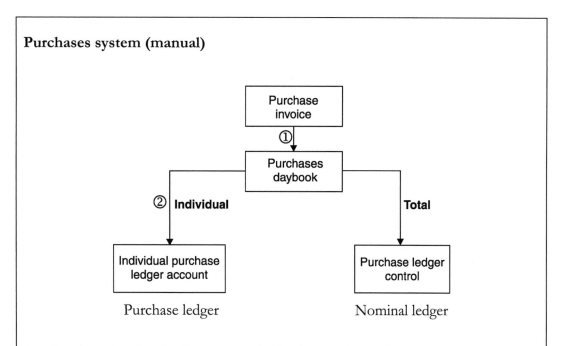

1. Purchase invoice details are recorded in the purchases daybook

2. Gross amounts of individual invoices/credit notes are posted to the purchase ledger

3. Totals are posted to the nominal ledger as follows:

	Dr	Cr
Purchase ledger control		xx
VAT	x	
Expense – 1	x	
Expense – 2 etc	x	

Computerised systems

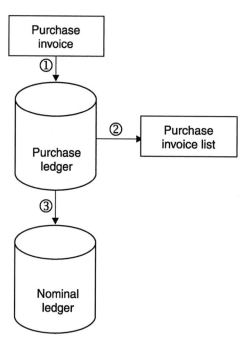

1. Purchase invoice details are recorded in the purchase ledger
2. A report is taken of purchase invoices/credit notes
3. The nominal ledger is updated from the purchase ledger

The sales system operates in a similar way.

Review

In this module you have learnt that:

*   Sale purchase daybooks record the credit invoices sent out/received by the business.

*   Information from the daybooks will need to be posted to both the individual accounts in the sales/purchase ledgers and various accounts in the nominal ledger, where double entry takes place.

*   Sales/purchase ledger control accounts in the nominal ledger record, in total, the same information recorded in detail in the sales and purchase ledgers.

*   Computerised systems have a rather different sequence of processing from manual systems.

*   Certain errors, common in manual systems, could not be made in a computerised system.

Answers

Introduction

1.

Category	Examples
Income	Sales, interest received
Expenses	Purchases, rent, wages
Assets	Property, debtors, bank
Liabilities	Loan, creditors

2. The *Debtors* account will record the total sales figure and the total cash received figure, leaving as a balance the total amount due from customers.

3. The sales ledger contains detailed information regarding transactions with individual customers (invoices, credit notes and payments), and resultant balances due by them.

4. The creditors ledger contains detailed information regarding transactions with, and amounts owing to individual suppliers.

5. Credit suppliers of both expenses and purchases are shown in the purchase ledger.

6. The best system of recording the sales ledger accounts:

   a. If there are a few accounts   In the nominal ledger
   b. Many accounts   In a separate sales ledger

Sales ledger

7. The ledger accounts for customers buying goods on credit.

8.   **A customer**

Increases	Decreases
Eg Goods invoiced	Eg Payments received Credit note

9. A cash sale is a sale where payment (cash or cheque) is received at the time of sale.

10. The accounting entries are: debit *Debtors*, credit *VAT* and *Sales* accounts

11. The double entry for items appearing in the sales ledger is in the nominal ledger *Debtors* account.

12. VAT is included in the amount posted to the sales ledger, as the customer owes both the value of goods/services invoiced and the related VAT to the other supplier.

13. The effect of a credit note is to reduce the amount owed by the customer.

14. A credit note would be issued when goods are returned.

15. The customer's account is credited, and the receipt should be matched (ticked off) with the related invoice(s). The balance due by the customer decreases.

16. The total of outstanding sales ledger accounts are represented in the trial balance by the *Debtors* account.

Purchase ledger

17. The purchase ledger contains accounts for each credit supplier..

18. The *Creditors* account is equal to the sum of the suppliers' accounts in the purchase ledger.

19.

A supplier

Decreases	Increases
Payments made Credit notes	Invoices received

20. The sequential numbering makes it easier for businesses to keep track of invoices received.

21.

Document	Accounting treatment
Supplier's invoice	Credit to supplier's account
Credit note	Debit to supplier's account
Cheque paid to supplier	Debit to supplier's account

22. They are ticked off when paid so that it is possible to see which items are outstanding (those unticked).

23. The *Purchase ledger control* account represents the total of the individual suppliers' accounts in the purchase ledger.

Sales invoices and credit notes

24.

Term	Description
Account no	Reference for a particular account
Invoice date	Determines when VAT becomes accountable, and when payment is due
VAT No	A VAT registered trader must show the VAT number
Details	Description is shown together with unit price and net sales value; sometimes a stock code is shown
VAT rate	Indicates the rate of VAT charged on each line of the invoice.
VAT analysis	Gives, for different rates of VAT, the net goods and VAT charged on them
Total VAT	Total VAT which is added to the net sales figure to give the total amount due by the customer
Payment terms	The period within which the invoice should be paid

25. Customers' accounts may be given an account number to make them easier to find.

26. Credit notes are negative invoices, and may cancel an invoice completely or offset part of an invoice.

27. Credit notes may be numbered in the same sequence as invoices with 'C/N' added.

28. Credit notes are often printed in red or the figures might be included within brackets.

29. The amounts are posted to a number of sales accounts so that a business can easily see the analysis of its sales.

Sales daybook – Posting the ledgers

30. A sales daybook is used to accumulate and total the sales invoices before they are entered in the ledgers.

31.

Term	Description
Invoice date	Date shown on the invoice
Invoice number	Sequential reference number
Customer name and account number	Given for reference purposes
Gross amount	The amount that will appear in a customer's sales ledger account
VAT	Figure from each invoice.
Net amount	The net amount is analysed over sales categories

32. Sequential numbers are used so that it is easy to check that no invoices are missing and it is easy to locate copy invoices at a later date.

33. The total of the gross amounts is posted to the debit of *Sales ledger control* account.

34. The output VAT will be posted to the credit of the *VAT* account.

35. Credit notes are normally entered as negative amounts.

36.

Date	Invoice number	Customer	Account number	Gross	VAT	Jewellery	C & W
Totals							

Posted to debit of sales ledger control account   Posted to credit of VAT account   Post to credit of relevant sales account

37. The cross-add checks that amounts have been correctly entered and summed.

38. An invoice omitted would not have been picked up.

39. The total of the sales invoices is posted to the debit of the *Sales ledger control* account.

40. They are ticked off to indicate that they have been posted to the individual sales ledger account.

41. Items to be shown an individual sales ledger account are:

- Date
- Details
- Amount of invoice

42. The difference is that in the second method a journal is used as an intermediary, and that items will then be ticked in the journal rather than the daybook.

43. The management should decide how often to update the organisation's sales ledger having regard to the number of invoices involved and the period of credit.

Purchase invoices and credit notes and posting the ledgers

44. Mr Allen numbers the invoice with the next number in his purchase invoice series.

45. Purchase invoices are recorded in the purchase daybook.

46.

Term	Description
Own invoice number	Mr Allen's reference number
Date	Date invoice sent; could also be a delivery date
Supplier's name and Account number	Each supplier may have an account code as well as name for reference
VAT	The total VAT from the invoice
Net amount	This amount will be analysed over the appropriate category of purchases/expenses

47. Sequential numbering and filing means that missing invoices can be easily spotted, and also invoices can be easily located in the future.

48. A despatch date will be included if the invoice relates to the supply of goods.

49. Purchase credit notes are often shown as negative amounts in the purchase daybook.

50.

Date	Invoice number	Supplier	Account number	Gross	VAT	Jewellery	C&W	Packaging	Ins
Totals									

Posted to credit of the *Purchase ledger control*   Posted to debit of *VAT* account   Post to debit of relevant expense accounts

Types of ledgers

51. Accounting records can be either manual or computerised.

52. Separate loose-leaf pages will be used for each customer or supplier so that additional pages can be added in the right place as and when required.

53. Computerised records are presented as follows:

    - 3 column format often used
    - Accounts are referred to by a code number
    - Accounts examined either on screen or in printed form.

54. As a result of ticking off items it is possible to see exactly which items are still outstanding.

55. Small businesses might only keep files of unpaid invoices instead of traditional ledgers.

56. The small business will add up all the unpaid invoices in the appropriate file.

Computerised sales and purchases ledgers

57. The order of processing invoices in a manual system is:

    - Enter details from invoice into the purchase daybook

      ° Gross
      ° VAT
      ° Net – analysed to appropriate analysis column

    - From the daybook post the gross amount of each invoice to the suppliers' accounts in the purchase ledger

    - Periodically, usually monthly, post the totals from the purchase daybook to the nominal ledger

      ° Cr *Purchase ledger control* with the gross total
      ° Dr *VAT* with the VAT total
      ° Dr *Purchases* and various expenses with total of analysis columns

58. The order of processing in a computerised system is:

    - Make an entry in the supplier's purchase ledger account (using the account code) directly from the invoice.

    - A report of invoices posted is taken from the purchase ledger system after the invoices have been posted – a computerised form of daybook.

    - The nominal ledger is updated, usually directly from the purchase ledger.

59. If the ledgers are not integrated, then a journal entry is put through the nominal ledger system in the same way as with a manual system.

60. If the purchase ledger and the nominal ledger are integrated then the journal entry is made automatically.

61.

Method	Description
Item-by-item	Nominal ledger is updated whenever a purchase invoice is entered
Batch	Updating occurs when a batch of invoices is entered
Monthly	The nominal ledger is updated at the end of the month

62. The first action is the production of sales invoices, which are then processed through a similar system to the purchase invoices. These invoices are often produced by the computer system.

63.

	Description of error
1	VAT entered incorrectly
2	Gross and net figures entered the wrong way round
3	Addition of columns incorrect
4	Same figure entered for gross and net
5	Invoice missing

64. During the period-end routine matched transactions may be cleared from the files. This was often done when storage was a problem in older systems.

65. Details of these transactions should either be kept on a copy disk or on a printout.

66. The two methods are:

- Open item account
- Balance forward account

67. In the open item account system all unmatched transactions are carried forward individually.

68. In the balance forward system full transaction details are not carried forward, only the balance, and possibly an ageing.

69. This system is used in many computerised systems and is one in which, the transactions are kept for a full year, only being cleared out at the year-end.

70. The advantage of a full history method is that tracing movements on accounts is easier and detailed printouts are only required annually.

Returns daybooks

71. A returns inwards daybook records credit notes that have been sent to customers.

72. The nominal ledger will be have two groups of postings – one from the sales daybook and one from the returns inwards daybook.

73. A returns outwards daybook is where credit notes from suppliers are recorded.

74. In a computer system invoices and credit notes are usually entered in separate entry routines.

Module 14

Receipts and payments

Introduction

In Module 15 we will look at the recording of information in the cash book (which records all transactions going through the business *bank* account!). We will firstly have a look, in this module, at some of the practical aspects of dealing with receipts and payments.

In many businesses, nearly all transactions will go through the bank account. Customers will send in payment by cheque and the payment of suppliers and other items will be made by cheque. So that you can understand the timings involved, and be aware of possible risks, for example, of a customer's cheque bouncing, we take a look at the whole banking and clearing system.

Cheques, however, will not be the only mechanism of receiving/paying money through the business bank account. Becoming increasingly important are other methods such as BACS, CHAPS and Switch, as well as the traditional standing order and direct debit methods of making payments. These various methods are all explained.

In other businesses most of the receipts will be in the form of cash (eg retail shops). This has special risks that must be controlled. As part of this control, the cash received should all be banked and not used to make payments (any small payments, as in any other business, can be made from the petty cash). Many traditional 'cash businesses' accept other types of payment. Cheques, with an associated cheque guarantee card, will often be the means for paying for a 'cash sale'. (Remember the odd use of terminology here – a 'cash sale' is one where no credit is given – payment is made at the time of sale.) Also commonly met now are settlements by Switch, using an EFTPOS (electronic funds transfer at point of sale) system, or by credit card. The mechanism of dealing with these systems is also explained.

Once you are familiar with the practicalities involved in the making of payments and the various ways in which receipts might come in, you can progress to the next module where we will deal with the recording of these figures.

Learning objectives

The objectives of this module are to ensure you:

- Are familiar with the different ways in which:
  - ° Receipts might come in to a business
  - ° Payments can be made by a business

- Know how to lodge receipts into a bank account and make payments from it.

- Become familiar with the documentation relating to receipts and payments.

- Understand that effective control must be exercised over both the receipts and payments in a business.

- Are aware of some useful computer reports relating to debtors and creditors.

Note form questions

Cash and cheque receipts

The following questions relate to Module 14 Section 2 of AAT Bookkeeping Certificate

1. What is a bank overdraft?

    ....

2. What criteria must a business and the bank have agreed to in relation to a bank overdraft?

    ....

    ....

3. Give two methods that will help a business control its cash.

    ....

    ....

4. Explain why a payment made by cheque is more secure than by cash.

    ....

    ....

5. Why are bank charges higher if cash is used instead of cheques?

    ....

6. What should be written on a cheque stub when a cheque is issued?

    ....

    ....

7. Fill in below the description and relevance of items contained on a cheque.

	Description and relevance
Date	
Payee	
Amount	
Sort code	
Cheque number	
Signature	
Crossing	

8. What is a post-dated cheque?

9. When can post-dated cheques be banked?

10. How long are cheques valid for?

11. What should happen if the words and numbers on a cheque are different?

12. Give a feature about cheques which make them easy to process by computer.

13. What helps the banking system speed up the processing of cheques?

BPP
PROFESSIONAL EDUCATION

14. What does the term 'drawer' mean?

----

15. What does the term 'clearing' mean?

----

16. How long does it take to clear a cheque?

----

17. What happens if a cheque is 'bounced'?

----

18. What is cheque guarantee card?

----

19. What two things should be checked by the recipient when a cheque guarantee card is used?

----

20. What should the recipient do when offered a cheque guarantee card?

----

21. What can happen if the cheque is written for more than the card limit?

If you are having difficulties go back to Module 14 Section 2 of the disc.

Debit and credit card receipts

The following questions relate to Module 14 Section 3 of AAT Bookkeeping Certificate.

22. What are the two types of plastic card?

23. Explain how a credit card operates.

24. How does a debit card operate?

25. In the table below fill in the description of items found on a credit card.

	Description
Bank name	
Mastercard or Visa	
Number	
Dates	
User's name	
Signature	
£50 cheque guarantee	
Magnetic strip	
Hologram	

26. Explain how a manual credit card system operates.

27. What checks should a trader make to avoid using stolen or misused cards?

28. What is EFTPOS?

29. How is the EFTPOS system used for a credit card payment?

30. What is a 'switch card'?

31. What is a PIN?

32. What system operates when goods bought using a credit card are returned?

33. What system operates when goods bought using a debit card are returned?

34. How can goods bought over the telephone be paid for?

If you are having difficulties go back to Module 14 Section 3 of the disc.

Other receipts

The following questions relate to Module 14 Section 4 of AAT Bookkeeping Certificate.

35. In the table below, fill in three other methods that could be used for the settlement of debts and note how they are operated.

Method	Operation

36. Give one advantage and one disadvantage of using telegraphic transfer.

....

....

37. Give three other methods of arranging the transfer of funds mentioned in Section 4.

....

....

....

If you are having difficulties go back to Module 14 Section 4 of the disc.

Banking receipts

The following questions relate to Module 14 Section 5 of AAT Bookkeeping Certificate.

38. Why is control of receipts important in a cash business?

....

39. List three items that are recorded on the till or cash register.

....

....

....

40. In relation to the production of the till receipt, what is the difference between a sale made for cash and one by a credit card?

41. What type of keyboard might be used in a fast-food outlet?

42. Describe what might happen in a more sophisticated cash register.

43. Suggest four items of information that might be available from a cash register at the end of the day?

44. What is the 'analysis of sales by category' used for?

45. What are the 'totals by method of payment' used for?

46. What is a cash float?

---

47. What should the trader do with cash taken from the till?

---

48. What is a cash sales summary book?

---

49. What does the trader do when banking receipts?

---

50. What happens to the two-part credit card vouchers kept by the trader?

---

51. How are the credit card vouchers banked by the trader?

---

52. Suggest types of business that might not have cash registers.

---

53. What type of records might a business keep instead of a cash register?

If you are having difficulties go back to Module 14 Section 5 of the disc.

Receipts from debtors

The following questions relate to Module 14 Section 6 of AAT Bookkeeping Certificate.

54. What is a customer statement and when are statements usually sent out?

....

....

55. What is a remittance advice?

....

....

56. How can the trader encourage customers to identify which invoices are being paid?

....

....

57. Why is it important that a customer sends a remittance advice when using credit transfer as the method of payment?

....

....

If you are having difficulties go back to Module 14 Section 6 of the disc.

Control and security over receipts

The following questions relate to Module 14 Section 7 of AAT Bookkeeping Certificate.

58. In relation to sales and receipts from customers, give three risks that a business could be subject to?

....

....

....

59. When is theft most likely to occur?

....

60. Suggest three invalid methods of payments that a business might be subject to.

-----

61. Give three procedures that a trader could use to avoid theft of cash.

-----

62. What should a trader do if the till is short of cash compared to the total on the till register?

-----

63. What might have happened if the till has too much cash compared to the total on the till register?

-----

64. Give three security features that might be built into a till.

-----

65. Where should an organisation keep its safe?

-----

66. Why should cash be taken to the bank at different times of the day?

-----

67. List six additional safeguards that a large organisation might employ.

----

68. Give two procedures that a firm could carry out in order to minimise the risk of not getting paid by credit customers.

If you are having difficulties go back to Module 14 Section 7 of the disc.

Methods of payment

The following questions relate to Module 14 Section 8 of AAT Bookkeeping Certificate.

69. List six methods that could be used to make a payment.

----

70. What is the advantage for an organisation of sending out their bills with a pre-printed bank giro credit form?

------

71. What type of expense might be paid by standing order?

------

72. What is a standing order mandate?

------

73. What is a direct debit?

------

74. How may a business be given authority to collect funds by direct debit?

------

75. What type of payments could be made by direct debit?

------

76. What is BACS?

------

77. How does BACS work?

----

78. What is an advantage of using BACS?

----

79. What is an essential security feature of telephone or Internet banking?

----

80. When might it be useful to have a company credit card?

----

81. How is it possible to withdraw cash from a bank using a pre-crossed cheque?

----

82. Explain why it is better to bank receipts in full.

----

83. How are small payments for the business often made?

If you are having difficulties go back to Module 14 Section 8 of the disc.

Purchase ledger payments

The following questions relate to Module 14 Section 9 of AAT Bookkeeping Certificate.

84. Why are the debits and credits on the statement from the supplier and those on the purchase ledger account reversed?

85. What other differences could there be between the statement from the supplier and the purchase ledger account?

86. When would a customer compile a remittance advice?

87. What method, other than a remittance advice, might a customer use when sending a cheque to a supplier?

88. How is possible to identify which invoices are outstanding?

89. What analysis might a computerised system provide that will help a customer decide which invoices to pay?

90. Which invoices are normally paid if the business does not have a cash flow problem?

91. What is an aged debtors list?

92. Give two ways a computer system can help an organisation make payments to suppliers.

If you are having difficulties go back to Module 14 Section 9 of the disc.

Control over payments

The following questions relate to Module 14 Section 10 of AAT Bookkeeping Certificate.

93. Give two risks a business could encounter in the purchases system?

94. What must a business put in place in order to avoid these risks?

95. List below five matters that could go wrong with a purchase invoice.

96. Who should check purchase invoices?

97. In a large business who might be the authorising official?

....

98. What two documents should an invoice for goods be checked against?

....

....

99. Against what should an invoice for services be checked?

....

....

100. What should happen once an invoice has been fully checked?

....

101. What is an invoice stamp?

....

102. What is prevented by segregation of duties?

....

103. When might it be impossible to use segregation of duties?

....

104. Suggest four other payments a business might make which do not have external evidence such as invoices?

....

....

....

105. What procedure should be carried out for these other payments?

106. List five items that should be shown on a cheque requisition form.

107. List four items of expenses a sales person could claim by agreement with the employer.

108. What procedure should be followed when claiming expenses?

109. What procedure should be followed to ensure that the petty cash is controlled?

If you are having difficulties go back to Module 14 Section 10 of the disc.

SUMMARY

Most business transactions will be channelled through the business's bank current account. Many payments/receipts are in the form of a cheque.

It will take a few days for a cheque to clear.

A cheque will:

- Be paid into the payee's (receiver's) branch of their bank.
- Be transferred through the Banking System.
- Be removed from the drawer's account (in 2/3 days time).

Payments made by credit card:

- Can be immediately banked by the receiver.
- Will appear on the credit card statement of the payer for the appropriate month.
- Require to be paid by the payer to the credit card company 2/3 weeks after the issue of the statement.

Debit cards payments are immediately:

- Banked by the receiver.
- Removed from the account of the payer.

Under EFTPOS (Electronic Funds Transfer at Point Of Sale) system, the retailer is linked into the credit card and banking system. Transfers by credit and debit cards are processed automatically.

Business receipts/payments may be in the format of:

- Cash
- Cheques
- Credit card
- Banker's draft
- Bank giro credit/credit transfer/BACS
- Telegraphic transfer
- Standing order
- Direct debit

A **banker's draft** is a bank's own cheque drawn on themselves.

A **standing order** is an instruction to the bank to make payments of a specified amount, at particular intervals, to the payee detailed.

A **direct debit payment** is a payment by the bank as requested by the payee. Authority must previously have been given to the bank by the payer.

Cash must be particularly rigorously controlled in a business:

- All business takings should be banked intact

- Cash at the end of day should be squared with the till totals

- Cash should be kept in a safe and banked as soon as possible

- Banking times/people should be varied

- Cash payments should be either be:

  ° From petty cash (small amounts)
  ° From cash withdrawn specially (eg wages)

A **remittance advice** will detail invoices being paid

A computerised purchase ledger system will usually:

- Produce an aged creditors list
- Produce a list of outstanding invoices
- Print remittance advices, possibly with attached cheques

A computerised sales ledger will usually:

- Produce an aged debtors list
- Produce a list of overdue invoices

All payments should be properly authorised and supported by appropriate documentation. This may be:

- Fully checked/signed invoices.
- Authorised cheque requisition forms with supporting documentation.
- Authorised staff expense forms.
- Authorised petty cash vouchers.

Review

In this module you have learnt that:

- Business receipts and payments may be made in many different ways.

- The least secure method of making payments or receiving money is in the form of cash.

- The business bank account should be central to the business's system of payments/receipts. This bank account will be part of the banking system which enables funds to be transferred from one person's accounts to another.

- Control over receipts and payments is extremely important in a business, particularly where there is a large amount of cash involved.

- Proper documentation must be used in the business. Computer reports and printouts will be helpful in running the receipts/payments systems.

Answers

Cash and cheque receipts

1. A bank overdraft occurs when a business borrows money from a bank on a day-to-day short-term basis.

2. The overdraft must be agreed in advance, and the business must not exceed the agreed limit.

3. Two of the methods are:

    *   All receipts, in whatever form, should be banked intact

    *   All payments, except for very small items, should be made through the bank account

4. Cash can be stolen, whereas when a cheque is made out to a payee and 'crossed', it must be paid into the payee's account.

5. Banks charge more for banking cash than for banking cheques.

6. A cheque stub should contain the main details of the cheque, particularly payee and amount. This will later be used as a basis of making a permanent record of the transaction.

7.

	Description and relevance
Date	Cheques cannot be processed through the bank before the date written on it.
Payee	The person or business to whom the cheque is being written
Amount	This is the amount being paid, written on the cheque both in words and numbers
Sort code	Identification of the paying bank and branch
Cheque number	Identification for each cheque
Signature	A cheque must be signed by an authorised signatory for it to be valid
Crossing	Crossing limits the cheque to be paid into the bank account of the person named only

8. Post-dated cheques are written for payment at some specified later date; not on receipt by the payee.

9. Post-dated can only be banked after the date on the cheque.

10. Cheques are only valid for 6 months after the date on the face of the cheque.

11. If the words and numbers are different the bank will refuse to honour the cheque.

12. The account number, sort code and cheque number on a cheque are machine readable.

13. The machine-readable numbers help the banking system speed up cheque processing.

14. The drawer is the person who writes and signs the cheque or the account the cheque will be debited to by the bank.

15. 'Clearing' is the process by which a payment made by a cheque etc is transferred through the banking system from the payer's account to the payee's account.

16. It normally takes three business days to clear a cheque.

17. A cheque 'bounces' when the bank refuses to honour it due to lack of funds available.

18. A card that can guarantee a cheque will be honoured by the bank.

19. The following should be checked:

    - Card is within valid dates
    - Signature matches the one on the cheque

20. The recipient should write the card number on the back of the cheque.

21. If the cheque is written for more than the limit, then the cheque card will not guarantee the cheque.

Debit and credit cards

22. The two types of plastic card are:

    - Credit cards
    - Debit cards

23. A credit card operates in the following way.

    - Goods are charged to the holder's account, but are not paid for immediately by the holder

    - Account holders receive monthly statements from the credit card company detailing purchases made

    - The holder pays the balance to the credit card company within a specified time, usually 2-3 weeks

    - If balance is unpaid then interest is charged

24. A debit card is a card that takes funds immediately from the bank.

25.

	Description
Bank	Bank or building society that has issued that card
Mastercard or Visa	Type of credit card
Number	Unique number that identifies each card
Dates	Dates within which the credit card is valid
User's name	The name of the user User's name, card number and dates are raised characters that can be imprinted
Signature	To be valid a card must be signed
£50 cheque guarantee	Some credit cards also act as a cheque guarantee card
Magnetic strip	The card details can be read electronically from magnetic strip on back of the card
Hologram	Helps card security – not easy to forge

26. A manual credit card system operates as follows:

    - Card is fitted into a slot in a small machine
    - 3 or 4 part transaction voucher is fitted on top and a roller is pushed over the voucher
    - An imprint is made on voucher of number, name and dates
    - Imprint also made of supplier's details from raised characters on the plate
    - Voucher removed from machine and signed
    - Voucher should be checked with the signature on the card
    - Top copy given to customer, the rest in the till

27. Checks should include:

    - Check signature on voucher with that on the card
    - Check that signature strip is smooth; if raised it may have been tampered with
    - Check card number against list of stolen cards
    - Check that date is within start and expiry date on the card
    - Check shop authorisation limit has not been exceeded
    - Ring credit card company for authorisation number if concerned or over authorisation limit
    - Check that details have come through all copies of the voucher

28. Electronic Funds Transfer at Point of Sale is a small terminal and telephone line which the retailer uses to connect to the banking and credit card systems

29. The EFTPOS is used in the following ways.

    - Credit card is either swiped or inserted in a slot on the terminal
    - Details on card read off the magnetic strip
    - Transaction details either keyed in or transferred automatically if till is linked
    - Short delay whilst terminal connects to credit card company for authorisation
    - If authorisation received the terminal will receive an authorisation code; otherwise the transaction will be refused.
    - Once agreed a two-part receipt is issued; customer will sign the both copies; the top one of which is taken away
    - Bottom copy kept in till
    - Funds will be automatically transferred to the retailer's account.

30. A 'switch card' is a debit card which takes funds straight out of the payer's bank account.

31. A Personal Identification Number that allows access to a bank account.

32. The system is the same as the original sale except that 'refund' will be entered on the transaction slip.

33. If a debit card has been used then the funds will transferred automatically back to the customer's account.

34. These goods can be paid for by giving appropriate credit card details over the telephone.

Other receipts

35.

Method	Operation
Banker's draft	Bank issue a cheque from the bank itself
Bank giro credit or credit transfer	Money transferred from the customers account direct to the seller's account
Telegraphic transfer	Instruction from paying bank to recipient's bank by telephone

36. Advantage – quick
Disadvantage – costly

37. Other methods are:

- Bankers Automated Clearing Service (BACS)
- Standing order
- Direct debit

Banking receipts

38. Control of receipts is important because cash can easily go astray.

39. The following are recorded on the till or cash register:

- Amount of cash sales
- Category of goods
- VAT rate

40. For cash sales a till receipt will be produced immediately, and for credit card the sale through the till will not be completed until the card payment has been fully processed.

41. Keyboards in fast-food outlets often store the item description and price.

42. In more sophisticated systems the following might happen:

- Tills are linked to a central computer
- Items have their own code number and price maintained centrally
- Sales are either keyed in, or bar code read
- On completion of the sale the till picks up the price and reduces stock

43. The following information might be generated by a cash register – sales figures broken down into:

- Sale/refund amounts
- Breakdown by sales category
- VAT amount for each VAT code
- Total received by method of payment

44. The information is used to produce an analysis of sales in the accounting records.

45. The information is used to check that the trader has the correct amount of cash, cheques and card receipts.

46. A cash float is a small amount of cash kept in the till for giving change.

47. The cash taken from the till should either be put in a safe or banked immediately.

48. A cash sales summary book contains a daily analysed summary of receipts.

49. The trader totals up the takings, and completes the paying-in slip for cash and cheques – details of quantities of cash and individual cheques are required. The cash, cheques and paying-in slip are taken to the bank.

50. One copy of the credit card voucher is banked by the trader the other is retained by the trader.

51. The credit card vouchers are included on a separate paying-in slip and taken to the bank.

52. Types of business that might not have cash registers are:

    - Small businesses
    - Businesses with a few high value receipts

53. A business might just keep cash received sheets that list all receipts.

Receipts from debtors

54. Statements are details of what a credit customer owes and are normally sent out at the end of each month.

55. A remittance advice is sent by a customer with a cheque detailing which invoices are being paid.

56. A trader can send out a two-part statement/remittance advice; the remittance advice part should then be returned with the payment.

57. It is important to send a remittance advice otherwise the supplier would know nothing of the receipt until he gets his bank statement.

Control and security over receipts

58. Three risks are:

    - Theft by either a staff member or member of the public
    - Acceptance of some invalid method of payment
    - Sale on credit to someone who does not pay

59. This risk is greatest where there is a large amount of cash involved.

60. Invalid methods of payments include:

    - Forged notes or coins
    - Acceptance of cheques which later bounce
    - Acceptance of invalid cheque or credit card eg out of date

61. A trader could use the following:

    - A cash till that keeps a permanent record of all sales rung up

- Keep unbanked cash in a safe
- Take cash to the bank at different times

62. The trader should check if any of the following have occurred:

  - Refunds given but not recorded
  - Expenses paid but not recorded or stolen
  - Cash stolen

63. If there is too much cash then sales might not have been rung up on the till.

64. Security features built into a till:

  - Cash drawer can only be opened by a staff member when a sale is rung up
  - Access keys limit operations available to different people
  - Analysis of sales by staff member

65. A safe should be kept out of view, and there should be as few as keys as possible.

66. If cash is taken at different times there is less likelihood of it being a target for a robbery.

67. A large organisation might:

  - Place staff behind protective glass
  - Employ security guards
  - Use outside security firms to take money to the bank
  - Bank cash in a night safe rather than keeping it on the premises
  - Incorporate a strong box into the till
  - Use chutes to send cash to strong rooms

68. A firm could use the following methods:

  - Obtain credit references before allowing credit to a customer
  - Check age of debtors' balances

Methods of payment

69. Six payment methods are:

  - Cheque
  - Standing order or direct debit
  - BACS
  - Other bank payment, eg bankers draft or telegraphic transfer
  - Cash
  - Credit card

70. Advantages are that it is more secure than having large number of payments coming in envelopes through their post box, and also the funds are cleared when they arrive.

71. An expense which is the same amount each month, eg a hire purchase payment.

72. A standing order mandate is a written instruction to the bank giving it full instructions regarding the payment.

73. A direct debit arises when the recipient of the money contacts the payer's bank asking for a specific sum of money.

74. The paying trader has to give the bank details about who has authority to collect the funds.

75. Mobile phone bills and leasing payments are often paid by direct debit.

76. Bankers Automated Clearing Service.

77. BACS works as follows:

    - Business acquires bank details of its suppliers
    - The amounts will be filled in by the business
    - The forms will be sent to the bank either manually or electronically
    - Payment transferred through the banking/clearing system
    - Arrive at recipient two or three days later as cleared funds.

78. BACS is quicker and more secure than many other forms of payment.

79. An essential security feature is that the system is password controlled.

80. A company credit card might be useful when buying items from businesses with whom you do not have credit.

81. In order to withdraw cash, the crossing must be removed by scoring through the 'A/c payee only', writing 'cash' and an authorised signatory initialling the alteration.

82. If cash is banked in full better control is kept.

83. Small payments are usually made from petty cash.

Purchase ledger payments

84. The debits and credits are reversed as the statement is expressed from the supplier's point of view and the purchase ledger account is from the customer's point of view.

85. There might be timing differences for example a cheque that has been sent at the end of a month might not yet have been processed, or invoices may be missing or withheld because of a query.

86. A remittance advice would be prepared if the customer did not receive one from his supplier.

87. A note of invoices being paid might be sent with the cheque.

88. If invoices and cash have been ticked then any unticked items will represent the outstanding amount.

89. The computerised system will help by analysing accounts over current, 30 days etc.

90. The business would probably pay anything over one month old.

91. A list of each of the debtors' balances analysed according to the age of the debt.

92. Computer systems can help organisations by producing remittance advices with a tear-off cheque and also a list of outstanding invoices.

Control over payments

93. Two risks are:

    - The business being invoiced for something it should not be, or being charged the wrong amount

    - Employees arranging payments that can be diverted to themselves

94. The business must put in place a proper system of authorisation, payment and recording.

95. Matters could include:

    - Supplier sending the invoice to the wrong person
    - Wrong price being charged
    - Goods charged for, but have not been received
    - Goods received (or some of them) were faulty and sent back so a credit note is due
    - Invoice is totally fictitious; produced by an employee who thinks he can get it paid

96. An invoice should be checked by someone in authority who has knowledge of that particular purchase.

97. The authorising official might be a departmental head.

98. The invoice should be checked against:

    - Delivery note
    - Purchase order

99. These invoices should be checked against any available confirmation including contracts and correspondence.

100. The invoice should be signed or initialled by the authorised person.

101. A stamp which is filled with the details required such as codes for the nominal ledger.

102. If segregation of duties happens no one person is able to take control of a complete operation, eg the processing and payment of a purchase invoice.

103. Segregation of duties might not be possible in a small business.

104. A business might need to make the following payments:

    - Payment in advance, where credit has not been arranged with a supplier
    - Payment of an air fare, where no account is held with a travel agent
    - Payment of VAT to Customs and Excise
    - Payment to Companies House of annual return fee

105. For these other payments an authorised person should fill in a cheque requisition form.

106. The following should be shown on a cheque requisition form:

- Details of cheque required
- Reason for cheque being required
- Documentation attached and to follow
- Details of where the cheque should be sent
- Signature of authorised person

107. The sales person may claim back the following:

- Entertaining customers
- Part of home telephone
- Petrol/mileage
- Trade Association magazine/subscription

108. Here is the procedure that should be followed:

- Employee should fill in a company expense claim form
- Attach receipts, including proper VAT receipts if applicable
- The form should be signed by the employee and someone in authority

109. The procedure for petty cash is that:

- Only authorised officials should have access to the petty cash

- Numbered petty cash vouchers should be made out for each payment

- Vouchers should be authorised and supported by independent invoices where possible.

Module 15

The cash book and petty cash

Introduction

As mentioned in the introduction to the last module, it is another odd piece of accounting terminology that the cash book records all transactions going through the business **bank** account. The cash book is a very important part of the accounting records. Indeed, many small businesses that do not find it necessary to keep sales and purchase ledgers, may keep no other main records than the cash book: their accountants would prepare their accounts annually from the cash book.

We consider here, however, a full manual system (and later a computerised system) where sales, purchase and nominal ledgers are maintained. You have already seen how invoice information finds its way into the sales and purchase ledgers via the daybooks. Receipts from credit customers and payments to credit suppliers will find their way into the sales and purchase ledgers via the cash book.

The cash book is often split into two parts, as we will deal with it here – the cash receipts book and the cash payments book. On the receipts side, most of the money coming into the business will usually be from customers. This may be from only credit customers, or from only cash customers, or it may be a mixture of both, depending on the nature of the business. Remember that, for credit sales, the sale itself has already been recorded, so all that matters in the cash book is to record the fact that a debt has been settled. For cash sales, however, the type of sale itself, and any associated VAT, will need to be recorded in the cash book, for later posting to the nominal ledger. Any other sundry receipts, such as interest or grants received, would similarly need to be analysed out so that they will finish up in the right accounts in the nominal ledger.

Similarly, the cash payments book will record a mixture of payments to credit suppliers and other payments. There will usually be many more other items than on the receipts side, as a business will tend have many non-purchase ledger payments (eg wages and drawings).

You will get some practice here in recording items in the cash book, as you might well do in any manual system. You will then take the figures, as appropriate, into the sales, purchase and nominal ledgers.

The final part of this module deals with cash discount – not now commonly encountered. This is where you can settle an invoice by payment of less than the full invoice value if it is paid within a certain specified time, by deducting a discount for early payment. It is important that this discount is properly recorded in the books, otherwise invoices that are fully settled would show as only part-paid.

As we have considered several times before, it is extremely important that accounting information is correct. This is particularly important when it comes to information on the bank position. Fortunately this information can be easily checked as the bank provides statements detailing what they have seen going through the account. The process of checking the cash book against the bank statement is covered in the next module.

At the end of the module we look at the use and recording of petty cash, and see how it can best be controlled using the imprest system.

BPP
PROFESSIONAL EDUCATION

Learning objectives

At the end of this module you will:

- Be able to record bank receipts and payments in the cash book.

- Understand the postings from the cash book to the ledgers in a manual system.

- Realise that the postings will be different in an integrated computerised system.

- Know how to deal with cash discounts.

- Understand the keeping of petty cash using the imprest system.

Note form questions

The cash book

The following questions relate to Module 15 Section 2 of AAT Bookkeeping Certificate.

1. Where are receipts and payments both recorded?

---

2. Other than payments to suppliers, what payments might a business make?

---

3. In which book will the business record its payments?

---

4. Where will receipts be recorded?

---

5. Detail the type of items recorded in the cash payments book.

---

6. What is recorded in the petty cash book?

---

7. What type of receipts are recorded in the cash receipts book?

---

8. What are the four functions of a cash book?

---

9.   What is a cash sale?

----

10. What layout is commonly used in a manual cash book?

----

11. How often is the cash book normally totalled?

----

12. List three different forms of cash book that can be used.

If you are having difficulties go back to Module 15 Section 2 of the disc.

Cash payments book – Recording payments

The following questions relate to Module 15 Section 3 of AAT Bookkeeping Certificate.

13. In the table below fill in a description for each of the column heading of a cash payments book.

Column	Description
Date	
Cheque no	
Payee	
A/c no	
Bank	
P/L, wages, petty cash, drawings, VAT, sundries	

14. In the table below enter the information that should be shown in the cash payments book for the following transactions.

> 1. April 2 – Mr Allen writes a cheque number 345264 for £784 to Time Trading, one of the purchase ledger creditors (account T1).
>
> 2. April 4 – Mr Allen uses cheque number 345265 to withdraw £120 to pay wages.
>
> 3. April 6 – Mr Allen writes himself cheque number 345266 for £800 for his own personal use.
>
> 4. April 12 – Mr Allen cashes cheque number 345267 for £100 with which he is going to start a petty cash float.
>
> 5. April 12 – Mr Allen buys some jewellery from Opal Traders. He does not have an account with them so at the time of purchase it is a cash purchase. The goods cost £500 + £50 VAT = £550 which he pays with cheque 3435268.
>
> 6. April 13 – Mr Allen starts writing a cheque to the Inland Revenue but enters the wrong amount. He decides to cancel this cheque and write another one.
>
> 7. April 13 – Mr Allen writes cheque no 345270 to the Inland Revenue for £151 to pay the March PAYE and NI.

Item no	Date	Cheque no	Payee	A/c	Bank	Analysis eg P/L wages etc
1						
2						
3						
4						
5						
6						
7						

15. What should be included in the *Sundries* column in a cash payments book?

If you are having difficulties go back to Module 15 Section 3 of the disc.

Cash payments book – Posting the ledgers

The following questions relate to Module 15 Section 4 of AAT Bookkeeping Certificate.

16. In the table below enter the name of each of the ledgers to which cash payments will be posted, describing which accounts will be posted.

Ledger	Accounts posted

17. On April 2 Mr Allen writes a cheque number 345264 for £784 to Time Trading, one of the purchase ledger creditors. What entry will be made in the purchase ledger?

18. In the space below write which ledger the totals of the cash payments book are posted to, whether the item is a debit or credit, and the name of the relevant ledger account.

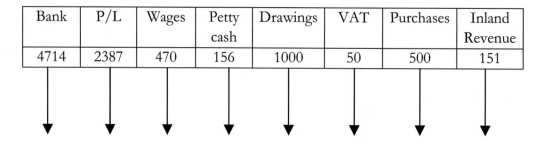

Bank	P/L	Wages	Petty cash	Drawings	VAT	Purchases	Inland Revenue
4714	2387	470	156	1000	50	500	151

If you are having difficulties go back to Module 15 Section 4 of the disc.

Cash payments book – Keeping the records

The following questions relate to Module 15 Section 5 of AAT Bookkeeping Certificate.

19. What should be filled in at the same time as the cheque is written?

---

20. What should happen to the details on the stub?

---

21. How is it possible to know which purchase invoices have been paid?

---

22. Explain what happens if a business does not keep a cash book?

If you are having difficulties go back to Module 15 Section 5 of the disc.

Cash receipts book – Recording receipts

The following questions relate to Module 15 Section 6 of AAT Bookkeeping Certificate.

23. What is recorded in the cash receipts book?

---

24. In the table below fill in a description for each of the column headings of a cash receipts book.

Column	Description
Date	
Ref no	
Description	
A/c no	
Bank	
Cash sales, VAT, sundries	

BPP PROFESSIONAL EDUCATION

25. In the table below enter the information that should be shown in the cash receipts book for the following transactions.

> 1. April 4 – Mr Allen receives and banks a cheque for £420 from Mrs Ritchie, one of his sales ledger customers (account R2).
>
> 2. April 6 – Mr Allen banks the week's cash sales. From his till rolls he can tell that £460 is in respect of jewellery sales while £230 was the amount received for the sales of clocks and watches. VAT on the total is £69.
>
> 3. April 10 – Mr Allen receives and banks a cheque for £1,250 from Time Trading, one of his credit customers (account T4).
>
> 4. April 12 – Mr Allen receives and banks a rent refund from his former landlord Mr Blanc

Item no	Date	Description	A/c	Bank	S/L	VAT	Cash Sales - Jwlry	Cash Sales – C & W	Sundries
1									
2									
3									
4									

If you are having difficulties go back to Module 15 Section 6 of the disc.

Cash receipts book – Posting the ledgers

The following questions relate to Module 15 Section 7 of AAT Bookkeeping Certificate.

26. In the table below enter the two ledgers to which cash receipts will be posted, and describe what accounts will be posted.

Ledger	Accounts posted

27. What postings will be made for Mrs Ritchie and Time Trading from the cash receipts book above?

-----

28. In the space below name the account and ledger where the totals of the cash receipts book are posted and whether each item is a debit or credit.

Bank	S/L	VAT	Cash sales – jwlry	Cash sales – C & W	Sundries
4900	1770	280	1940	860	50 (rent)

29. Show the full journal postings of the cash receipts book for April.

30. From what two sources are amounts posted to the *Purchases* account?

----

31. Describe the entries in the *Sales ledger control* account in respect of sales and receipts from customers.

----

32. What should be agreed to the *Sales ledger control* account balance?

----

33. From which two sources are amounts posted to the credit of the *Sales* accounts?

If you are having difficulties go back to Module 15 Section 7 of the disc.

Cash receipts book – Keeping the records

The following questions relate to Module 15 Section 8 of AAT Bookkeeping Certificate.

34. What is the pay-in counterfoil used for?

----

35. How would a proprietor know the up to date position with debtors?

----

36. Describe how the layout of the cash receipts book could be changed if a business received a number of receipts each day.

----

37. Why is it sensible to have this additional column?

----

38. What additional records might be kept if cash sales are only banked weekly?

----

39. In deciding a system of recording receipts, what three criteria should be taken into account?

If you are having difficulties go back to Module 15 Section 8 of the disc.

Examples – Errors

The following questions relate to Module 15 Section 10 of AAT Bookkeeping Certificate

40. In the table below describe the five errors in Mr Allen's cash book for May.

Error

41. What is a suspense account?

----

42. What should happen to the balance on a suspense account?

If you are having difficulties go back to Module 15 Section 10 of the disc.

Cash discount

The following questions relate to Module 15 Section 11 of AAT Bookkeeping Certificate.

43. What does the term 'cash discount' mean?

---

44. How is cash discount calculated?

---

45. What is trade discount?

---

46. Using the invoice in Section 11.2 of the software, fill in below the description of the terms listed.

Term	Description
Wholesale price (cost to retailer)	
Total due	
Settlement terms	

47. How is trade discount recorded on an invoice?

---

48. How is VAT calculated when a cash discount is offered?

---

49. Does the VAT figure change if the cash discount is not taken?

---

50. If, when paying an invoice, a customer takes advantage of cash discount, a balance of the discount will be left on the sales ledger account. What accounting entries remove this balance?

....

51. Why is it necessary to credit the sales ledger control with the same amount?

....

....

52. Where is *Discount allowed* usually shown in the profit and loss account?

....

53. What happens in the purchaser's accounting records when they have taken advantage of the cash discount?

....

....

54. Where is *Discount received* usually shown in the profit and loss account?

....

....

If you are having difficulties go back to Module 15 Section 11 of the disc.

Cash discount – Recording in the books

The following questions relate to Module 15 Section 12 of AAT Bookkeeping Certificate.

55. How can cash discounts be recorded in the cash payments book?

....

....

....

56. How will the transaction be posted to the purchase ledger?

....

57. How will the discount be posted to the nominal ledger?

----

58. Explain how a discount allowed can be recorded in the cash receipts book.

----

59. How will a customer receipt and discount be recorded in the nominal ledger?

----

60. How will the transaction be posted to the sales ledger?

If you are having difficulties go back to Module 15 Section 12 of the disc.

Computerised systems

The following questions relate to Module 15 Section 14 of AAT Bookkeeping Certificate.

61. Give three variations that can be used when dealing with computerised ledger accounts?

----

62. Describe the operation of a manual cash book with non-integrated sales and purchase ledgers.

----

63. If a manual cash book is maintained with integrated sales and purchase ledgers how will the system operate?

-----

64. How will a fully integrated system differ from that described in question 63?

-----

65. Describe three different ways in which purchase ledger payments may be updated in the nominal ledger.

-----

66. How might a computerised system operate if the computer produces the cheques?

-----

67. How will the system operate for cash receipts in a computerised system?

If you are having difficulties go back to Module 15 Section 14 of the disc.

Petty cash

The following questions relate to Module 15 Section 15 of AAT Bookkeeping Certificate.

68. Give three examples of items that it would be unusual to pay by cheque.

-----

69. What should be the size of the petty cash float?

BPP *PROFESSIONAL EDUCATION*

70. What evidence should be kept of payments made out of petty cash?

----

71. How is the petty cash float reimbursed?

----

72. In which book will a record be kept of petty cash transactions?

----

73. What two methods can be used to reimburse petty cash?

----

74. What is the imprest system?

----

75. Why should cash sales not be used to make cash payments?

----

76. How can the petty cash book be used to keep a check on the cash in the imprest system?

----

77. Explain how postings are made from the petty cash book.

----

78. What should the amount of cash in the petty cash box be equal to?

----

79. How should small miscellaneous receipts be dealt with?

----

80. What should be posted periodically to the cash account in the nominal ledger?

If you are having difficulties go back to Module 15 Section 15 of the disc.

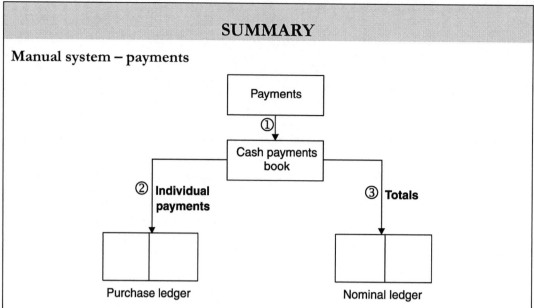

SUMMARY

Manual system – payments

1. Payment details are entered in the cash payment book.

2. Individual amounts paid to purchase ledger suppliers, together with any associated discount, are entered in the supplier accounts in the purchase ledger.

3. Totals are posted to the nominal ledger.

	Dr	Cr
Bank		xx
Discount received		x
P/L control	xx	
Wages	x	
....	x	

Manual system - receipts

```
                    ┌──────────────┐
                    │   Receipts   │
                    └──────────────┘
                          ①│
                           ▼
                    ┌──────────────┐
                    │ Cash receipts│
                    │     book     │
                    └──────────────┘
          ②│Individual              ③│Totals
           │receipts                 │
           ▼                         ▼
      ┌─────┬─────┐             ┌─────┬─────┐
      │     │     │             │     │     │
      └─────┴─────┘             └─────┴─────┘
       Sales ledger              Nominal ledger
```

1. Receipt details are entered in the cash receipts book.

2. Individual amounts received from credit customers, together with any associated discount, are entered in the customer accounts in the sales ledger.

3. Totals are posted in the nominal ledger.

	Dr	Cr
Bank	x	
Discount allowed	x	
Sales ledger control		x
VAT		x
Sales		x
- - -		x

Manual cash book, integrated ledgers

1. Individual receipts and payments are entered in the customer and supplier accounts in the sales and purchases ledgers.

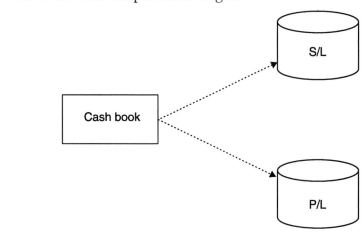

2. Amounts are transferred automatically from the sales and purchase ledgers to the nominal ledger.

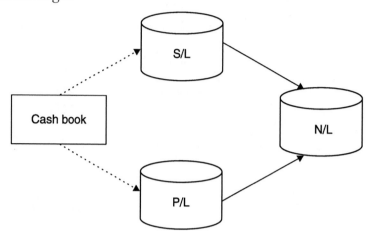

Receipts		
	Dr	Cr
Bank	xx	
Discount allowed	x	
S/L control		xx

Payments		
	Dr	Cr
Bank		xx
Discount received		x
P/L control	xx	

3. Totals for the remaining receipts and payments are posted by manual input to the nominal ledger.

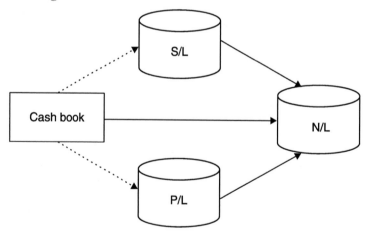

Receipts		
	Dr	Cr
Bank	xx	
VAT		x
Sales		x
Other		x
- - - -		x

Payments		
	Dr	Cr
Bank		x
Wages	x	
Drawings	x	
Other	x	
- - - -	x	

Fully computerised system

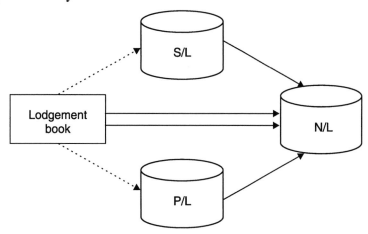

1. Individual receipts and payments are entered in the customer and supplier accounts in the sales and purchase ledgers

2. Amounts are transferred automatically from the sales and purchase ledgers to the nominal ledger

Receipts	Dr	Cr	Payments	Dr	Cr
Bank	xx		Bank		xx
Discount allowed	x		Discount Received		x
S/L control		xx	P/L control	xx	

3. Other receipts and payments are entered directly into the nominal ledger (possibly via a cash book module).

Petty cash

Periodically the amount of cash spent is reimbursed to take the balance of cash back to the preset level – the value of the imprest.

At any point:

Cash balance + Cash spent (since last reimbursement) = Imprest

Review

In this module you have learnt that:

- Bank receipts and payments are recorded in the cash book, often in an analysed format.

- Various figures from the cash book are posted to the:
    - sales ledger
    - purchase ledger
    - nominal ledger.

- Computerised systems will operate in a slightly different way to manual systems. The operation will vary from one system to another.

- Cash discounts are sometimes given for early settlement of an invoice. This discount must be recorded in both the sales/purchase ledger and the nominal ledger.

- A petty cash float is often kept for making small cash payments. The best method of operation is the imprest system.

Answers

The cash book

1. Receipts and payments are recorded in the cash book.

2. A business will make other payments such as wages and proprietor's drawings.

3. Payments will be recorded either in the cash book or the cash payments book.

4. Receipts will be recorded in the cash book or the cash receipts book.

5. The cash book contains cheque payments of the business and other payments that have gone through the business bank account.

6. Small payments made in cash are recorded in the petty cash book.

7. All receipts, both cash and cheques, are recorded in the cash receipts book.

8. The four functions of the cash book are:

    *   To record and briefly explain the bank transactions

    *   To show the amounts that will appear in due course on the bank statement

    *   To record receipts from debtors and payments to creditors for subsequent posting to their sales ledger and purchase ledger accounts.

    *   To accumulate and total all bank receipts and payments for subsequent posting to the nominal ledger

9. A cash sale is a 'non-credit' sale.

10. The cash book is normally in analysed format with the left hand page recording receipts (or debits to the *Bank* account) and the right hand side recording payments (or credits to the *Bank* account).

11. The cash book is normally totalled at least once a month.

12. Different forms of cash book are:

    *   Cash book that acts as the nominal ledger *Bank* account and incorporates the bank balance to be included on the trial balance

    *   Separate cash receipts and cash payments books are kept due to there being more receipts or payments

    *   Cash payments book that contains columns for both cash and bank payments and a combined analysis of expenditure

Cash payments book – Recording payments

13.

Column	Description
Date	The date the payment was made.
Cheque no	Number of the cheque for future reference and checking against the bank statement.
Payee	The person to whom the payment was made. Possibly some brief description will be included.
A/c no	Where applicable, purchase ledger account number to make posting of purchase ledger easier.
Bank	Amount of cheque that will in due course be shown on the bank statement.
P/L, wages, petty cash, drawings, VAT, sundries	Analysis columns – there will be columns for frequently used categories of expenses.

14.

Item no	Date		Cheque no	Payee	A/c	Bank	Analysis
1	April	2	345264	Time Trading	T1	784	P/L
2		4	265	Wages		120	Wages
3		6	266	J Allen		800	Drawings
4		12	267	Cash		100	Petty cash
5		12	268	Opal Traders		550	VAT 50 Sundries (Purchases) 500
6		13	269	Cancelled			
7		13	270	Inland Revenue		151	Sundries (I.R.)

15. The *Sundries* column should contain items that are not very frequent. A description of the item should also be included.

Cash payments book – Posting the ledgers

16.

Ledger	What is posted
Purchase ledger	Individual supplier accounts
Nominal ledger	Expense accounts, asset accounts and liabilities account

17. The amount will be debited to Time Trading and ticked against the related invoice.

18.

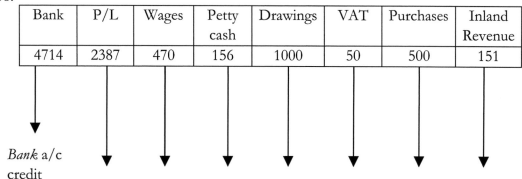

Bank	P/L	Wages	Petty cash	Drawings	VAT	Purchases	Inland Revenue
4714	2387	470	156	1000	50	500	151

Bank a/c credit

All these items would have been posted to the debit of the individual accounts in the nominal ledger

Cash payments book – Keeping the records

19. Details of the cheque should be written on the cheque stub.

20. The details should be entered in the cash payments book.

21. Details of the invoices paid should be included on the cheque stub or included on a copy remittance advice.

22. The business's bank statements, cheque stubs etc will be handed to their accountant.

Cash receipts book – Recording receipts

23. The cash receipts book records all receipts banked in the main business bank account.

24.

Column	Description
Date	The date the money was received
Ref no	The number of paying in counterfoil if sequentially numbered
Description	Detail of the sender of money and/or some description
A/c no	Details of sales ledger debtor if relevant
Bank	Amount of receipt or banking
Cash sales, VAT, sundries	Analysis columns – there will be analysis for subsequent posting to nominal ledger

25.

Item no	Date	Description	A/c	Bank	S/L	VAT	Cash Sales - Jwlry	Cash Sales - C & W	Sundries
1	April 4	Mrs Richie	R 2	420	420				
2	April 6	Cash sales		759		69	460	230	
3	April 10	Time Trading	T 4	1250	1250				
4	April 12	Mr Blanc		50					50 Rent refund

Cash receipts book – Posting the ledgers

26.

Ledger	What is posted
Sales ledger	Individual customer accounts
Nominal ledger	Income and *Debtors* accounts (and possibly some others)

27. The amounts received would be posted to the credit of Mrs Ritchie and Time Trading and the receipts ticked off with the relevant invoices.

28.

Bank	S/L	VAT	Cash sales - jwlry	Cash sales – C & W	Sundries
4900	1770	280	1940	860	50 (rent)

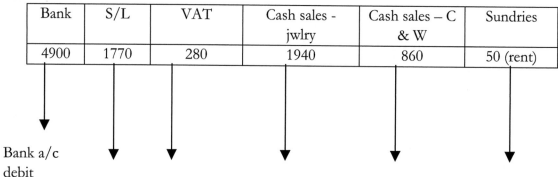

Bank a/c debit

All these items would have been posted to the credit of the individual accounts in the nominal ledger

29. The full journal is:

		Dr	Cr
April 30	Bank	4900	
	S/L Control		1770
	VAT		280
	Sales – jewellery		1940
	Sales – C & W		860
	Rent		50
		4900	4900

Posting of the cash receipts book for April

30. The two sources are credit purchases from the purchase daybook, and cash purchases from the cash payments book.

31. Debit total sales invoiced from sales daybook, and credit total receipts from cash receipts book.

32. The total of the list of all the individual sales ledger account balances should be agreed to the *Sales ledger control* account balance.

33. The two sources are credit sales from the sales daybook and cash sales from the cash receipts book.

Cash receipts book – Keeping the records

34. The pay-in counterfoil records details of amounts banked and is used as the basis for writing up the cash receipts book.

35. The up to date position could be ascertained by looking at the sales ledger accounts if they are regularly posted up to date.

36. Another column would be required in the cash receipts to show the total of each banking.

37. It is advantageous when checking the cash book to the bank statement as the totals of each banking will be clearly shown.

38. If cash sales are banked weekly then a subsidiary record showing daily cash sales might be kept.

39. The following criteria should be taken into account:

   - Frequency and level of cash business
   - Frequency and level of credit sales
   - Carefulness of the proprietor

Examples – Errors

40.

Error
Incorrect analysis – transposition of figure
VAT incorrectly analysed
Purchase ledger column incorrectly added
Purchase ledger receipt analysed as a cash purchase
Cheque omitted

41. A suspense account contains differences such as a trial balance difference and items under query.

42. The balance on the suspense account should be investigated as early as possible and cleared by journal entry.

Cash discount

43. Cash discount is an allowance for paying an invoice within a certain number of days.

44. Cash discount is calculated as a percentage of the invoice value.

45. Trade discount is the allowance made by a manufacturer or wholesaler to a trader. This discount usually takes the form of a fixed percentage off the list price of the goods. It will often be shown on the invoice.

46.

Term	Description
Wholesale price	List price less trade discount
Total due	Net + VAT
Settlement terms	Details of the discount available for payment within a specified period

47. Trade discount may not be shown on an invoice. The price of the goods may shown net of trade discount. Alternatively, the invoice may show the list price, trade discount, and wholesale price to the retailer.

48. VAT is calculated on the cost of the goods assuming the cash discount is taken.

49. The VAT remains the same irrespective of whether the cash discount is taken or not.

50. The accounting entries are:

    • Sales ledger (memorandum) – credit customer account

    • Nominal ledger (double entry)

        – credit *Sales ledger control* account
        – debit *Discount allowed*

51. The entry in the nominal ledger is required to maintain double entry; the entry in the sales ledger account being purely memorandum.

52. *Discount allowed* will be shown as a business expense.

53. The accounting entries will be debit the supplier's account (memorandum); credit *Discount received*, and debit the *Purchase ledger control* account (double entry).

54. *Discount received* can either be shown after gross profit being added with other sundry income, or it can be shown as a negative expense, or netted off against *Discount allowed*.

Cash discount – Recording in the books

55. An additional column to record cash discount received can be included in the cash payments book. The discount is posted to debit the supplier account and will be included in totals posted to the nominal ledger.

56. The payment, plus the discount, will be included as debits in the supplier's account.

57. The discount will be included as part of the total monthly posting to debit the *Purchase ledger control* and credit the *Discount received* account.

58. The cash receipts book can have a memorandum column for *Discount allowed*.

59. The entries will be debit *Bank*, credit *Sales ledger control* with the amount received, and debit *Discount allowed*, and credit *Sales ledger control* with the discount allowed.

60. Both the receipt and discount will be credited to the customer's account.

Computerised systems

61. The following three methods can be used:

    • Manual cash book, non-integrated sales and purchase ledgers
    • Manual cash book, integrated sales and purchase ledgers
    • Computerised cash book, fully integrated system.

62. The system would operate as follows:

    - The cash book would be written up manually as previously described
    - Sales and purchase ledgers will be posted separately
    - Journal entries to update the sales purchase and cash book information will be keyed into the computerised nominal ledger.

63. The system would operate as follows:

    - The cash book as before

    - Information input into the sales and purchase ledgers will be automatically updated in the nominal ledger

64. Other receipts and payments will be keyed into the computerised cash book along with the appropriate nominal ledger code to complete the double entry.

65. The three methods are:

    - Item-by-item – where each payment in the purchase ledger is automatically input to the nominal ledger.

    - Batch totals – where the posting to the nominal ledger is updated periodically for the total of a batch of payments.

    - Monthly totals – where the nominal update is done at the end of each month

66. When a batch of such cheques has been completed, a listing of payments will be produced, and the totals updated in the cash book.

67. The system will operate in the same manner as cash payments.

68. Examples that are usually inappropriate to pay by cheque include window cleaning, milk and stamps.

69. The petty cash float should be as small as possible consistent with the size and needs of the business.

70. Evidence for petty cash payments should be a numbered petty cash voucher for each payment supported if possible by a cash invoice.

71. The petty cash float should be reimbursed by drawing a cheque for cash.

72. Petty cash transactions should be recorded in the petty cash book.

73. Petty cash can be reimbursed by either:

    - Drawing a regular amount from the bank
    - Regular replacement of amounts paid out

74. A petty cash float is set up. Periodically the level of cash is made up to that same figure again.

75. In order to control the amount of cash received, cash sales should always be banked intact.

76. At any point in time, payments recorded in the petty cash book since the last reimbursement, plus cash in hand equal the original imprest balance.

77. The analysis columns will be totaled and these totals posted to the debit of the nominal ledger expense accounts, and credited to *Petty cash*.

78. The actual petty cash should be equal to the balance in the petty cash book.

79. Small miscellaneous receipts should be included in the petty cash book, and posted, in due course, to the nominal ledger.

80. The payments and sundry receipts will be posted to the cash account in the nominal ledger.

Module 16

Bank reconciliations

Introduction

It is important that a business knows how much it has (or does not have) in the bank. It should be regularly checking the cash book against the statements provided by the bank. As we pointed out when you were first introduced to debits and credits, the bank produces its statements from its own point of view, while you will be looking at the *Bank* account in your own records from your point of view. Thus debits on the bank statement represent money coming out of the bank account – credits in your own records (and vice versa). This is explained more fully in the module!

You will work through an example of checking the cash book against a given bank statement, using Mr Allen's cash book from the last module. Differences will fall into two categories – they will either be errors/omissions that require correcting in the records, or they will simply be timing differences (this most often happens with cheques, which can take some time from the date of issue, until they reach the bank account). Occasionally there may also be bank errors which require correction by the bank!

Once all necessary corrections have been made, and timing differences identified, you should be able to reconcile the cash book or nominal ledger *Bank* balance with that showing on the bank statement. This gives good external verification of one of the very important figures in the nominal ledger.

The next module will continue with the idea of controls and checks in the system, looking at the reconciliation of the *Sales* and *Purchase ledger control* account balances.

Learning objectives

By the end of this module you will:

- Be aware of the differences to expect when comparing a cash book against the bank statement.

- Know how and when to correct the cash book/nominal ledger.

- Be able to prepare a bank reconciliation.

Note form questions

Introduction

The following questions relate to Module 16 Section 2 of AAT Bookkeeping Certificate.

1.   How can the balance on the *Bank* account be confirmed?

   ....

2.   What is this agreement called?

   ....

3.   How often are bank statements received?

   ....

4.   What other method can be used to obtain bank information?

   ....

If you are having difficulties go back to Module 16 Section 2 of the disc.

Bank statements

The following questions relate to Module 16 Section 3 of AAT Bookkeeping Certificate.

5.   If the *Bank* account in the trader's nominal ledger carries a credit balance, where will it be shown on the balance sheet?

   ....

6.   If there is a £300 debit in a trader's nominal ledger *Bank* account, why would this appear as a credit on the bank statement received from the bank?

   ....

   ....

7.   In what format are bank statements usually produced?

   ....

   ....

8. In the table below, fill in descriptions for the items listed.

Item	Description
Account number	
Bank sorting code	
Date	
Description	
Debits/credits	
Balance	

9. What happens to customers' cheques after the bank has honoured them?

If you are having difficulties go back to Module 16 Section 3 of the disc.

Checking the bank statement – Payment

The following questions relate to Module 16 Section 4 of AAT Bookkeeping Certificate.

10. Why can it take up to a week from writing the cheque until it appears on the bank statement?

----

11. How is the bank reconciliation of the payments side started?

----

12. What are outstanding cheques?

----

13. When would cheques outstanding at the end of April be expected to go through the bank account?

----

14. What happens to outstanding cheques at the end of the month?

....

15. List five items that could be unticked on the bank statement, after entries had been checked to the cash book.

....

....

....

16. How can a computer system help in recording these unticked items?

....

If you are having difficulties go back to Module 16 Section 4 of the disc.

Checking the bank statement – Receipts

The following questions relate to Module 16 Section 5 of AAT Bookkeeping Certificate.

17. How is the bank reconciliation started on the receipts side?

....

18. What are outstanding lodgements?

....

....

19. List two receipts that might be unticked on the bank statements.

....

....

20. What procedure should be followed in preparing a bank reconciliation?

If you are having difficulties go back to Module 16 Section 5 of the disc.

Correction of the cash book

The following questions relate to Module 16 Section 6 of AAT Bookkeeping Certificate.

21. What is the most appropriate way to correct the cash book?

----

22. If the cash book has already been posted, what two methods could be used to correct entries?

If you are having difficulties go back to Module 16 Section 6 of the disc.

The bank reconciliation

The following questions relate to Module 16 Section 8 of AAT Bookkeeping Certificate.

23. What two types of transactions might be affected by timing differences when trying to reconcile the bank balance with the bank statements?

----

24. What is the format used when preparing the bank reconciliation?

25. How would the above reconciliation change if the bank balance is overdrawn?

If you are having difficulties go back to Module 16 Section 8 of the disc

Miscellaneous points

The following questions relate to Module 16 Section 10 of AAT Bookkeeping Certificate

26. What is a 'bounced' cheque?

------

27. Give three reasons for a bank dishonouring a cheque?

------

28. What procedure is followed when a cheque is dishonoured?

------

29. What accounting entries need to be made when a cheque has been dishonoured?

----

30. What is the time within which a cheque must be presented?

----

31. What could the payee do if a cheque is out of date?

----

32. What should the payer do after six months?

----

33. Where should bank errors be adjusted?

If you are having difficulties go back to Module 16 Section 10 of the disc.

SUMMARY

Differences between the cash book and bank statements are (mostly) either:

    a.   Errors or omissions in the cash book

    b.   Timing differences

In preparing a bank reconciliation the following steps are required:

    1.   Check off the cash book against the bank statement

    2.   Correct the cash book/nominal ledger for any errors/omissions

    3.   Prepare the reconciliation

Format of Bank reconciliation

Bank reconciliation at xx

	£
Balance per bank statement at xx	x
Add: Outstanding lodgements	x
Less: Outstanding cheques	(x)
Balance per nominal ledger at xx	x

Review

In this module you have learnt that:

- It is important to verify the balance recorded in the nominal ledger *Bank* account, by checking off individual items in the cash book against the bank statement.

- There will usually be several differences found between the entries in the cash book and those on the bank statement. Differences may be:

    –   Cash book errors

    –   Bank errors

    –   Timing differences

- After correction of any cash book errors, the nominal ledger *Bank* balance should be able to be reconciled with the balance on the bank statement.

Answers

Introduction

1.   The *Bank* balance can be confirmed by agreeing with the bank statements.

2.   This agreement is called a bank reconciliation.

3.   Bank statements are often received on a monthly basis, but may be more frequently.

4.   It is possible to receive daily updates using modem communication or by Internet banking.

Bank statements

5.   A credit bank balance will be shown as a current liability.

6.   The *Bank* account, as maintained in the books of the trader, is a statement of how the item appears from the business point of view, whilst the bank statement reflects how the items appear from the bank's point of view. If the trader has money in the bank (debit balance) this is an asset to him, but a liability to the bank, as they owe him £300.

7.   Bank statements are usually produced in 3-column format to show debits (withdrawals), credits (pays-in) and balance.

8.

Item	Description
Account number	Unique number for a customers' account
Bank sorting code	Indicates the particular bank and branch
Date	The date transactions go through the account. The statement will include transactions for a particular period.
Description	Brief description of transaction
Debit/credits	Debits are payments and credits are receipts
Balance	Balance is calculated at the end of each day

9.   The cheques are retained by the bank, but can be requested by the customer.

Checking the bank statement – Payment

10.   The cheque will need to be signed, posted to and received by the supplier who will then bank it, before it goes through the banking system.

11.   Payments that appear in the bank account and on the bank statements are ticked off.

12.   Outstanding (unpresented) cheques are cheques that have been included in the *Bank* account, but which have not yet worked their way through the banking system to appear on the bank statements before the end of the month.

13.   Cheques outstanding at the end of April will probably go through the bank account early in May.

14.   Outstanding cheques need to be included in the bank reconciliation.

15. The following items could be unticked:

    - Cheque that were unpresented in an earlier reconciliation
    - Direct debits
    - Bank transfers
    - Bank interest
    - Standing orders

16. A computer system can help by setting up recurring payments, so that items such as standing orders are not forgotten about.

Checking the bank statement – Receipts

17. It is started by ticking receipts that appear in the *Bank* account and on the bank statements.

18. Outstanding lodgements are items that have been paid into the bank account, which have not appeared on the bank statement.

19. The following items could be unticked:

    - Bank deposit interest

    - Credit transfers from customers who have transferred funds into the company bank account

20. The procedure is:

    - Correct the bank account for errors and omissions.

    - Prepare a bank reconciliation that agrees the *Bank* balance with the bank statement once timing differences have been taken into account.

Correction of the cash book

21. The easiest way is to check the cash book to the bank statement and to include any adjustments *before* postings are made from the cash book to the nominal ledger.

22. The entries could be corrected either by using a journal entry or making additional entries in the cash book.

The bank reconciliation

23. The two types of transactions affected by timing differences are:

    - Outstanding cheques
    - Outstanding lodgements

24. The format for the bank reconciliation is:

Balance per bank statement	x
+/- Timing differences	x
Balance per nominal ledger *Bank* account	x

25. If the bank balance is overdrawn the bank reconciliation would start with a negative figure.

Miscellaneous points

26. A 'bounced' cheque is a one which is not honoured by the bank on which it is drawn.

27. The reasons for dishonouring a cheque could be:

    - The cheque is not signed.
    - The words and figures on a cheque do not agree.
    - There are insufficient funds in the customer's account and the customer's bank is not prepared for the account to be overdrawn.

28. The procedure is:

    - The bank will debit the account where the cheque was originally presented.
    - The supplier and usually the bank will then get in touch with the customer to try to rectify the problem.

29. The dishonoured cheque will appear as a payment in the cash payment book and will be posted to the customer's account to reinstate the amount as being still due.

30. A cheque must be presented within 6 months of the date of issue.

31. The payee could ask for a replacement cheque.

32. The payer should cancel the original payment in the books after 6 months.

33. Bank errors should be adjusted on the bank statement balance being used in the bank reconciliation.

Module 17

Control accounts and bad debts

Introduction

We continue further here with sales and purchase ledgers and the corresponding control accounts in the nominal ledger. You have seen how invoices, and their settlement, are originally recorded in the books and find their way from there into the appropriate accounts in the sales or purchase ledgers. There may, however, be other entries required in these ledgers – to be entered as adjustments. The main ones are bad debts in the sales ledger and contras, where an amount in the sales ledger is set against an amount in the purchase ledger. The recording of these adjustments will need to be made in both the individual accounts in the sales and/or purchase ledgers and in the control accounts in the nominal ledger (where double entry, as always, must be maintained).

When it is known that a debt will never be received, it is written off as a bad debt. Rather trickier are doubtful debts. Here, the debt is not to be written off, so no entry is made in the sales ledger. Instead, a provision is made in the nominal ledger. In the first year, the full amount of the provision is charged against profits, and is set against the *Debtors* figure in the balance sheet. Something that is explained in the module, but you may need to think about a bit, is the fact that, in subsequent years, it is only the **change** in the provision that goes to the profit and loss account.

The final part of the module deals with the control aspect of the sales and purchase ledger systems. A list of individual customer balances from the sales ledger should total to the same figure showing in the *Sales ledger control* account in the nominal ledger. If the figures are different, something must be wrong. After a revision of the manual accounting system, you will be taken through various errors that might or might not cause such a difference. There will also be several examples for you to complete. These examples can be quite tricky, but they are a very good test of your understanding of the system.

This module concludes our investigation of practical accounting. By this stage you should have a good understanding of both how and why transactions are recorded in particular ways in the accounting system, whether it is manual or computerised. You should also have a good awareness of errors that could occur, and the checks that should be carried out to minimise these. The final module looks at the end result of all the bookkeeping/accounting you have learnt – the final accounts are looked at in a bit more detail for various types of business.

Learning objectives

By the end of this module you will:

* Know how to write off bad debts and record contras between sales and purchase ledgers.

* Know how to make and adjust a provision for doubtful debts, and why this may be necessary.

* Be aware of the need to exercise prudence in situations of uncertainty.

* Be able to correct differences between the control accounts and the subsidiary ledgers.

* Realise that many differences between the control accounts and the corresponding lists of balances cannot occur in a computerised system.

Note form questions

Posting of the ledgers

The following questions relate to Module 17 Section 2 of AAT Bookkeeping Certificate.

1. Summarise the postings that are made to the individual sales ledger accounts and also to the *Sales ledger control* account in respect of credit sales and customer receipts transactions.

	Debit	Credit
Sales ledger control		
Sales ledger accounts		

2. Summarise the postings that are made to the individual purchase ledger accounts and also to the *Purchase ledger control* account in respect of credit purchase transactions.

	Debit	Credit
Purchase ledger control		
Purchase ledger accounts		

If you are having difficulties go back to Module 17 Section 2 of the disc.

Bad debts

The following questions relate to Module 17 Section 3 of AAT Bookkeeping Certificate.

3. What is a common period of credit allowed to customers?

4. Why might a customer put off paying a debt?

5. What can a business do if a customer does not pay a debt?

6. In what two circumstances might a business decide not to take legal action?

....

....

7. Why might such a decision be taken in the case of a small debt?

....

8. Explain why a business could be overstating its assets with regard to *Debtors*.

....

9. What is a bad debt written off?

....

10. What accounting entries are required to be made when a bad debt is written off?

....

....

11. What is the effect of your entry in question 10?

....

....

....

12. In which accounting book should the adjustment be recorded?

....

13. When a bad debt is written off what adjustment is required for VAT?

....

....

....

14. What accounting entries are required to record this recoverable VAT?

---

15. Why is it possible to reclaim VAT on a bad debt from the HMRC by a registered trader?

---

16. What accounting entries are required if a bad debt is recovered?

---

17. What is the VAT position if a bad debt is recovered?

If you are having difficulties go back to Module 17 Section 3 of the disc.

Doubtful debts – Making provisions

The following questions relate to Module 17 Section 4 of AAT Bookkeeping Certificate.

18. In what two slightly different ways might a business be doubtful about the collectability of its debts?

---

19. Explain why it is important that at this stage the sales ledger balances are unadjusted for any potential bad debts?

---

20. What is a provision for doubtful debts?

---

21. How is the provision for doubtful debts shown on the balance sheet?

---

22. What happens to the other half of the accounting entry for doubtful debts?

-----

23. What are the accounting entries necessary to create a bad debt provision?

-----

24. What would be included within an account called *Bad and doubtful debts*?

-----

25. For the two situations indicated in the table below, state whether the individual customer's accounts are affected

Accounting for	Sales ledger accounts affected
Bad debts written off	
Provision for doubtful debts	

If you are having difficulties go back to Module 17 Section 4 of the disc.

Doubtful debts – Provision required

The following questions relate to Module 17 Section 5 of AAT Bookkeeping Certificate.

26. Explain four methods that could be used to estimate the provision for doubtful debts.

-----

27. What is a specific bad debt provision?

-----

28. What is a partial provision for specific debts?

....

....

29. What is a general bad debt provision?

....

30. How can a computerised system help in the assessment of the provision?

....

31. What is an aged debtors list?

....

....

32. How can the aged debtors list be used to produce a provision for doubtful debts?

....

....

33. Why does the amount of the provision for doubtful debts affect the net profit figure?

....

....

If you are having difficulties go back to Module 17 Section 5 of the disc.

Doubtful debts – Subsequent years (1) and (2)

The following questions relate to Module 17 Sections 6 and 7 of AAT Bookkeeping Certificate.

34. What happens to the provision for doubtful debts in subsequent years?

....

....

35. Why do the *Bad debts* account and *Increase in provision for doubtful debts* (expense) account not contain a balance at the beginning of an accounting period?

....

....

36. Explain what can happen to the existing provision for doubtful debts in subsequent years.

....

37. What is the procedure required to make an adjustment to the provision for doubtful debts?

....

....

38. Explain another way to record the adjustment to the provision for doubtful debts.

....

....

39. What are the accounting entries in a subsequent year for writing off the bad debts and then reducing the provision for doubtful debts?

....

....

....

40. Explain why the treatment of doubtful debts is an example of the concept of prudence.

....

....

....

....

If you are having difficulties go back to Module 17 Sections 6 and 7 of the disc.

Sales and purchase ledger adjustments

The following questions relate to Module 17 Section 9 of AAT Bookkeeping Certificate.

41. How would amounts be written off a purchase ledger account?

----

42. What is a contra item in the context of sales and purchase ledgers?

----

43. How are contra entries dealt with?

----

44. Does the use of a computerised system change the way adjustments are made?

If you are having difficulties go back to Module 17 Section 9 of the disc.

Control account – Errors

The following questions relate to Module 17 Section 10 of AAT Bookkeeping Certificate.

45. How is a business able to ensure that its individual sales and purchase ledger balances agree with the appropriate control account?

----

46. List below the procedure of recording credit sales transactions in a manual sales system.

47. List below the process of recording credit purchases in a manual purchases system.

48. How can differences arise between the control accounts and the individual ledger account balances?

49. Where can the error(s) occur?

50. How is it possible to ascertain whether errors exist?

....

....

51. What needs to be considered for each error?

....

....

52. Complete the table below showing the effect of errors on the control accounts and lists of balances.

Category	Control a/c correct Yes/No	List of balances correct Yes/No	Correction required
Entries recorded correctly in the daybook or cash book, but transferred incorrectly to an individual ledger account			
Entries recorded incorrectly in the daybook or cash book			
Entries recorded in the individual ledger accounts correctly, but not posted to the control a/c			
The balances in the individual accounts transferred incorrectly from the ledger to the list of balances			
Incorrect addition of the cash book or daybook			

If you are having difficulties go back to Module 17 Section 10 of the disc.

Errors – Worked examples

The following questions relate to Module 17 Section 11 of AAT Bookkeeping Certificate.

53. In the table below suggest how the error listed could be corrected.

Error	Correction
Debit balance listed as a credit balance	
Transposition error in listing	

54. In a computerised accounting system why do fewer errors occur?

----

55. What are the principles suggested in the software that should be used to correct errors?

If you are having difficulties go back to Module 17 Section 11 of the disc.

SUMMARY

Bad debts

The balance in the *Sales ledger control (Debtors)* account may need to be reduced so that the balance sheet shows the amount expected to be recovered from those debtors.

Bad debt – where a debt which is known to be irrecoverable.

A customer (memo only)				Sales ledger control			
Bal b/f	x	Bad debts	x	Bal b/f	xx	Bad debts	x

	Dr	Cr	
Bad debts	x		(Net)
VAT	x		(VAT)
S/L control		x	(Gross)
S/L customer account (memo)		x	

Provision for doubtful debts (DD)– where it is thought that not all of the money will be recovered from debtors:

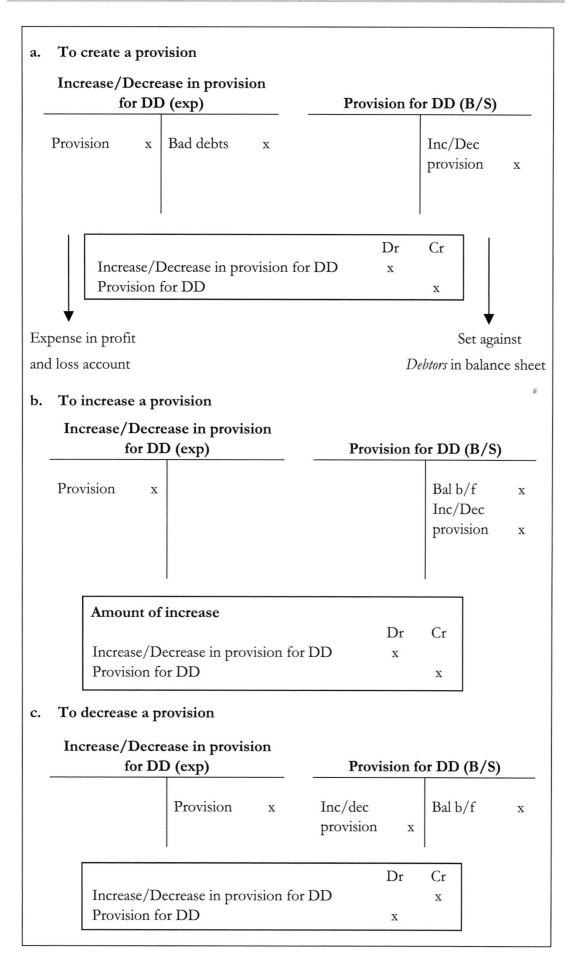

a. To create a provision

Increase/Decrease in provision for DD (exp)				Provision for DD (B/S)		
Provision	x	Bad debts	x		Inc/Dec provision	x

	Dr	Cr
Increase/Decrease in provision for DD	x	
Provision for DD		x

Expense in profit and loss account

Set against *Debtors* in balance sheet

b. To increase a provision

Increase/Decrease in provision for DD (exp)		Provision for DD (B/S)	
Provision	x	Bal b/f	x
		Inc/Dec provision	x

Amount of increase

	Dr	Cr
Increase/Decrease in provision for DD	x	
Provision for DD		x

c. To decrease a provision

Increase/Decrease in provision for DD (exp)		Provision for DD (B/S)		
	Provision	x	Inc/dec provision	x	Bal b/f	x

	Dr	Cr
Increase/Decrease in provision for DD		x
Provision for DD	x	

Specific provision – a **provision** which is calculated with reference to particular debts that are thought not to be recoverable.

General provision – a provision that is calculated by considering the overall debt with no reference to any particular debts.

Prudence – In situations of uncertainty, a degree of caution should be exercised when judgments and estimates are made.

Reconciliation of control account and list of balances

At all times

- *Sales ledger control* account balance should equal the total of the list of individual sales ledger balances.

- *Purchase ledger control* account balance should equal the total of the list of individual purchase ledger balances.

Differences should be investigated and errors corrected.

When an error is found, decide if the correction required is:

 a. to the list of balances only; or
 b. to the control account only; or
 c . to both

and correct accordingly

Many errors that occur in manual systems cannot occur in computer systems (the possibilities will vary from one system to another)

Review

In this module you have learnt that:

- The *Debtors* figure in the balance sheet should represent the amount expected to be recoverable from debtors.

- Debts known to be irrecoverable should be written off as bad debts. If the full amount of debtors is still not expected to be recoverable, a provision for doubtful debts should be a made.

- At all times the balance in the control accounts in the nominal ledger should equal the total of the lists of balances from the subsidiary ledgers (sales and purchase ledgers).

- In a manual system, it is very easy for errors to arise, making the control account not equal the total of the list of balances. Such differences should be investigated and corrected.

- In a computer system, many of the common errors in a manual system will not be possible.

Answers

Posting of the ledgers

1.

	Debit	Credit
Sales ledger control	**Total** sales	**Total** receipts from customers
Sales ledger accounts	**Individual** sales invoices	Receipts from **individual** customers

2.

	Debit	Credit
Purchase ledger control	**Total** payments to suppliers	**Total** purchases
Purchase ledger accounts	Payments to **individual** suppliers	**Individual** purchase invoices

Bad debts

3. A common period of credit is a month from the date of sale.

4. A customer in financial difficulties might put off paying invoices.

5. A business can:

   - Telephone, send letters and statements
   - Instruct a solicitor to take legal action

6. Two circumstances where a business might decide not to take legal action are:

   - If the debt is small
   - The customer has no funds to make the payment

7. With a small debt the cost of collection might exceed the debt itself.

8. A business may be overstating its assets if *Debtors* include an amount that will never be received.

9. A bad debt is an amount written off a debtors account.

10. The accounting entries are:

    - Debit *Bad debts* account and credit *Sales ledger control*
    - Credit also required (memorandum only) to the individual debtor account

11. The effect of the entries in question 10 is to reduce the debtor (an asset) on the balance sheet, and include a bad debts account as an expense in the profit and loss account at the end of the accounting period.

12. The adjustment should be recorded as a journal entry.

13. If the business is not registered for VAT no adjustment will be required.

    If the business is registered for VAT then related VAT could be reclaimed from the Customs and Excise so long as the debt is more than six months old.

14. The accounting entries are debit *VAT*, credit *Sales ledger control* with the VAT recoverable. The net bad debt expense will debit *Bad debts* and credit *Sales ledger control.*

15. It is possible to reclaim the VAT, as the VAT charged on the invoice will have been paid over to Customs and Excise but never been received from the customer.

16. The accounting entries are debit *Bank*, credit *Bad debts recovered* (or *Bad debts*).

17. The VAT on the bad debt recovered must be repaid to the Customs and Excise.

Doubtful debts – Making provisions

18. The business might be concerned that:

    - Specific customers might not pay.
    - Some, at present unidentifiable, customers will not eventually make full payment.

19. The balances must be left unadjusted as the business is not yet sure that full recovery will not be possible, and the debtors are still being pursued for payment in full.

20 A provision for doubtful is an estimate of debts that might not be recovered.

21. The provision for doubtful debts is shown as a deduction from *Debtors* on the balance sheet.

22. The other half of the entry will be shown as an expense in the profit and loss account.

23. The accounting entries are debit *Increase in provision for doubtful debts*, credit *Provision for doubtful debts.*

24. The account *Bad and doubtful debts* includes bad debts written off and any increase in provision for doubtful debts.

25.

Accounting for	Sales ledger accounts affected
Bad debts written off	Yes
Provision for doubtful debts	No

Doubtful debts – Provision required

26. Four methods are:

    - Make full provision for specific debts
    - Make partial provision for specific debts
    - Make a general provision, not related to any specific debts
    - Provide for specific debts, plus a further general provision.

27. A specific bad debt provision is one that is provided against the debts of specific customers, whose creditworthiness is in doubt.

28. Identify specific debts that might not pay – then assume a percentage will pay (say 50%).

29. A general bad debt provision is one that does not apply to specific balances.

30. A computerised system can produced an aged debtors list.

31. An aged debtors list will analyse outstanding balances over the length of time the debt has been outstanding.

32. From the aged debtors list it is possible to decide on the make up of a provision – x% of certain debts, x% of all debts, or x% of debts over 3 months old.

33. An increase in the provision shows as an expense in the profit and loss account, thus reducing profit.

Doubtful debts – Subsequent years (1) and (2)

34. The provision will be carried forward and adjusted to reflect the situation each year.

35. The two accounts do not show a balance as they are both expense accounts which were cleared to zero at the end of the last accounting year.

36. In subsequent years the provision can be either increased or decreased.

37. The procedure is:

    - Write off any debts known to be irrecoverable.

    - Estimate the provision now required and increase/decrease the existing provision accordingly.

38. (a) reverse opening provision

    (b) include closing provision

    (rather than simply adjusting for the charge in the provision).

39. The write off of bad debts – debit *Bad debts* and credit *Sales ledger control* + credit to individual sales ledger accounts (memo only).

    Reduction in the provision is debit *Provision for doubtful debts* (B/S) and credit *Increase/decrease in Provision for doubtful debts* (P&L) with the amount of the reduction required in the provision.

40. In providing for a doubtful debt, the expense of non-recovery is recognised and charged to the profit and loss account when the provision is made. The subsequent writing off of a debt previously provided for has no further effect on profit. A degree of caution is being exercised in this situation of uncertainty.

Sales and purchase ledger adjustments

41. The accounting entries would be credit to expense account, debit to *Purchase ledger control* and the individual purchase ledger account.

42. A contra arises when the same business is both a supplier and a customer and has transactions in both the sales and purchase ledger. An amount due *by* the business is offset against an amount due *to* them.

43. The balance on one account will be offset against the balance on the other. If the supplier account has the higher balance the difference will be paid over; if the customer account has the higher balance the difference will be received.

44. Adjustment are made in the same manner. In an integrated system, making the adjustment in the individual sales and purchase ledger accounts will initiate the corresponding postings to the control accounts.

Control account – Errors

45. By ensuring that whenever a posting is made to an individual account it is also made to the control account (in total) and visa versa.

46. The procedure is:

     • Invoices are recorded in the sales daybook.

     • Invoices are posted individually to the customer accounts in the sales ledger (debit).

     • The totals of the invoices for a month are posted to credit of the *Sales and VAT accounts* in the nominal ledger. The gross total of invoices will debit the *Sales ledger control.*

     • Receipts from customers are recorded in the cash receipts book (along with any other receipts).

     • Individual customer receipts are posted to the customer accounts in the sales ledger (credit).

     • Cash receipts book totals for the month are posted to debit of the *Bank* account in the nominal ledger. Customer receipts credit the *Sales ledger control.*

     • Adjustments are posted by journal entry to both the individual accounts in the sales ledger and the control account in the nominal ledger.

47. The procedure is:

     • Invoices are recorded in the purchases daybook.

     • Invoices are posted individually to the supplier accounts in the purchase ledger (credit).

     • The totals of the invoices for a month are posted to the debit of the appropriate purchase or expense accounts in the nominal ledger. The gross total of invoices will credit the *Purchase ledger control.*

     • Payments to suppliers, together with all other bank payments are recorded in the cash payments book.

     • Individual supplier payments are posted to the supplier accounts in the purchase ledger (debit).

- Cash payments book totals for the month are posted to the nominal ledger. Supplier payments debit the *Purchase ledger control*.

- Posting of adjustments, via the journal, to both *Purchase ledger control* account in the nominal ledger and individual supplier accounts in the purchase ledger.

48. Differences can occur if the sum of the individual postings made does not correspond with the total postings made to the control accounts.

49. The errors can occur in the individual postings, or the total postings, or both.

50. It is possible to know that errors exist if the balance on the control account does not equal the sum of the balances on the individual ledger accounts.

51. For each error the following need to be considered:

- Is the control account correct?
- Is the total of the list of balances correct?

52.

Category	Control a/c correct Yes/No	List of balances correct Yes/No	Correction required
Entries recorded correctly in the daybook or cash book, but transferred incorrectly to an individual ledger account	Yes	No	List of balances to be corrected
Entries recorded incorrectly in the daybook or cash book	No	No	Both control a/c & list of balances require correction
Entries recorded in the individual ledger accounts correctly, but not posted to the control a/c	No	Yes	Control a/c only requires correction
The balances in the individual accounts transferred incorrectly from the ledger to the list of balances	Yes	No	List of balances to be corrected
Incorrect addition of the cash book or daybook	No	Yes	Control a/c to be corrected

Errors – Worked examples

53. In the table below suggest how the error listed could be corrected.

Error	Correction
Debit balance listed as a credit balance	Only adjustment required is to change the balance to a debit balance
Transposition error in listing	Change the balance to the correct figure on the listing

54. Subsidiary ledgers are usually integrated with the nominal ledger in a computerised system. Thus any entry in an individual customer/supplier account will be correctly updated in the control accounts. There should also not be any errors in the listing of balances.

55. The principle involved is:

    1) Follow through the description of the error to see if it affects the list of balances and/or the balance per the control account and decide:

       ° Is the balance per the control account correct?
       ° Is the total per the list of balances correct?

    2) Make the necessary correction. In some questions you may be required just to adjust the balance per the control account or the total per the list to arrive at the correct figure. In other cases a journal entry may be required to correct the error.

Module 18

Final accounts

Introduction

As you saw right back at the start of the package, there are many different types of business. They may differ in the ways they are structured or in the area in which they operate. We have followed through the transactions, books and accounts of Mr Allen, a sole trader in a retail business. In this module we look at some variations of this.

Some organisations, such as clubs and societies, are not in existence to make a profit. The accounts of these non-profit seeking organisations will be slightly different to those of Mr Allen. For example, they will usually produce a receipts and payments account, or preferably, an income and expenditure account in place of a profit and loss account.

One of the main things that will cause variations in accounts is the ownership of a business. Mr Allen was a sole-trader, owning his business himself. A variation on this is a partnership, when the business is owned by two or more people. The accounts are very similar to those of the sole-trader, but the profit will need to be split amongst the partners and they will each need their own capital accounts.

Rather different will be the accounts of the limited company, which is a separate legal entity. The owners are the shareholders, who, in a large company may have nothing at all to do with the running of the company. There is a lot of legislation in place regarding the set-up, running and reporting of limited companies. We take a look here at some of the important aspects of this legislation and the format of the accounts as they would be produced for the shareholders.

On completion of this module you will realise that much of what you have learnt already applies in any business situation, and also be aware of variations that will apply in different types of business set-ups.

Well done in reaching the last module! You have covered a lot of ground and will have learnt a lot by this stage. Hopefully you will be able to prove this in the exam – good luck!

Learning objectives

The objectives of this module are to ensure you:

- Understand the differences between receipts and payments accounts and income and expenditure accounts.

- Are aware of the differences in the accounts of sole traders and partnerships.

- Understand a company's share capital reserves and long-term liabilities.

- Know how a company's internal accounts are drawn up.

- Are aware of the format of published accounts and the legislation governing them.

Note form questions

Non-profit seeking organisations

The following questions relate to Module 18 Section 2 of AAT Bookkeeping Certificate.

1. What is a non-profit seeking organisation?

    ....

2. What type of income and expenditure might such an organisation have?

    ....

    ....

3. Who usually looks after the finances of non-profit making organisations?

    ....

4. What does the treasurer do at the organisation's AGM?

    ....

    ....

5. What is the simplest form of annual financial summary?

    ....

6. What is a receipts and payments account?

    ....

    ....

7. In what two different formats can receipts and payments accounts be produced?

    ....

    ....

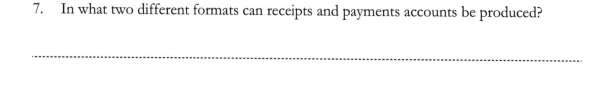

8.   What are the disadvantages of a receipts and payments account?

9.   Which documents is it better for a non-profit seeking organisation to produce?

10.   Why is it inappropriate for a non-profit making organisation to produce a trading and profit and loss account?

11.   What is the main difference between an income and expenditure account and a profit and loss account?

12.   How does the balance sheet of a non-profit seeking organisation differ from that of a trading organisation?

13. With reference to the accounts of a non-profit seeking organisation, fill in the table below the description for the items listed.

Item	Description
Subscription	
Bar profit	
Expenditure	
Surplus for the year	
Subscriptions due	
Subscription in advance	
Accumulated fund	

14. On an income and expenditure account, why are subscriptions shown as the amount **due** for the year rather than the amount actually **received**?

15. Where will subscriptions in arrears be shown in the balance sheet of a non-profit seeking organisation?

16. Where will subscriptions in advance be shown in the balance sheet of a non-profit seeking organisation?

If you are having difficulties go back to Module 18 Section 2 of the disc.

Sole trader

The following questions relate to Module 18 Section 3 of AAT Bookkeeping Certificate.

17. What is a sole trader's gross profit?

18. What is a sole trader's net profit?

19. What is a sole trader's net current assets?

----

20. What is a sole trader's net assets?

----

21. What is a sole trader's capital employed?

----

22. In which two places could the balance sheet of a sole trader show the long-term liabilities?

----

23. What will be included in the amount shown as due to the Inland Revenue for a sole trader?

----

24. Where should loan repayments due in the next year be shown on a sole trader's balance sheet?

If you are having difficulties go back to Module 18 Section 3 of the disc.

Partnerships

The following questions relate to Module 18 Section 4 of AAT Bookkeeping Certificate.

25. Why might a number of people wish to be in business together?

----

26. Where should details of profit shares be laid down?

----

27. If there is no partnership agreement which Act governs the running of a partnership?

28. What additional ledger accounts will be needed for a partnership?

29. In a partnership, what happens to the profit at the end of the year?

30. How is a sole trader's closing balance capital calculated?

31. What are drawings?

32. A partnership usually maintains two accounts for each partner. What are they and what are they used for?

33. Where are details of the profit sharing arrangements usually found?

34. In the table below, detail the four main methods of splitting profit and briefly describe, and explain the reason for, each method.

Method	Description

35. Why are partners' salaries not an expense of the business?

---

36. Where is the split of profit between the partners shown?

---

37. What happens to a sole trader or partner if the business is unable to pay its debts?

---

38. What is the rule on the number of persons able to be a partner?

If you are having difficulties go back to Module 18 Section 4 of the disc.

Limited companies – Capital and reserves

The following questions relate to Module 18 Section 5 of AAT Bookkeeping Certificate.

39. What is limited liability?

40. What is often the difference in the shareholders' involvement in a small company and a large company?

41. What is a board of directors?

42. What are the directors required to do each year?

43. What is contained within the published accounts?

44. Whose responsibility is it to produce the accounts?

45. Who are the main shareholders in large public companies?

46. What is a share?

---

47. What new category of accounts will be shown in the capital section of a company's balance sheet?

---

48. How is the profit generated during the year disclosed?

---

49. What does the term 'nominal value' mean?

---

50. What does the term 'share premium' mean?

---

51. What is the accounting entry if share capital is issued at a premium?

---

52. What is a dividend?

---

53. How is the dividend normally calculated?

---

54. A quoted dividend percentage is a percentage of

---

55. What is an undistributable reserve?

56. What is a distributable reserve?

57. Who are the members of a company?

58. What rights do the members have?

59. What other types of shareholders might a company have?

60. What type of dividend is a preference shareholder entitled to?

61. What is authorised capital?

62. What is issued share capital?

63. What type of loans can a company raise?

64. What does it mean when debentures are redeemable?

---

65. What happens when debentures are irredeemable?

---

66. In the table below, fill in the differences between shares and debentures.

	Debentures	**Shares**
Voting rights		
Return on investment		
Security		
On liquidation		

If you are having difficulties go back to Module 18 Section 5 of the disc.

Limited companies – Accounts

The following questions relate to Module 18 Section 6 of AAT Bookkeeping Certificate.

67. What is the historical cost convention?

---

68. In what circumstances might the historical cost convention not be used?

---

69. In some countries why is it necessary to use some form of current cost accounting?

---

70. What modification to the use of historic costs is commonly used in the UK?

....

71. Can companies carry out only occasional revaluations?

....

72. How is a revaluation recorded in the accounting records?

....

....

73. Why is this revaluation not included in the profit and loss account?

....

....

74. Where is the revaluation reserve shown on the balance sheet?

....

75. What are the four main differences between the profit and loss account of a sole trader and that of a company?

	Differences
1	
2	
3	
4	

76. Write a description beside each item in the table below.

Term	Description
Directors' remuneration	
Audit fee	
Debenture interest	
Taxation	
Preference dividend	
Interim dividend	
Final proposed	
Retained profits	

77. What is an executive director?

78. What is a non-executive director?

79. What must be included within the corporation tax figure?

80. When will the proposed final dividend be paid?

81. Give two reasons why a company might not pay a dividend.

82. Where will the liabilities for taxation and dividends be shown?

....

83. In relation to a company's balance sheet, give descriptions of each of the items listed below.

Term	Description
Cost/valuation	
Property	
Tax liabilities	
Current liabilities	
Debentures	
Proposed dividends payable	
Share premium	
Revaluation reserve	
Profit and loss account	

84. What accounting entries are required to enter the tax liability and the proposed dividends?

....

....

....

If you are having difficulties go back to Module 18 Section 6 of the disc.

Limited companies – Legislation

The following questions relate to Module 18 Section 7 of AAT Bookkeeping Certificate.

85. To whom must a company send its published accounts?

....

....

86. What legislation governs the format of published accounts?

----

87. What is the Accounting Standards Committee (ASC)?

----

88. What are SSAPs?

----

89. What is the ASB?

----

90. What are FRSs?

----

91. What rules are companies quoted on the Stock Exchange required to comply with?

----

92. What was the subject area of SSAP 2?

----

93. What are the two categories used by FRS 18 to categorise accounting concepts?

----

94. What are two accounting concepts?

----

95. What are two desirable concepts?

----

96. What is the going concern concept?

----

97. Give an example of the use of the going concern concept.

----

98. What is the accruals concept?

----

99. Give three examples of the application of the accruals concept.

----

100. What is the consistency/comparability quality?

----

101. Why is comparability important?

----

102. What is the prudence quality?

----

103. Give an example of the use of prudence.

----

104. What is disaggregation?

----

105. Give an example of disaggregation.

----

106. In the table below, fill in details of the SSAPs and FRSs listed.

Accounting standard	Details
SSAP 4	
SSAP 13	
FRS 1	
FRS 3	
FRS 14	
FRS 18	

107. What are international accounting standards?

----

108. What is a group?

BPP
PROFESSIONAL EDUCATION

109. What are consolidated accounts?

....

110. What type of adjustments might be required in the preparation of the consolidated accounts?

....

....

111. One of the Companies Act criteria for a 'small' company relates to turnover. What is this level of turnover?

....

If you are having difficulties go back to Module 18 Section 7 of the disc.

Limited companies – Published accounts

The following questions relate to Module 18 Section 8 of AAT Bookkeeping Certificate.

112. In the table below, draft a published profit and loss account.

Name of company
Profit and loss account for the year ended..........

Notes		£'000	£'000

113. In the table below, explain which figures in the internal accounts make up the item in the published accounts, and say what further details will be given.

Published accounts	Internal accounts
Turnover	
Cost of sales	
Gross profit	
Administrative expenses/distribution costs	
Operating profit	
Interest	
Profit on ordinary activities before taxation	
Taxation	
Profit attributable to ordinary shareholders	
Ordinary dividend	
Retained profit for the year	
Earnings per share	
Continuing operations	

114. In the table below draft a published balance sheet

Name of company
Balance sheet at ....

Notes		£'000

115. In the table below explain which figures in the internal accounts make up the item in the published accounts, and say what further detail will need to be disclosed.

Published accounts	Internal accounts
Tangible assets	
Stocks	
Debtors	
Creditors due in one year	
Net current assets/Total assets less current liabilities	
Creditors – due after one year	
Capital and reserves	
Signature	

116. What will be shown in the notes to the accounts?

If you are having difficulties go back to Module 18 Section 8 of the disc.

SUMMARY

Non-profit seeking organisations may draw up a:

Receipts and payments account

This is effectively a cash book summary, showing opening balances, receipts, payments and closing balances.

Income and expenditure account

This is drawn up in the same way as a profit & loss account, but it calculates a surplus/deficit rather than a profit/loss.

This will usually accompanied by a balance sheet

	£
Subscription received	xx
– Subscriptions in arrears last year	(x)
+ Subscriptions in advance last year	x
+ Subscriptions in arrears this year	x
– Subscriptions in advance this year	(x)
Subscriptions to I&E account	xx

Partnership profit and loss account

NET PROFIT			xx
APPROPRIATED:	**Partner 1**	**Partner 2**	
Interest on capital	x	x	
Interest on drawings	(x)	(x)	
Salaries	x	x	
Balance of profits	(x%) x	(y%) x	
	x	x	
			xx

Partnership balance sheet

	Partner 1	Partner 2	
			XXX
CAPITAL ACCOUNTS	X	X	XX
CURRENT ACCOUNTS			
Opening balance	X	X	
Interest on capital	X	X	
Salaries	X	X	
Balance of profits	X	X	
	X	X	
Drawings	(X)	(X)	
Interest on drawings	(X)	(X)	
	X	X	XX
			XXX

Company profit and loss account

		XX
Net profit before taxation		XX
Taxation		X
Net profit after taxation		XX
Dividends:		
Preference dividends	X	
Ordinary dividends		
Interim paid	X	
Final proposed	X	
		X
Retained profit for year		XX

Company balance sheet

	XX
CAPITAL AND RESERVES	
Share capital	X
Share premium	X
Revaluation reserve	X
Profit and loss account	X
	XX

Limited companies: published accounts

Published accounts are governed by:

Companies Act 1985
Statements of Standard Accounting Practice (SSAPs)
Financial Reporting Standards (FRSs)

Published profit and loss account

Turnover		XX
Cost of sales		X
Gross profit		XX
Administrative expenses	X	
Distribution costs	X	
		XX
Operating profit		X
Interest		X
Profit on ordinary activities before taxation		X
Taxation		X
Profit on ordinary activities after taxation		X
Dividends		X
Retained profit for the year		X

Published balance sheet

Fixed assets		
Tangible assets		X
Current assets		
Stock	X	
Debtors	X	
Cash at bank and in hand	X	
	X	
Creditors : amounts falling due within one year	X	
Net current assets		X
Total assets less current liabilities		X
Creditors: amounts falling due after more than one year		(x)
		XX
Capital and reserves		
Called up share capital		X
Share premium		X
Revaluation reserve		X
Profit and loss account		X
		XX

Review

In this module you have learnt that:

- A non-profit seeking organisation may prepare a receipts and payments account, but an income and expenditure account and balance sheet (or statement of affairs) will give better information.

- The accounts of a partnership will need to show how the profit (or loss) is split amongst the partners. Details of each partner's capital investment must also be kept, perhaps in fixed capital accounts with annual movements being made in their current accounts.

- There are several advantages (and some disadvantages) to operating as a limited company instead of as a sole trader or partnership. There are many regulations to be complied with by the limited company.

- A sole trader or partnership's capital will be replaced by the share capital and reserves of a limited company. A company may also be partly financed by loans or debentures.

- A company's published accounts must follow the format laid down in the Companies Act and comply with other requirements of the Act and various accounting standards.

Answers

Non-profit seeking organisations

1. An organisation which does not operate with a view to making profit.

2. Income is usually subscriptions or fees, and expenses are those connected with the running of the club.

3. The treasurer usually looks after the finances of non-profit making organisations.

4. At the AGM the treasurer will present the members with information about the finances of the organisation.

5. The receipts and payments account is the simplest form of annual financial summary.

6. The receipts and payments account is a summary of the organisation's cash book.

7. Receipts and payments accounts can be produced in double-sided form or in vertical format.

8. The receipts and payments account does not give any indication of whether or not the club is covering its costs, nor is there any indication of its assets and liabilities.

9. A non-profit making organisation would be better producing an income and expenditure account and a balance sheet.

10. A non-profit making organisation is not in existence to trade and generate profits.

11. On an income and expenditure account the net figure will be surplus or deficit instead of a profit or loss.

12. The balance sheet of a non-profit seeking organisation will have accumulated funds instead of capital to which will be added (subtracted) accumulated surplus (deficit). The balance sheet itself is often referred to as a statement of affairs.

13.

Item	Description
Subscription	Amount due by a member for the year.
Bar profit	Profit from the operation of the bar. This should be supported by a detailed profit and loss account of the bar takings less expenses.
Expenditure	Calculated according to the normal rules.
Surplus for the year	Equivalent to profit.
Subscriptions due	These will only be included if it is certain that they will be received.
Subscriptions in advance	Subscriptions received for the next year.
Accumulated fund	Equivalent of capital.

14. The statement is an income and expenditure account rather than a receipts and payments account, and must therefore include all **income due for the period**.

15. Current assets.

16. Current liabilities.

Sole trader

17. The gross profit is the difference between sales and cost of sales.

18. The net profit is the difference between the income and expenditure.

19. The net current assets are current assets less current liabilities.

20. The net assets are assets less liabilities.

21. A sole trader's capital employed is the closing balance of capital (equal to assets less liabilities).

22. The long-term liabilities can be shown as an addition to capital or as a deduction in the assets section of the balance sheet.

23. This will be the PAYE and NI due by the sole trader for the business's employees.

24. Loans repayable in the next year should be shown as a current liability.

Partnerships

25. By combining together they are able to combine expertise or capital as well as sharing risk.

26. Details of share of profits should be included within a partnership agreement.

27. In the absence of a partnership agreement the running of the partnership is governed by the Partnership Act 1890.

28. In a partnership ledger accounts will be needed for the capital and drawings for each partner.

29. The profit must be split – the appropriate amount being transferred to each partner's capital account.

30.

Capital at beginning of the year	X
Add: Additional capital contributed	X
Add: Profit for the year	X
Less: Drawings	(X)
Capital at the end of the year	X

31. Drawings are amounts taken out of the business by the sole trader – goods, assets taken from the business or personal bills paid by the business.

32. Two accounts, and their use, usually kept by a partnership for each partner are:

| Capital account | Long-term capital contributed to the business |
| Current account | Accumulated profit less drawings |

33. Profit sharing arrangements are usually found in the partnership agreement.

34.

Method	Description
Interest on capital	Partners are rewarded for leaving capital in the business by giving them interest at an agreed rate on their capital balances.
Interest on Drawings	Penalty to partners by charging them interest on their drawings. Not commonly used.
Partners' salaries	Partners may have a fixed salary that is apportioned to them. This may be as a reward for working in the business to different extents, or some partners may be given a higher fixed 'salary' and lower share of the balance of profits.
Share of the residue	After apportioning the profits in any of the above ways as agreed by the partners, the balance will be split amongst them in their profit-sharing ratios.

35. Partners' salaries are an appropriation of profit – one means of splitting the net profit amongst the partners.

36. The split of profit is shown in the appropriation account.

37. If the business is unable to pay its debts the sole trader or partner is personally liable, and their personal assets could be used.

38. Only 20 partners are permitted except in the case of certain professional partnerships.

Limited companies – Capital and reserves

39. Limited liability allows a business to be incorporated with the liability limited to the amount they have contributed, or are due to contribute as share capital.

40. The owners of small companies are often involved in running the business, whilst with large companies the owners have nothing at all to do with the company.

41. A board of directors is elected by the shareholders to run the company on their behalf.

42. The directors report annually to the shareholders by the production of the published accounts.

43. The published accounts consist of the profit and loss account and balance sheet in a prescribed format together with various other reports and notes.

44. It is the directors' responsibility to produce the accounts.

45. The main shareholders are investing institutions – insurance companies, pension funds, etc.

46. A share is part of the share capital of a company.

47. In a company, the capital section of the balance sheet includes *Capital* and *Reserves*.

48. The profit generated is included within the *Profit and loss account* balance on the balance sheet in the category of reserves.

49 Nominal value is the face value of the shares.

50. Share premium is the excess over the nominal value that is paid when the shares are first issued.

51. The accounting entry is debit *Bank* with proceeds of issue, credit *Share capital* with the nominal value of the shares and credit *Share premium* with the difference – the premium.

52. A dividend is the return on the shareholders' investment.

53. The dividend is normally calculated as a percentage or the amount per share.

54. The dividend is a percentage of the nominal value of the shares.

55. An undistributable reserve is a capital reserve that cannot be returned to the shareholders in the form of a dividend, eg share premium.

56. A distributable reserve is a reserve that has arisen from the generation of profit and can therefore be distributed to the shareholders e.g. profit and loss account.

57. The members of a company are the ordinary shareholders of the company.

58. The members have the right to vote at general meetings.

59. A company might also have preference shareholders.

60. A preference shareholder is entitled to fixed rate of dividend.

61. Authorised capital is the total amount of capital a company can issue. This is set at incorporation, but may subsequently be changed.

62. Issued share capital is the amount of share capital a company has issued.

63. A company can raise debentures, loan stock or loan capital.

64. When debentures are redeemable they will be repaid by certain dates or between certain dates.

65. The debentures would only be repaid on liquidation if there are funds available.

66.

	Debentures	Shares
Voting rights	Able to attend meetings, but not vote.	Right to attend meetings and vote.
Return on investment	Debenture interest is an expense of the business.	Dividend is a distribution of profits.
Security	Usually secured on the assets.	No security.
On liquidation	Due to security likely to receive some investment back.	Risky.

Limited companies – Accounts

67. The historical cost convention is the recording of items at their historical cost.

68. The historical cost convention might not be used in countries where there is high inflation.

69. A form of current cost accounting is necessary to give assets a realistic value.

70. The modification to historic costs commonly used in the UK is the revaluation of property.

71. Valuations must be kept up to date.

72. The increase in value is debited to the *Asset* account and credited to a *Revaluation reserve*.

73. It is not included as it is not a realised profit; the realisation concept says that only realised profits can be included in the profit and loss account.

74. The revaluation reserve is shown with other reserves such as *Share premium* account.

75.

	Differences
1	Different expenses such as *Directors' remuneration*
2	Appropriation of profits eg *Dividends*
3	Capital section of the balance sheet is different – now includes reserves
4	Current liabilities will contain extra items such as proposed dividends.

76.

Term	Description
Directors' remuneration	Includes all payments for the directors' services – salaries, fees, bonuses and employer's NI.
Audit fee	The remuneration paid the auditor for carrying out the audit.
Debenture interest	Interest on the debentures – one of the expenses of the company.
Taxation	Corporation tax – a liability of the company which must therefore be shown on the balance sheet.
Preference dividend	% paid to preference shareholders.
Interim dividend	A dividend paid during the year to the ordinary shareholders.
Final proposed dividend	Dividend based on the results for the year; to be agreed by shareholders at AGM.
Retained profits	Profit retained in the business after everything has been appropriated.

77. An executive director is a full-time employee of the company.

78. A non-executive director is an outsider who is elected to the board to bring in some further experience.

79. The corporation tax figure should include the charge for this year together with any adjustment for previous years.

80. The proposed final dividend will be paid after the AGM.

81. A company might not pay a dividend if:

- There are insufficient profits.
- Cash is needed to fund the current business or expansion.

82. The liabilities will be shown as current liabilities.

83.

Term	Description
Cost/valuation	Heading to allow for inclusion of property at valuation.
Property	May now be shown at valuation - revalued property must be depreciated.
Tax liabilities	Will include VAT, PAYE and NI, and corporation tax.
Current liabilities	Amount to be paid within the next 12 months.
Debentures	Long-term loans repayable within certain dates.
Proposed dividends payable	Amounts due to shareholders for dividends.
Share premium	Amount of the premium on the original issue of shares.
Revaluation reserve	Increase in property value.
Profit and loss account	Total of accumulated profits retained since the business was incorporated.

84. The accounting entries are:

    - Tax – debit taxation (profit and loss account), credit tax liability (balance sheet)

    - Dividends – debit proposed dividend (profit and loss account) and credit proposed dividend (balance sheet)

Limited companies – Legislation

85. The published accounts must be sent to shareholders, debenture holders and the Registrar of Companies.

86. The legislation governing the format of published accounts is the Companies Act 1985, amended by the Companies Act 1989, together with various Statutory Instruments.

87. The ASC was a committee set up in an effort to standardise the method of treatment of items which could be dealt with in different ways.

88. SSAPs are Statements of Standard Accounting Practice and deal with the treatment of accounting issues.

89. The ASB is the Accounting Standards Board and it superseded the ASC.

90. FRSs are Financial Reporting Standards some of which have superseded SSAPs.

91. Companies quoted on the Stock Exchange are required to comply with the Financial Services Authority Listing Rules.

92. SSAP 2 dealt with the Disclosure of Accounting Policies.

93. Two categories are:

    - accounting concepts
    - desirable qualities

94. Two accounting concepts are going concern and accruals.

95. Two desirable qualities are consistency/comparability and prudence.

96. The going concern concept – the enterprise will continue in existence for the foreseeable future.

97. It is appropriate to state assets at their written down value rather than their break-up value.

98. The accruals or matching concept – revenues and costs are accrued (recognised when they are earned or incurred, not as they are received or paid); they are matched with one another as far as possible and dealt with in the profit and loss account of the period to which they relate.

99. Examples are accruals, prepayments and depreciation.

100. The consistency/comparability quality is that there is consistency of accounting treatment and disclosure.

101. The comparability is important so that there can be meaningful comparison from one period and another.

102. Prudence should be exercised only where there is a level of uncertainty about either the existence or amount at which accounting entries should be measured.

103. The provision for doubtful debts is an application of prudence.

104. Disaggregation is that netting off is not allowed.

105. An example of disaggregation is that if a loan has been obtained to purchase an asset, the two items must be shown separately.

106.

Accounting standard	Details
SSAP 4	Treatment of government grants – grants should be matched against the expenditure.
SSAP 13	Accounting for research & development – research expenditure must be written off in year; in certain cases development expenditure may be carried forward and matched against future revenues.
FRS 1	Companies (except small companies) must produce a cash flow statement in their accounts.
FRS 3	Turnover and operating profit should be split into that arising from: continuing operations, acquisitions, discontinued operations.
FRS 14	Quoted companies must disclose a figure for earnings per share.
FRS 18	Entity should judge the appropriateness of accounting policies to its circumstances against the objectives of: • comparability • relevance • reliability • understandability.

107. International accounting standards are similar to SSAPs/FRSs.

108. A group occurs where one company owns a large proportion of the shares of another company.

109. Consolidated accounts are accounts which show the results of all group companies.

110. In consolidated accounts it might be necessary to exclude sales from one company to another.

111. One of the criteria for a 'small' company is for turnover to be less than £2.8m.

Limited companies – Published accounts

112. Name of company Wholesale Supplies Ltd
Profit and loss account for the year ended 2006

Notes		£'000	£'000
2	Turnover		5,876
	Cost of sales		2,863
	Gross profit		3,013
	Administrative expenses	1,506	
	Distribution costs	1,180	
			2,686
3	Operating profit		327
4	Interest		60
	Profit on ordinary activities before taxation		267
5	Taxation		75
	Profit on ordinary activities after taxation		192
6	Preference dividends		10
	Profit attributable to ordinary shareholders		182
6	Ordinary dividends		27
	Retained profit for the year		155
	Earnings per share		12.1p
Note. All figures relate to continuing operations			

113.

Published accounts	Internal accounts
Turnover	Sales with basis of calculation.
Cost of sales	Figure from internal accounts.
Gross profit	Figure from internal accounts.
Administrative expenses/distribution costs	Need to split the expenses between the two headings.
Operating profit	Profit earned before taking account of financing costs.
Interest	Total of all the interest costs – analysed in a note.
Profit on ordinary activities before taxation	Net profit before tax.
Taxation	A note will explain the basis of the calculation of the tax charge.
Profit attributable to ordinary shareholders	Profit left for ordinary shareholders after all other items have been removed.
Ordinary dividend	Details of dividend including split between interim paid and final proposed.
Retained profit for the year	Final profit figure being retained in the company.
Earnings per share	For a quoted company; needs to be a note explaining the calculation.
Continuing operations	Acquisitions and discontinued operations need to be split out.

114. Name of company Wholesale Supplies Ltd
     Balance sheet at 2006

Notes		£000
7	FIXED ASSETS	
	Tangible assets	1,259
	CURRENT ASSETS	
8	Stock	289
9	Debtors	657
		946
10	CREDITORS : amounts due within one year	711
	NET CURRENT ASSETS	235
	TOTAL ASSETS LESS CURRENT LIABILITIES	1,494
11	CREDTIORS: amounts due after one year	422
		1,072
	CAPITAL AND RESERVES	
12	Called up share capital	425
13	Share premium	120
13	Revaluation reserve	147
13	Profit and loss account	380
		1,072
Signature		

115.

Published accounts	Internal accounts
Tangible assets	Total net value of the fixed assets with a breakdown into categories.
Stocks	Note will give a breakdown and accounting policy.
Debtors	Includes trade debtors, prepayments and sundry debtors – note giving breakdown.
Creditors due in one year	Total of current liabilities plus current portion of long-term liabilities.
Net current assets/Total assets less current liabilities	Net assets is lower than on internal balance sheet because of the inclusion here of current portion of long-term liabilities.
Creditors – due after one year	Includes all long-term liabilities except amounts due to be repaid within one year.
Capital and reserves	Notes will show the details of the share capital and movements in reserves.
Signature	Balance sheet must be signed by at least one director.

116. The notes will give information and explanations of items shown in the profit and loss
     account and balance sheet.

Unit 3

Additional question

The following question is based on an integrated example relating to all modules of the software. It is a fairly complex example building up to a profit and loss account and balance sheet for a limited company. Unless you are very confident, you may not wish to attempt this exercise without some tutorial assistance. (Your exam will not include anything of this standard.)

1. Using the opening trial balance of Cuckoo Clocks Ltd (Appendix A) design a coding system for each of the accounts in the nominal ledger, sales ledger and purchase ledger.

2. Open T accounts for the balances on the opening trial balance. Confirm the accuracy of your postings by extracting a trial balance.

3. Using the attached information make entries in the following books of prime entry:

    *   Purchase daybook (Appendix B contains purchase invoices and credit note)
    *   Sales daybook (Appendix C contains sales invoices and credit note)
    *   Cash received book (Appendix D contains bank receipts)
    *   Cash payments book (Appendix E contains bank payments)
    *   Petty cash book (Appendix F contains petty cash details)
    *   Salaries and wages book (Appendix G contains salaries and wages details)

4. Post from the above books of prime entry to the nominal, sales and purchase ledgers.

5. Extract and agree a trial balance and control accounts to listings.

6. Reconcile the bank account with the attached bank statement (Appendix H).

7. Prepare journals to make the following adjustments and enter in the T accounts:

    a. Complete the recording of new van purchase, which cost £5,500. One of the old vans was taken in part-exchange with a value of £1,500. This van had originally cost £3,000 two years ago and had been depreciated at 25% using the reducing balance method.

    b. Repair invoice for £250 had been incorrectly included in *Fixtures and fittings*.

    c. Bank entries found as a result of reconciling the bank account.

8. Draw up journal entries and make the appropriate postings in the T accounts to reflect the following amounts that Cuckoo Clock Ltd owed at the end of September, but for which no invoices had been received by the year-end.

	£
• Electricity	250
• Petrol	141
• Van repair	442
• Loan interest outstanding	300

    • The audit fee estimated at £2,500, for the year to 30 September 2005.

9. Draw up journal entries for the following prepayments and adjustments and post to the T accounts:

    • Council tax of £8,400 had been paid in May for the year to 31 March 2006, and

    • Insurance of £2,500 had been paid for the year to 31 December 2005, and £1,200 was paid for insurance to 30 September 2006 shortly before the year-end.

    • £300 for van licences and insurance related to the period 1 October to 31 December 2005.

    • The directors have decided that they will be unable to recover the outstanding account from PQ, which should therefore be written off. (There was no VAT on this invoice.)

10. Depreciation is to be calculated using the following rates. Draw up journal entries and post to the T accounts:

• Fixtures and fittings	10% on cost
• Computer equipment	$33\frac{1}{3}\%$ on cost
• Vans	25% on reducing balance

11. Make the necessary adjustment for opening and closing stock using stock adjustment accounts as explained on 6.6 in module 6. The stock at 30 September 2005 amounted to £96,887.

12. Prepare the profit and loss account for the year ended 30 September 2005, and the balance sheet at that date, for internal use.

13. Prepare the financial statements of Cuckoo Clocks Ltd using the Companies Act layout and including:

    • The estimate for corporation tax is £45,000.
    • A dividend of 40p per ordinary share is proposed by the directors.

14. Balance off the T accounts at 30 September 2005, closing off income and expense accounts to the profit and loss account, and take out a final trial balance.

Appendix A

The following trial balance relates to the accounting entries of Cuckoo Clocks Ltd at 23 September 2005, one week before the year-end of 30 September 2005.

Code number		Debit £	Credit £
	Freehold Property	234,000	
	Fixtures and fittings at cost	22,000	
	Fixtures and fittings – acc. depreciation (to 1 October 2004)		4,400
	Computer equipment at cost	3,500	
	Computer equipment – acc. depreciation (to 1 October 2004)		1,750
	Van	6,000	
	Van – acc. depreciation (to 1 October 2004)		3,500
	Stock (at 1 October 2004)	174,780	
	Debtors control	34,020	
	Creditors control		35,670
	Bank account		12,654
	Petty cash	250	
	VAT		13,799
	PAYE and national insurance		2,208
	Sales - clocks		345,821
	Sales - watches		457,892
	Purchases – clocks	164,345	
	Purchases – watches	200,114	
	Advertising	2,439	
	Wages and national insurance	48,567	
	Directors' salaries	47,786	
	Council tax	12,000	
	Water rates	2,762	
	Insurance	5,785	
	Light and heating	2,348	
	Van licence and insurance	1,990	
	Van repairs and fuel	2,344	
	Travelling expenses	786	
	Postage and carriage	1,433	
	Repairs and renewals	298	
	Audit and accountancy	250	
	Cleaning	598	
	Sundry expenses	698	
	6% Loan		10,000
	Loan interest	300	
	Profit and loss account (at 1 October 2004)		86,699
	Ordinary 25p shares		5,000
	Packaging	10,000	
		979,393	979,393

Sales ledger

Details of the outstanding sales ledger balances at 23 September 2005 are as follows:

Code number	Customer	Total balance	Outstanding invoices			
		£	£	£	£	£
	A Ltd	6,789	2,345	1,123	980	2,341
	GH	3,672	1,890	235	668	879
	X	12,990	5,890	3,491	3,609	
	BB	4,761	2,361	1,400	1,000	
	TJ	3,789	1,100	567	2,122	
	PQ Inc	2,019	2,019			
		34,020				

Purchase ledger

Details of the outstanding purchase ledger balances at 23 September 2005 are as follows:

Code number	Supplier	Total balance	Outstanding invoices			
		£	£	£	£	£
	Clocks Unlimited	16,890	5,670	4,396	6,824	
	Watches for Ever	5,763	321	3,965	250	1,227
	Cuckoos	3,873	2,670	1,203		
	Speaking Clocks	4,440	2,220	1,000	1,220	
	New Watches	2,983	1,500	1,483		
	Big Ben Clocks	1,721	1,721			
		35,670				

Appendix B

Purchases for the period 24 September to 30 September 2005

Invoices

Date	Invoice number	Supplier	Gross	VAT	Clocks	Watches	Packing material
			£	£	£	£	£
24/9	1467	Clock Unlimited	6,447	960	5,487		
24/9	1468	Watches for Ever	1,085	162		923	
24/9	1469	Cuckoos	9,085	1,353	7,732		
24/9	1470	Clock Unlimited	3,274	488	2,786		
26/9	1471	Clock Unlimited	1,303	194	1,109		
28/9	1472	Speaking Clocks	1,515	226	1,289		
28/9	1473	Watches for Ever	2,349	350		1,999	
28/9	1474	New Watches	791	118		673	
28/9	1475	Big Ben Clocks	1,170	174	996		
28/9	1476	Clock Unlimited	405	60	345		
28/9	1477	Packaging Ltd	1,175	175			1,000
28/9	1478	Watches for Ever	536	80		456	

Credit note

			£	£	£
24/9	CN115	Clock Unlimited	(536)	(80)	(456)

Appendix C

Credit sales for the period 24 September 2005 to 30 September 2005

Invoices

Date	Invoice number	Customer	Gross	VAT	Clocks	Watches	
			£	£	£	£	
24/9	15211	A Ltd	1,707	254	700	753	
24/9	15212	X	6,902	1,028	5,874		
24/9	15213	BB	410	61		349	
24/9	15214	A Ltd	5,392	803	2,389	2,200	
26/9	15215	GH	1,459	217	675	567	
26/9	15216	X	9,293	1,384	6,678	1,231	
26/9	15217	TJ	1,516	226	1,290		
27/9	15218	ZZ	924	138		786	
27/9	15219	BB	1,069	159	342	568	
28/9	15220	GH	1,025	153	872		
29/9	15221	A Ltd	1,153	172		981	
29/9	15222	GH	2,052	306	1,290	456	
30/9	15223	MN	1,706	243	679	784	*
30/9	15224	GH	5,613	836	1,295	3,482	

Credit note

			£	£	£
30/9	CN 560	BB	402	60	342

*VAT adjusted due to possibility of 5% cash discount

Appendix D

Cash receipts

For the period 24 September to 30 September 2005

Date	Description	Bank	Cash sales	
			Watches	Clocks
		£	£	£
24/9	A Ltd	3,468		
25/9	GH	1,890		
26/9	X	5,890		
26/9	Cash sales	3,498	2,389	1,109
27/9	Cash sales	6,540	4,590	1,950
28/9	TJ	1,100		
29/9	GH	235		
29/9	A Ltd	3,321		
30/9	X	3,491		
30/9	Cash sales	9,845	3,386	6,459

Additionally the amount outstanding was received on 30 September from the new customer MN subject to a one off introductory cash discount of 5%.

All cash sales figures include VAT at 17.5%.

Appendix E

Bank payments

For the period 24 September to 30 September 2005

Date	Cheque No	Payee	Amount	Details
			£	
24/9	12345	Clocks Unlimited	16,890	
24/9	12346	Watches for Ever	4,286	
24/9	12347	Cuckoos	2,670	
24/9	12348	Speaking Clocks	2,220	
24/9	12349	Big Ben Clocks	1,721	
26/9	12350	New Van	4,000	Part exchange of van
26/9	12351	Insurance	1,200	For year to 30 September 2006
30/9	12352	Wages	Amount from wages book	
30/9	12353	Salaries	Amount from salaries book	
30/9	12354	Petrol	250	Including VAT at 17.5%
30/9	12355	Petty cash	Amount from petty cash book	

Appendix F

Petty cash payments

Date	Description	Voucher No	£
23/9	Balance b/d		
24/9	Postage	65	20
24/9	Tea and coffee	66	6
25/9	Bus fares	67	5
26/9	Window cleaning	68	10
27/9	Parcel	69	11
28/9	Taxi	70	12
29/9	Postage	71	25

The petty cash balance was reimbursed using the imprest system on 30 September.

Appendix G

Salaries and wages

Wages for week ending 30 September 2005				
	Gross	Tax	Employees NI	Employer's NI
	£	£	£	£
R Andrews	168	30	9	9
A Hayes	124	21	5	5
T Slough	150	33	8	8
T Ealing	180	38	10	10
Salaries for month ending 30 September 2005				
J Perry	2,000	250	168	168
T Perry	2,000	278	168	168

Appendix H

Bank Statement		Statement of Current Account		

Bank of Birds
Birdcage Walk
Leeds

	Account number	239854
	Branch Code	34 76 29
	Page no	67
	Date	30 September 2005

Cuckoo Clocks Ltd

Date	Description	Debits £	Credit £	Balance £
2005				
23 Sept	Balance from statement 66			12,654 o/d
24 Sept	Lodgment		3,468	9,186 o/d
25 Sept	Lodgment		1,890	7,296 o/d
26 Sept	Lodgment		9,388	2,092
28 Sept	12345	16,890		14,798 o/d
28 Sept	Lodgment		6,540	8,258 o/d
	Lodgment		1,100	7,158 o/d
29 Sept	12346	4,286		11,444 o/d
	12348	2,220		13,664 o/d
	Lodgment		3,556	10,108 o/d
	12350	4,000		14,108 o/d
30 Sept	Lodgment		3,491	10,617 o/d
	12347	2,670		13,287 o/d
30 Sept	BACS	468		13,755 o/d
	BACS	3,156		16,911 o/d
	12355	89		17,000 o/d
	Bank charges	51		17,051 o/d
	Bank interest	126		17,177 o/d
	Direct debit – water rates	67		17,244 o/d

Unit 3 Answers

1. Coding system

Coding system for the nominal ledger accounts of Cuckoo Clocks Ltd. The first two numbers relate to the category of the item in the financial statement (10 relates to fixed assets), the third number the sub-category(1 for freehold property), and the final number to depreciation (9 for depreciation).

Code number		Debit £	Credit £
1010	Freehold property	234,000	
1020	Fixtures and fittings at cost	22,000	
1029	Fixtures and fittings – acc. depreciation (to 1 October 2004)		4,400
1030	Computer equipment at cost	3,500	
1039	Computer equipment – acc. depreciation (to 1 October 2004)		1,750
1040	Van	6,000	
1049	Van – acc. depreciation (to 1 October 2004)		3,500
2010	Stock (at 1 October 2004)	174,780	
2020	Debtors control	34,020	
3010	Creditors control		35,670
2030	Bank account		12,654
2040	Petty cash	250	
3020	VAT		13,799
3030	PAYE and national insurance		2,208
5010	Sales - clocks		345,821
5020	Sales - watches		457,892
6010	Purchases - clocks	164,345	
6020	Purchases - watches	200,114	
7010	Advertising	2,439	
7020	Wages and national insurance	48,567	
7021	Directors' salaries	47,786	
7030	Council tax	12,000	
7031	Water rates	2,762	
7040	Insurance	5,785	
7050	Light and heating	2,348	
7060	Van license and insurance	1,990	

BPP
PROFESSIONAL EDUCATION

Code number		Debit	Credit
		£	£
7061	Van repairs and fuel	2,344	
7062	Travelling expenses	786	
7070	Postage and carriage	1,433	
7080	Repairs and renewals	298	
7090	Audit and accountancy	250	
8010	Cleaning	598	
8020	Sundry expenses	698	
3040	6% Loan		10,000
8030	Loan interest	300	
4010	Profit and loss account (at 1 October 2004)		86,699
4020	Ordinary 25p shares		5,000
8040	Packaging	10,000	
		979,393	**979,393**

Coding system for the sales ledger accounts

Code number	Customer	Total balance	Outstanding invoices			
		£	£	£	£	£
A1	A Ltd	6,789	2,345	1,123	980	2,341
G1	GH	3,672	1,890	235	668	879
X1	X	12,990	5,890	3,491	3,609	
B1	BB	4,761	2,361	1,400	1,000	
T1	TJ	3,789	1,100	567	2,122	
P1	PQ Inc	2,019	2,019			
		34,020				

Coding system for the purchase ledger accounts

Code number	Supplier	Total balance	Outstanding invoices			
		£	£	£	£	£
C1	Clocks Unlimited	16,890	5,670	4,396	6,824	
W1	Watches for Ever	5,763	321	3,965	250	1,227
C2	Cuckoos	3,873	2,670	1,203		
S1	Speaking Clocks	4,440	2,220	1,000	1,220	
N1	New Watches	2,983	1,500	1,483		
B1	Big Ben Clocks	1,721	1,721			
		35,670				

2.   T accounts

T accounts after the inclusion of opening balances and postings from the books of prime entry:

NOMINAL LEDGER

1010 — Freehold property

23/9	Bal b/d	234,000			

1020 — Fixtures & fittings – cost

23/9	Bal b/d	22,000			

1029 — Fixtures & fittings – acc. depreciation

			23/9	Bal b/d	4,400

1030 — Computer equipment – cost

23/9	Bal b/d	3,500			

1039 — Computer equipment – acc. depreciation

			23/9	Bal b/d	1,750

1040 — Vans – cost

23/9	Bal b/d	6,000			
26/9	Cash Payments Book	4,000			

1049 — Vans – acc. depreciation

			23/9	Bal b/d	3,500

2010 — Stock

23/9	Bal b/d	174,780			

2020 — Debtors control account

23/9	Bal b/d	34,020	30/9	Cash Received Book	21,101
30/9	Sales Daybook	39,819			

3010 — Creditors control account

30/9	Cash Payments Book	27,787	23/9	Bal b/d	35,670
			30/9	Purchase Daybook	28,599

2030 — Bank account

30/9	Cash Received Book	40,911	23/9	Bal b/d	12,654
			30/9	Cash Payments Book	36,950

2040 **Petty cash**

| 23/9 | Bal b/d | 250 | 30/9 | Petty Cash Book | 89 |
| 30/9 | Cash Payments Book | 89 | | | |

3020 **VAT**

30/9	Purchase Daybook	4,260	23/9	Bal b/d	13,799
30/9	Cash Payments Book	37	30/9	Sales Daybook	5,920
			30/9	Cash Received Book	2,961

3030 **PAYE and NI**

			23/9	Bal b/d	2,208
			30/9	Wages - tax	122
			30/9	NI - employee's	32
			30/9	NI - employer's	32
			30/9	Salaries - tax	508
			30/9	NI - employee's	336
			30/9	NI - employer's	336

5010 **Sales - clocks**

			23/9	Bal b/d	345,821
			30/9	Sales Daybook	21,742
			30/9	Cash Received Book	8,821

5020 **Sales - watches**

			23/9	Bal b/d	457,892
			30/9	Sales Daybook	12,157
			30/9	Cash Received Book	8,101

6010 **Purchases - clocks**

| 23/9 | Bal b/d | 164,345 | | | |
| 30/9 | Purchase Daybook | 19,288 | | | |

6020 **Purchases - watches**

| 23/9 | Bal b/d | 200,114 | | | |
| 30/9 | Purchase Daybook | 4,051 | | | |

7010 **Advertising**

| 23/9 | Bal b/d | 2,439 | | | |

7020   **Wages and NI**

23/9	Bal b/d	48,567
30/9	Wages	622
30/9	NI	32

7021   **Directors' salaries**

23/9	Bal b/d	47,786
30/9	Salaries	4,000
30/9	NI	336

7030   **Council tax**

| 23/9 | Bal b/d | 12,000 |

7031   **Water rates**

| 23/9 | Bal b/d | 2,762 |

7040   **Insurance**

| 23/9 | Bal b/d | 5,785 |
| 30/9 | Cash Payments Book | 1,200 |

7050   **Light and heating**

| 23/9 | Bal b/d | 2,348 |

7060   **Van licence and insurance**

| 23/9 | Bal b/d | 1,990 |

7061   **Van repairs and fuel**

| 23/9 | Bal b/d | 2,344 |
| 30/9 | Cash Payments Book | 213 |

7062   **Travelling expenses**

| 23/9 | Bal b/d | 786 |

7070   **Postage and carriage**

| 23/9 | Bal b/d | 1,433 |
| 30/9 | Petty Cash Book | 56 |

7080   **Repairs and renewals**

| 23/9 | Bal b/d | 298 | | | |

7090   **Audit and accountancy**

| 23/9 | Bal b/d | 250 | | | |

8010   **Cleaning**

| 23/9 | Bal b/d | 598 | | | |
| 30/9 | Petty Cash Book | 10 | | | |

8020   **Sundry expenses**

| 23/9 | Bal b/d | 698 | | | |
| 30/9 | Petty Cash Book | 23 | | | |

3040   **6% Loan**

| | | | 23/9 | Bal b/d | 10,000 |

8030   **Loan interest**

| 23/9 | Bal b/d | 300 | | | |

4010   **Profit and loss account**

| | | | 23/9 | Bal b/d | 86,699 |

4020   **Ordinary 25p shares**

| | | | 23/9 | Bal b/d | 5,000 |

8040   **Packaging**

| 23/9 | Bal b/d | 10,000 | | | |
| 30/9 | Purchase Daybook | 1,000 | | | |

8050   **Discount allowed**

| 30/9 | Cash Received Book | 73 | | | |

3050   **Salaries and wages control**

| 30/9 | Cash Payments Book | 3,624 | 30/9 | Net wages | 468 |
| | | | 30/9 | Net salaries | 3,156 |

374

SALES LEDGER

A1   **A Ltd**

23/9	Bal b/d	2,345	24/9	Cash Received Book	3,468
		1,123	29/9	Cash Received Book	3,321
		980			
		2,341			
		6,789			
24/9	Sales Daybook	1,707			
24/9	Sales Daybook	5,392			
29/9	Sales Daybook	1,153			

G1   **GH**

23/9	Bal b/d	1,890	25/9	Cash Received Book	1,890
		235	29/9	Cash Received Book	235
		668			
		879			
		3,672			
24/9	Sales Daybook	1,459			
28/9	Sales Daybook	1,025			
29/9	Sales Daybook	2,052			
30/9	Sales Daybook	5,613			

X1   **X**

23/9	Bal b/d	5,890	26/9	Cash Received Book	5,890
		3,491	30/9	Cash Received Book	3,491
		3,609			
		12,990			
24/9	Sales Daybook	6,902			
26/9	Sales Daybook	9,293			

B1   **BB**

23/9	Bal b/d	2,361	30/9	Sales Daybook	402
		1,400			
		1,000			
		4,761			
24/9	Sales Daybook	410			
27/9	Sales Daybook	1,069			

T1   **TJ**

23/9	Bal b/d	1,100	28/9	Cash Received Book	1,100
		567			
		2,122			
		3,789			
26/9		1,516			

BPP
PROFESSIONAL EDUCATION

P1		PQ Inc			
23/9	Bal b/d	2,019			

M1		MN			
30/9	Sales Daybook	1,706	30/9	Cash Received Book	1,706

Z1		ZZ			
27/9	Sales Daybook	924			

PURCHASE LEDGER

C1		Clocks Unlimited			
23/9	Purchase Daybook	536	23/9	Bal b/d	5,670
24/9	Cash Payments Book	16,890			4,396
					6,824
					16,890
			23/9	Purchase Daybook	6,447
			24/9	Purchase Daybook	3,274
			26/9	Purchase Daybook	1,303
			28/9	Purchase Daybook	405

W1		Watches for Ever			
24/9	Cash Payments Book	4,286	23/9	Bal b/d	321
					3,965
					250
					1,227
					5,763
			23/9	Purchase Daybook	1,085
			28/9	Purchase Daybook	2,349
			28/9	Purchase Daybook	536

C2		Cuckoos			
24/9	Cash Payments	2,670	23/9	Bal b/d	2,670
					1,203
					3,873
			24/9	Purchase Daybook	9,085

S1		Speaking Clocks			
24/9	Cash Payments Book	2,220	23/9	Bal b/d	2,220
					1,000
					1,220
					4,440
			28/9	Purchase Daybook	1,515

NI   **New Watches**

		23/9	Bal b/d	1,500
				1,483
				2,983
		28/9	Purchase Daybook	791

B1   **Big Ben Clocks**

24/9	Cash Payments Book	1,721	23/9	Bal b/d	1,721
			28/9	Purchase Daybook	1,170

P1   **Packaging Ltd**

		28/9	Purchase Daybook	1,175

All the opening balances above should be checked to the opening trial balance given in the question.

3. Books of prime entry

Purchase Daybook

Date	Invoice no	Supplier	A/c no	Gross	VAT	Clocks	Watches	Packing material
				£	£	£	£	£
24/9	1467	Clocks Unlimited	C1	6,447	960	5,487		
24/9	1468	Watches for Ever	W1	1,085	162		923	
24/9	CN115	Clocks Unlimited	C1	(536)	(80)	(456)		
24/9	1469	Cuckoos	C2	9,085	1,353	7,732		
24/9	1470	Clocks Unlimited	C1	3,274	488	2,786		
26/9	1471	Clocks Unlimited	C1	1,303	194	1,109		
28/9	1472	Speaking Clocks	S1	1,515	226	1,289		
28/9	1473	Watches for Ever	W1	2,349	350		1,999	
28/9	1474	New Watches	N1	791	118		673	
28/9	1475	Big Ben Clocks	B1	1,170	174	996		
28/9	1476	Clocks Unlimited	C1	405	60	345		
28/9	1477	Packaging Ltd	P1	1,175	175			1,000
28/9	1478	Watches for Ever	W1	536	80		456	
				28,599	4,260	19,288	4,051	1,000
Nominal ledger postings				3010 Cr	3020 Dr	6010 Dr	6020 Dr	8040 Dr

Sales daybook

Date	Invoice no	Customer	A/c	Gross	VAT	Clocks	Watches
				£	£	£	£
24/9	15211	A Ltd	A1	1,707	254	700	753
24/9	15212	X	X1	6,902	1,028	5,874	
24/9	15213	BB	B1	410	61		349
24/9	15214	A Ltd	A1	5,392	803	2,389	2,200
26/9	15215	GH	G1	1,459	217	675	567
26/9	15216	X	X1	9,293	1,384	6,678	1,231
26/9	15217	TJ	T1	1,516	226	1,290	
27/9	15218	ZZ	Z1	924	138		786
27/9	15219	BB	B1	1,069	159	342	568
28/9	15220	GH	G1	1,025	153	872	
29/9	15221	A Ltd	A1	1,153	172		981
29/9	15222	GH	G1	2,052	306	1,290	456
30/9	15223	MN	M1	1,706	243	679	784
30/9	15224	GH	G1	5,613	836	1,295	3,482
30/9	CN 560	BB	B1	(402)	(60)	(342)	
				39,819	5,920	21,742	12,157
Nominal ledger postings				2020 Dr	3020 Cr	5010 Cr	5020 Cr

Cash received book

Date	Description	Discount	Bank	S/L	Sales ledger	VAT	Cash sales Watches	Cash sales Clocks
			£		£	£	£	£
24/9	A Ltd		3,468	A1	3,468			
25/9	GH		1,890	G1	1,890			
26/9	X		5,890	X1	5,890			
26/9	Cash sales		3,498			521	2,033	944
27/9	Cash sales		6,540			974	3,906	1,660
28/9	TJ		1,100	T1	1,100			
29/9	GH		235	G1	235			
29/9	A Ltd		3,321	A1	3,321			
30/9	X		3,491	X1	3,491			
30/9	Cash sales		9,845			1,466	2,882	5,497
30/9	MN	73	1,633	M1	1,706			
		73	40,911		21,101	2,961	8,821	8,101
Nominal ledger postings		8050	2030 Dr		2020 Cr	3020 Cr	5010 Cr	5020 Cr

Cash payments book

Date	Cheque no	Payee	A/c no	Bank	P/L	Wages & salaries	Petrol	VAT	Sundries
				£	£	£	£	£	£
24/9	12345	Clocks Unlimited	C1	16,890	16,890				
24/9	12346	Watches for Ever	W1	4,286	4,286				
24/9	12347	Cuckoos	C2	2,670	2,670				
24/9	12348	Speaking Clocks	S1	2,220	2,220				
24/9	12349	Big Ben Clocks	B1	1,721	1,721				
26/9	12350	New van	1040	4,000					4,000
26/9	12351	Insurance	7040	1,200					1,200
30/9	12352	Wages		468		468			
30/9	12353	Salaries		3,156		3,156			
30/9	12354	Petrol		250			213	37	
30/9	12355	Petty cash	2040	89					89
				36,950	27,787	3,624	213	37	5,289
Nominal ledger postings				2030 Cr	3010 Dr	3050 Dr	7061 Dr	3020 Dr	

BPP
PROFESSIONAL EDUCATION

Petty cash book

Date	Description	Voucher no	Dr	Cr	Postage	Cleaning	Sundries	Bal.
			£	£	£	£	£	£
23/9	Balance b/d							250
24/9	Postage	65		20	20			230
24/9	Tea and coffee	66		6			6	224
25/9	Bus fares	67		5			5	219
26/9	Window cleaning	68		10		10		209
27/9	Parcel	69		11	11			198
28/9	Taxi	70		12			12	186
29/9	Postage	71		25	25			161
30/9	Cash from bank		89		56	10	23	250
			89	89	56	10	23	
Nominal ledger postings				2040 Cr	7070 Dr	8010 Dr	8020 Dr	

Salaries and wages book

Wages book

Date	Employee	Gross	Tax	NI - employees	Net	NI - employers
		£	£	£	£	£
30/9	R Andrews	168	30	9	129	9
	A Hayes	124	21	5	98	5
	T Slough	150	33	8	109	8
	T Ealing	180	38	10	132	10
		622	122	32	468	32
Nominal ledger postings		7020	3030	3030	3050	7020 & 3030

Salaries book						
30/9	J Perry	2,000	250	168	1,582	168
	T Perry	2,000	258	168	1,574	168
		4,000	508	336	3,156	336
Nominal ledger postings		7021	3030	3030	3050	3030 & 7021

4. You will find the entries required by question 4 in the ledgers set out as the answer to question 2.

5. Trial balance

Trial balance after books of prime entry have been posted to the ledgers:

Code number		Debit	Credit
		£	£
1010	Freehold property	234,000	
1020	Fixtures and fittings at cost	22,000	
1029	Fixtures and fittings – depreciation to 1 October 2004		4,400
1030	Computer equipment at cost	3,500	
1039	Computer equipment – depreciation to 1 October 2004		1,750
1040	Van	10,000	
1049	Van – depreciation to 1 October 2004		3,500
2010	Stock at 1 October 2004	174,780	
2020	Debtors control	52,738	
3010	Creditors control		36,482
2030	Bank account		8,693
2040	Petty cash	250	
3020	VAT		18,383
3030	PAYE and NI		3,574
5010	Sales - clocks		376,384
5020	Sales - watches		478,150
6010	Purchases - clocks	183,633	
6020	Purchases - watches	204,165	
7010	Advertising	2,439	
7020	Wages and NI	49,221	
7021	Directors' salaries	52,122	
7030	Council tax	12,000	
7031	Water rates	2,762	
7040	Insurance	6,985	
7050	Light and heating	2,348	
7060	Van license and insurance	1,990	
7061	Van repairs and fuel	2,557	
7062	Travelling expenses	786	
7070	Postage and carriage	1,489	
7080	Repairs and renewals	298	
7090	Audit and accountancy	250	
8010	Cleaning	608	
8020	Sundry expenses	721	
3040	6% Loan		10,000
8030	Loan interest	300	
4010	Profit and loss account at 1 October 2004		86,699
4020	Ordinary 25p shares		5,000
8040	Packaging	11,000	
8050	Discount allowed	73	
		1,033,015	**1,033,015**

Sales ledger balances at 30 September 2005

		£
A1	A Ltd	8,252
G1	GH	11,696
X1	X	19,804
B1	BB	5,838
T1	TJ	4,205
P1	PQ Inc	2,019
Z1	ZZ	924
Balance per control account		**52,738**

Purchase ledger balances at 30 September 2005

		£
C1	Clock Unlimited	10,893
W1	Watches for Ever	5,447
C2	Cuckoos	10,288
S1	Speaking Clocks	3,735
N1	New watches	3,774
B1	Big Ben Clocks	1,170
P1	Packaging Ltd	1,175
Balance per control account		**36,482**

6. Bank reconciliation

Bank reconciliation at 30 September 2005

	£	£
Balance per statement 67		17,244 o/d
Less Unpresented cheques	1,721	
	1,200	
	250	3,171
		20,415 o/d
Add Lodgments not yet credited	9,845	
	1,633	(11,478)
		8,937 o/d
Balance per bank account		8,693 o/d
Add payments not yet entered		
Bank charges	51	
Bank interest	126	
Water rates	67	244
		8,937 o/d

7. Journals

			Debit	Credit
			£	£
7a	8060	Disposals	3,000	
	1040	Van – cost		3,000
		being transfer of cost of van taken in part exchange for a new van		
	1049	Van – acc. depreciation	1,313	
	8060	Disposals		1,313
		Being depreciation on 25% using the reducing balance method of the van disposed of		
	1040	Van - cost	1,500	
	8060	Disposals		1,500
		Being the proceeds for van taken in part exchange		
7b	7080	Repairs and renewals	250	
	1020	Fixtures and fittings - cost		250
		Being a repair invoice incorrectly posted to fixtures and fittings now corrected		
7c	8070	Bank charges and interest (charges)	51	
	8070	Bank charges and interest (interest)	126	
	7031	Water rates	67	
	2030	Bank		244
		Being items omitted from the bank account		

8. Journals - accruals

		Debit	Credit
		£	£
7050	Light and heating	250	
7061	Van repairs and fuel (petrol)	141	
7061	Van repairs and fuel (repair)	442	
8030	Loan interest	300	
7090	Audit and accountancy	2,500	
3060	Accruals		3,633
	Accruals at 30/9/05		

9. Journals – prepayments and adjustments

		Debit	Credit
		£	£
7030	Council tax		4,200
7040	Insurance		1,825
7060	Van licences and insurance		300
2050	Prepayments	6,325	
	Prepayments at 30/9/05		
8080	Bad debts	2,019	
2020	Debtors control		2,019
S/L P1	PQ Inc – Memo		2,019
	Write off of debt from PQ Inc		

10. Journals – depreciation

		Debit	Credit
		£	£
1029	Fixtures and fittings – acc. depreciation		2,175
8060	Depreciation	2,175	
	Depreciation for the year (10% × £21,750)		
1039	Computer equipment – acc. depreciation		1,167
8060	Depreciation	1,167	
	Depreciation for the year (1/3 × £3,500)		
1049	Vans – acc. depreciation		1,578
8060	Depreciation	1,578	
	Depreciation for the year (25% × [£8,500 - £2,187])		

11. Journals – stock

		Debit	Credit
		£	£
2010	Stock (B/S)		174,780
6100	Opening stock (P&L)	174,780	
	Adjustment for opening stock		
2010	Stock (B/S)	96,887	
6110	Closing stock (P&L)		96,887
	Adjustment for closing stock		

7-11. T accounts with adjustments posted:

NOMINAL LEDGER

1010 — **Freehold property**

23/9	Bal b/d	234,000	30/9	Bal c/d		234,000
		234,000				234,000
1/10	Bal b/d	234,000				

1020 — **Fixtures and fittings - cost**

23/9	Bal b/d	22,000	30/9	Repairs	250
			30/9	Bal c/d	21,750
		22,000			22,000
1/10	Bal b/d	21,750			

1029 — **Fixtures and fittings – acc. depreciation**

30/9	Bal c/d	6,575	23/9	Bal b/d	4,400
			30/9	Depreciation	2,175
		6,575			6,575
			1/10	Bal b/d	6,575

1030 — **Computer equipment - cost**

23/9	Bal b/d	3,500	1/10	Bal c/d	3,500
		3,500			3,500
30/9	Bal b/d	3,500			

1039 — **Computer equipment – acc. depreciation**

1/10	Bal c/d	2,917	23/9	Bal b/d	1,750
			30/9	Depreciation	1,167
		2,917			2,917
			1/10	Bal b/d	2,917

1040 — **Vans – cost**

23/9	Bal b/d	6,000	30/9	Disposals	3,000
26/9	Cash Payments Book	4,000	30/9	Bal c/d	8,500
30/9	Part exchange	1,500			
		11,500			11,500
1/10	Bal b/d	8,500			

1049 — **Vans – acc. depreciation**

30/9	Disposals	1,313	23/9	Bal b/d	3,500
30/9	Bal c/d	3,765	30/9	Depreciation	1,578
		5,078			5,078
			1/10	Bal b/d	3,765

2010 — **Stock**

23/9	Bal b/d	174,780	30/9	Opening stock (P&L)	174,780
30/9	Closing stock (P&L)	96,887	30/9	Bal c/d	96,887
		271,667			271,667
1/10	Bal b/d	96,887			

2020 — Debtors control account

23/9	Bal b/d	34,020	30/9	Cash Received Book	21,101
30/9	Sales Daybook	39,819	30/9	Bad debts	2,019
			30/9	Bal c/d	50,719
		73,839			73,839
1/10	Bal b/d	50,719			

3010 — Creditors control account

30/9	Cash Payments Book	27,787	23/9	Bal b/d	35,670
30/9	Balance b/d	36,482	30/9	Purchase Daybook	28,599
		64,269			64,269
			1/10	Bal b/d	36,482

2030 — Bank account

30/9	Cash Received Book	40,911	23/9	Bal b/d	12,654
30/9	Bal c/d	8,937	30/9	Cash Payments Book	36,950
		49,848		Journals	244
					49,848
			1/10	Bal b/d	8,937

2040 — Petty cash

23/9	Bal b/d	250	30/9	Petty Cash Book	89
30/9	Cash Payments Book	89	1/10	Bal c/d	250
		339			339
1/10	Bal b/d	250			

3020 — VAT

30/9	Purchase Daybook	4,260	23/9	Bal b/d	13,799
30/9	Cash Payments Book	37	30/9	Sales Daybook	5,920
30/9	Bal c/d	18,383	30/9	Cash Received Book	2,961
		22,680			22,680
			1/10	Bal b/d	18,383

3030 — PAYE and NI

30/9	Bal c/d	3,574	23/9	Bal b/d	2,208
			30/9	Wages - tax	122
			30/9	NI - employee's	32
			30/9	NI - employer's	32
			30/9	Salaries - tax	508
			30/9	NI - employee's	336
			30/9	NI - employer's	336
		3,574			3,574
			1/10	Bal b/d	3,574

5010 — Sales - clocks

30/9	P & L a/c	376,384	23/9	Bal b/d	345,821
			30/9	Sales Daybook	21,742
			30/9	Cash Received Book	8,821
		376,384			376,384

5020   Sales - watches

30/9	P & L a/c	478,150	23/9	Bal b/d	457,892
			30/9	Sales Daybook	12,157
			30/9	Cash Received Book	8,101
		478,150			478,150

6010   Purchases - clocks

23/9	Bal b/d	164,345	30/9	P & L a/c	183,633
30/9	Purchase Daybook	19,288			
		183,633			183,633

6020   Purchases - watches

23/9	Bal b/d	200,114	30/9	P & L a/c	204,165
30/9	Purchase Daybook	4,051			
		204,165			204,165

7010   Advertising

23/9	Bal b/d	2,439	30/9	P & L a/c	2,439
		2,439			2,439

7020   Wages and NI

23/9	Bal b/d	48,567	30/9	P & L a/c	49,221
30/9	Wages	622			
30/9	NI	32			
		49,221			49,221

7021   Directors' salaries

23/9	Bal b/d	47,786	30/9	P & L a/c	52,122
30/9	Salaries	4,000			
30/9	NI	336			
		52,122			52,122

7030   Council tax

23/9	Bal b/d	12,000	30/9	Prepayment	4,200
			30/9	P & L a/c	7,800
		12,000			12,000

7031   Water rates

23/9	Bal b/d	2,762	30/9	P & L a/c	2,829
30/9	Bank	67			
		2,829			2,829

7040   Insurance

23/9	Bal b/d	5,785	30/9	Prepayment	1,825
30/9	Cash Payments Book	1,200	30/9	P & L a/c	5,160
		6,985			6,985

7050   Light and heating

23/9	Bal b/d	2,348	30/9	P & L a/c	2,598
30/9	Accrual	250			
		2,598			2,598

7060   Van licence and insurance

23/9	Bal b/d	1,990	30/9	Prepayment	300
			30/9	P & L a/c	1,690
		1,990			1,990

7061   Van repairs and fuel

23/9	Bal b/d	2,344	30/9	P & L a/c	3,140
30/9	Cash Payments Book	213			
30/9	Petrol accrual	141			
30/9	Van repairs accrual	442			
		3,140			3,140

7062   Travelling expenses

23/9	Bal b/d	786	30/9	P & L a/c	786
		786			786

7070   Postage and carriage

23/9	Bal b/d	1,433	30/9	P & L a/c	1,489
30/9	Petty Cash Book	56			
		1,489			1,489

7080   Repairs and renewals

23/9	Bal b/d	298	30/9	P & L a/c	548
30/9	Fixtures and fittings	250			
		548			548

7090   Audit and accountancy

23/9	Bal b/d	250	30/9	P & L a/c	2,750
30/9	Accrual	2,500			
		2,750			2,750

8010   Cleaning

23/9	Bal b/d	598	30/9	P & L a/c	608
30/9	Petty Cash Book	10			
		608			608

8020   Sundry expenses

23/9	Bal b/d	698	30/9	P & L a/c	721
30/9	Petty Cash Book	23			
		721			721

3040   6% Loan

30/9	Bal c/d	10,000	23/9	Bal b/d	10,000
		10,000			10,000
			1/10	Bal b/d	10,000

8030 — **Loan interest**

23/9	Bal b/d	300	30/9	P & L a/c		600
30/9	Accrual	300				
		600				600

4010 — **Profit and loss account**

30/9	Bal c/d	269,665	23/9	Bal b/d	86,699
			30/9	Profit	182,966
		269,665			269,665
			1/10	Bal b/d	269,665

4020 — **Ordinary 25p shares**

30/9	Bal c/d	5,000	23/9	Bal b/d	5,000
		5,000			5,000
			1/10	Bal b/d	5,000

8040 — **Packaging**

23/9	Bal b/d	10,000	30/9	P & L a/c	11,000
30/9	Purchase Daybook	1,000			
		11,000			11,000

8050 — **Discount allowed**

30/9	Cash Received Book	73	30/9	P & L a/c	73
		73			73

3050 — **Salaries and wages control**

30/9	Cash Payments Book	3,624	30/9	Net wages	468
			30/9	Net salaries	3,156
		3,624			3,624

8060 — **Disposals**

30/9	Van - costs	3,000	30/9	Depreciation	1,313
			30/9	Part exchange	1,500
			30/9	P & L a/c	187
		3,000			3,000

3060 — **Accruals**

30/9	Bal c/d	3,633	30/9	Electricity	250
			30/9	Petrol	141
			30/9	Van repair	442
			30/9	Audit fee	2,500
			30/9	Loan interest	300
		3,633			3,633
			1/10	Bal b/d	3,633

2050 — **Prepayments**

30/9	Council tax	4,200	30/9	Bal c/d		6,325
30/9	Van licence & insurance	300				
30/9	Insurance	1,825				
		6,325				
1/10	Bal b/d	6,325				6,325

8060 — **Depreciation**

30/9	Fixtures	2,175	30/9	P & L a/c		4,920
30/9	Computers	1,167				
30/9	Vans	1,578				
		4,920				4,920

8070 — **Bank charges and interest**

30/9	Charges	51	30/9	P & L a/c	
30/9	Interest	126			
		177			177

8080 — **Bad debts**

30/9	PQ	2,019	30/9	P & L a/c	2,019
		2,019			2,019

6100 — **Opening stock (P&L)**

30/9	(Stock (B/S)	174,780	30/9	P & L a/c	174,780
		174,780			174,780

6110 — **Closing stock (P&L)**

30/9	P&L a/c	96,887	30/9	Stock (B/S)	96,887
		96,887			96,887

SALES LEDGER

A1   **A Ltd**

23/9	Bal b/d	2,345	24/9	Cash Received Book	3,468
		1,123	29/9	Cash Received Book	3,321
		980	30/9	Bal c/d	8,252
		2,341			
		6,789			
24/9	Sales Daybook	1,707			
24/9	Sales Daybook	5,392			
29/9	Sales Daybook	1,153			
		15,041			15,041
1/10	Bal b/d	8,252			

G1   **GH**

23/9	Bal b/d	1,890	25/9	Cash Received Book	1,890
		235	29/9	Cash Received Book	235
		668	30/9	Bal c/d	11,696
		879			
		3,672			
24/9	Sales Daybook	1,459			
28/9	Sales Daybook	1,025			
29/9	Sales Daybook	2,052			
30/9	Sales Daybook	5,613			
		13,821			13,821
1/10	Bal b/d	11,696			

X1   **X**

23/9	Bal b/d	5,890	26/9	Cash Received Book	5,890
		3,491	30/9	Cash Received Book	3,491
		3,609	30/9	Bal c/d	19,804
		12,990			
24/9	Sales Daybook	6,902			
26/9	Sales Daybook	9,293			
		29,185			29,185
1/10	Bal b/d	19,804			

B1   **BB**

23/9	Bal b/d	2,361	30/9	Sales Daybook	402
		1,400	30/9	Bal c/d	5,838
		1,000			
		4,761			
24/9	Sales Daybook	410			
27/9	Sales Daybook	1,069			
		6,240			6,240
1/10	Bal b/d	5,838			

T1   **TJ**

23/9	Bal b/d	1,100	28/9	Cash Received Book	1,100
		567	30/9	Bal c/d	4,205
		2,122			
		3,789			
26/9		1,516			
		5,305			5,305
1/10	Bal b/d	4,205			

P1   **PQ Inc**

23/9	Bal b/d	2,019	30/9	Bad debts	2,019
		2,019			2,019

M1   **MN**

30/9	Sales Daybook	1,706	30/9	Cash Received Book	1,706
		1,706			1,706

Z1   **ZZ**

27/9	Sales Daybook	924	30/9	Bal c/d	924
		924			924
1/10	Bal b/d	924			

Sales ledger balances at 30 September 2005

		£
A1	A Ltd	8,252
G1	GH	11,696
X1	X	19,804
B1	BB	5,838
T1	TJ	4,205
Z1	ZZ	924
Balance per control account		**50,719**

PURCHASE LEDGER

C1   **Clocks Unlimited**

Date	Description	Amount	Date	Description	Amount
23/9	Purchase Daybook	536	23/9	Bal b/d	5,670
24/9	Cash Payments Book	16,890			4,396
30/9	Bal c/d	10,893			6,824
					16,890
			23/9	Purchase Daybook	6,447
			24/9	Purchase Daybook	3,274
			26/9	Purchase Daybook	1,303
			28/9	Purchase Daybook	405
		28,319			28,319
			1/10	Bal b/d	10,893

W1   **Watches for Ever**

Date	Description	Amount	Date	Description	Amount
24/9	Cash Payments Book	4,286	23/9	Bal b/d	321
30/9	Bal c/d	5,447			3,965
					250
					1,227
					5,763
			23/9	Purchase Daybook	1,085
			28/9	Purchase Daybook	2,349
			28/9	Purchase Daybook	536
		9,733			9,733
			1/10	Bal b/d	5,447

C2   **Cuckoos**

Date	Description	Amount	Date	Description	Amount
24/9	Cash Payments	2,670	23/9	Bal b/d	2,670
30/9	Bal c/d	10,288			1,203
					3,873
			24/9	Purchase Daybook	9,085
		12,958			12,958
			1/10	Bal b/d	10,288

S1   **Speaking Clocks**

Date	Description	Amount	Date	Description	Amount
24/9	Cash Payments Book	2,220	23/9	Bal b/d	2,220
30/9	Bal c/d	3,735			1,000
					1,220
					4,440
			28/9	Purchase Daybook	1,515
		5,955			5,955
			1/10	Bal b/d	3,735

NI   **New Watches**

Date	Description	Amount	Date	Description	Amount
30/9	Bal c/d	3,774	23/9	Bal b/d	1,500
					1,483
					2,983
			28/9	Purchase Daybook	791
		3,774			3,774
			1/10	Bal b/d	3,774

B1 **Big Ben Clocks**

24/9	Cash Payments Book	1,721	23/9	Bal b/d	1,721
30/9	Bal c/d	1,170	28/9	Purchase Daybook	1,170
		2,891			2,891
			1/10	Bal b/d	1,170

P1 **Packaging Ltd**

30/9	Bal c/d	1,175	28/9	Purchase Daybook	1,175
		1,175			1,175
				Bal b/d	1,175

Purchase ledger balances at 30 September 2005

		£
C1	Clock Unlimited	10,893
W1	Watches for Ever	5,447
C2	Cuckoos	10,288
S1	Speaking Clocks	3,735
N1	New watches	3,774
B1	Big Ben Clocks	1,170
P1	Packaging Ltd	1,175
Balance per control account		**36,482**

12. Internal accounts

Cuckoo Clocks Ltd

Profit and loss account for the year ended 30 September 2005

	£	£
Turnover (376,384 + 478,150)		854,534
Opening stock	174,780	
Purchases (183,633 + 204,165)	387,798	
Closing stock	(96,887)	
Cost of goods sold		465,691
Gross profit		388,843
Advertising	2439	
Wages and national insurance	49,221	
Directors' salaries	52,122	
Council tax	7,800	
Water rates	2,829	
Insurance	5,160	
Lighting and heating	2,598	
Van licence and insurance	1,690	
Van repairs and fuel	3,140	
Travelling expenses	786	
Postage and carriage	1,489	
Repairs and renewals	548	
Audit and accountancy	2,750	
Cleaning	608	
Sundry expenses	721	
Loan interest	600	
Packaging	11,000	
Discount allowed	73	
Bank charges	177	
Depreciation	4,920	
Bad debts	2,019	
Disposal of fixed assets	187	152,877
Net profit		235,966

Cuckoo Clocks Ltd
Balance sheet at 30 September 2005

	£	£
FIXED ASSETS		
Freehold property	234,000	
Fixtures and fittings 21,750 – 6,575	15,175	
Computer equipment 3,500 – 2,917	583	
Van (8500 – 3,765)	4,735	
		254,493
CURRENT ASSETS		
Stock	96,887	
Debtors and prepayments 50,719+6,325	57,044	
Petty cash	250	
	154,181	
CREDITORS : amounts falling due within one year		
Creditors	36,482	
Bank	8,937	
VAT	18,383	
PAYE & NI	3,574	
Accruals	3,633	
	71,009	
NET CURRENT ASSETS		83,172
TOTAL ASSETS LESS CURRENT LIABILITIES		337,665
CREDTIORS: amounts falling due after one year		(10,000)
		327,665
CAPITAL AND RESERVES		
Called up share capital		5,000
Profit and loss account (86,699 + 235,966)		322,665
		327,665

13. Accounts in Companies Act format

Adjustments for tax and dividends

	Debit	Credit
	£	£
Taxation charge (P&L)	45,000	
Corporation tax liability (B/S)		45,000
Estimate of corporation tax charge		
Proposed dividend (P&L)	8,000	
Proposed dividend liability (B/S)		8,000
Dividend of 40p per share proposed (40p × 20,000 shares)		

9000   **Taxation charge (P&L)**

30/9	C/T liability	45,000	30/9	P&L a/c	45,000
		45,000			45,000

3070   **Corporation tax liability (B/S)**

30/9	Bal c/d	45,000	30/9	Taxation charge	45,000
		45,000			45,000
			1/10	Bal b/d	45,000

9100   **Proposed dividend (P&L)**

30/9	Proposed dividend	8,000	30/9	P&L a/c	8,000
		8,000			8,000

3080   **Proposed dividend liability (B/S)**

30/9	Bal c/d	8,000	30/9	Proposed dividend	8,000
		8,000			8,000
			1/10	Bal b/d	8,000

Cuckoo Clocks Ltd
Profit and loss account at 30 September 2005

Notes		£	£
	Turnover		854,534
	Cost of sales		465,691
	Gross profit		388,843
	Administrative expenses	145,958	
	Distribution costs	6,319	152,277
	Operating profit		236,566
	Interest		600
	Profit on ordinary activities before taxation		235,966
	Taxation		45,000
	Profit on ordinary activities after taxation		190,966
	Ordinary dividends		8,000
	Retained profit for the year		182,966

Cuckoo Clocks Ltd
Balance Sheet at 30 September 2005

Notes		£	£	£
	FIXED ASSETS			254,493
	Tangible assets			
	CURRENT ASSETS			
	Stock	96,887		
	Debtors	57,044		
	Cash and bank	250	154,181	
	CREDITORS : amounts falling due within one year (71,009 + 8,000 + 45,000)		124,009	
	NET CURRENT ASSETS			30,172
	TOTAL ASSETS LESS CURRENT LIABILITIES			284,665
	CREDTIORS: amounts falling due after one year			10,000
				274,665
	CAPITAL AND RESERVES			
	Called up share capital			5,000
	Profit and loss account 86,699 + 182,966			269,665
				274,665

14. Final trial balance

	Debit	Credit
	£	£
Freehold property	234,000	
Fixtures and fittings – cost	21,750	
Fixtures and fittings – acc. depreciation		6,575
Computer equipment – cost	3,500	
Computer equipment – acc. depreciation		2,917
Vans – cost	8,500	
Vans - acc. depreciation		3,765
Stock	96,887	
Debtors control account	50,719	
Creditors control account		36,482
Bank account		8,937
Petty cash	250	
VAT		18,383
PAYE & NI		3,574
Loan		10,000
Profit and loss account		269,665
Share capital		5,000
Accruals		3,633
Prepayments	6,325	
Taxation liability		45,000
Proposed dividend		8,000
	421,931	**421,931**

Glossary

Account number

The code number given to an account in the coding system.

Accounting bases

The methods developed for applying the *accounting concepts* to financial *transactions* and items, for example *depreciation* is a means of applying the *matching concept* to the purchase of *fixed assets*.

See also Accounting policies

Accounting concepts

FRS 18 (Accounting policies) sets out the accounting concepts and desirable qualities that should be applied in the production of accounts.

Going concern concept: an assessment should be made as to whether there are significant doubts about an entity's ability to continue as a going concern.

Accruals concept (matching concept): revenues and costs are accrued (recognised when they are earned or incurred, not as they are received or paid). They are matched with one another as far as comparably possible and dealt with in the profit and loss of the period to which they relate.

Consistency desirable quality: there is consistency of accounting treatment and disclosure of like items within each accounting period and from one period to the next.

Prudence desirable quality: requires that accounting policies take account of uncertainty in recognising and measuring assets, liabilities, gains, losses and changes to shareholders' funds. It is not necessary to exercise prudence where there is no uncertainty.

The *Companies Act* defines another concept:

'Disaggregation': Accounts are to be prepared with a minimum of netting off.

See also Statement of Standard Accounting Practice

Accounting bases

Accounting equation

$$\text{Capital} = \text{Assets} - \text{Liabilities}$$

or

$$\text{Capital} + (\text{Income} - \text{Expenses}) = \text{Assets} - \text{Liabilities}$$

See also Balance sheet

Accounting policies

The specific *accounting bases* selected by a business and used in the preparation of their *accounts*, for example the method of *depreciation* in use.

The objective against which an entity should judge the appropriateness of accounting policies to its particular circumstances are:

a) *relevance;*
b) *reliability;*
c) *comparability;* and
d) *understandability.*

Accounting records

The formal recording of the transactions of a business. Depending on the size and type of the business these may take several different forms.

See also Manual records and Computerised records

Accounting year/year-end

Accounts are generally prepared for a year up to the same date each year. This date is the business's year-end. The period of a year from one year-end to another is the accounting year.

Accounts

a) The profit and loss account and balance sheet of a business.
Sometimes referred to as the final accounts.

b) Often used to mean the *ledger accounts.*

Accruals

The *profit and loss account* should include all *expenses* incurred in the year whether or not they have been billed. Where an expense has been incurred, but not yet billed and therefore not yet included in the records, an adjustment must be made to include an estimate of the amount of the expense incurred. This extra amount included is an accrual or an accrued expense. The adjustment to include the accrual is to *debit* the expense account and *credit* the Accruals account (a *current liability*). The adjustment must be reversed in the following year - this will offset part of the amount of the invoice for the expense when it is received.

Accruals concept

See Accounting concepts

Accumulated depreciation

See Depreciation

AGM

See Annual General Meeting

Annual general meeting (AGM)

Many organisations will have AGM's, but this applies particularly to *companies.* At a company AGM the *published accounts* are presented to be approved by the *shareholders.*

Assets

The items owned by a business. These will include machinery, motor vehicles, stock, debtors and money at the bank.

See also Fixed assets, Current assets and Balance sheet

Authorised share capital

The maximum amount of *share capital* that a company can issue, as set at the incorporation of the *company*. This can later be increased if necessary.

Bad debts

It sometimes happens that *credit customers* do not pay the *invoices* issued to them. At the point where it is known that a credit customer is never going to make payment, the balance should be *written off* as a bad debt. This becomes an *expense* of the business.

See also Provision for doubtful debts

Balance

The balance in account will be the difference between the total amounts *debited* to the account and the total amounts *credited*. An excess of debits over credits gives a debit balance (*assets* and expenses). An excess of credits over debits gives a credit balance (*capital, liabilities, income*).

Some formats of *ledger accounts* show a running balance. In *T account* format no such running balance is shown - it must be calculated by balancing off the account. In so doing a balance will be inserted to be carried down (Bal c/d) and the calculated balance will be brought down in the account (Bal b/d). Sometimes the balance is brought forward from one page to another (Bal b/f).

Balance forward

See Open item

Balance sheet

A statement detailing the *assets, liabilities* and *capital* of the business. The two sections of the balance sheet, usually the assets section (assets less liabilities) and the capital section, should be equal.

See also Financial accounts and Management accounts

Bank

A business should lodge all *receipts* in, and make all *payments* from, a business bank account (with the exception of sundry small payments to be made from *petty cash*). Reference to the bank account could mean either the account being run at the bank itself or the *nominal ledger* account for the bank.

See also Lodgement and Bank reconciliation

Bank overdraft

A business may have money at the *bank,* or as frequently happens, it may have agreed with the bank to spend more than it has deposited In this case the business will have overdrawn its account and will have a bank overdraft. Technically bank overdrafts are repayable on demand and are classed as *current liabilities* even though they may be ongoing for many years.

Bank reconciliation

In general, because of timing differences, the *balance* showing in the *Bank* account in the *nominal ledger* will be different to the balance showing on the *bank statement.* The process of agreeing the two figures, taking account of these timing differences, is the bank reconciliation.

See also Outstanding cheques and Outstanding lodgements

Bank statement

Periodically, usually once a month, *banks* send to their customers a statement showing the balance in the account and details of the transactions going through the account. This is the bank statement.

See also Bank reconciliation

Batch

In entering information into a *computer system* it is often the case that a series of items of the same type are processed together. These items are grouped together as a batch. The total of the items in a batch is the batch total which may be used for control purposes. *Integration* will often be carried out for a batch of items together.

Bookkeeping

The process of recording the transactions of a business in the books of the business. The process will vary from one business to another, but will usually consist of the *books of original entry (cash book and daybooks)* and the *ledgers* or a set of computerised ledgers.

Books of original entry

The books in which the first recording of business transactions are made. They are generally the *sales daybook, purchase daybook and cash book*. Also termed the books of prime entry.

Capital

a)   The amount invested in a business by its owner(s).

b)   The capital cost of an item is the cost of the item excluding any interest charges to be paid if the item is being purchased on some form of deferred *credit*.

See also Balance sheet

Capital employed

This term can be used with slightly different definitions corresponding to the different definitions of *net assets*, as:

> Capital Employed = Net Assets

The capital employed is the finance being provided for the business. It can be taken as being that provided by the owner(s) only (the proprietor's capital employed), or it can be taken to include that provided by third parties as well, in which case *long-term liabilities* are also included.

The Proprietor's Capital Employed will be the balance in the capital account of a *sole trader*, the *shareholders' funds* in a *limited company*.

Cash book

The cash book records all the transactions going through the business *bank* account. Note that in the case of payments, this means cheque payments, not as the name suggests cash payments. Payments made in cash should come from *petty cash* and would be recorded in the petty cash book. The cash book is often kept is an analysed format.

Receipts and payments may be recorded on the two sides of the one book or the Cash Book may be split into the cash receipts book and the cash payments book.

See also Cross-add

Cash flow forecast

A projection of the *receipts* and *payments* and *bank* balance for a future period. Not to be confused with the historic *cash flow statement*.

Cash flow statement

A statement in *published accounts*, required by FRS1, showing the flow of cash for the year just finished. Not to be confused with a *cash flow forecast*.

Cash payments book

See Cash book

Cash receipts book

See Cash book

Cash sales

When a cash sale is made the *customer* is not given any *credit*, but is required to make payment immediately. Note that the term cash sale does not mean that the payment was made in cash rather than cheque. It really means non-credit sales.

See also Credit sales

Coding system

In a computer system accounts are given codes by which they will be accessed. It is important to code accounts in a logical manner to get meaningful reports from the system. In a manual system accounts may also be given codes to make locating them easier. In the *sales ledger* and *purchase ledger* the coding will probably be by alphabetic reference to the name. In the *nominal ledger* however the coding will probably be by reference to the category of account, for example all *fixed assets* may well be coded together.

Companies Acts

The legislation governing the running and reporting of limited companies.

See also Published accounts

Comparability

See Accounting concepts

Consistency concept

See Accounting concepts

Contra

Where the same body is both a *customer* and a *supplier* of a business it will have an account in both the *sales ledger* and the *purchase ledger*. A contra adjustment sets one balance against the other.

Control account

In the *nominal ledger* there will usually be various control accounts. In some way these accounts are providing a check on some aspect of the accounting system. The most common control accounts are the *sales ledger control account* and the *purchase ledger control account*.

Corporation tax

The tax levied on the profits of a *company*. It is an appropriation of the profits and a *liability* of the company.

Cost of sales

In a retail business the cost of sales will simply be the cost of buying in the items to be sold. In a manufacturing business the cost of sales will be the cost of making the items to be sold. This will be the cost of materials bought in together with the work done to the materials - this will include manufacturing wages and various expenses relating to production.

See also Gross profit and Trading account

Cr

or Cr: abbreviation for *credit*.

Credit

a)   The right hand side of the *double entry* system. Often denoted as Cr.

See also   Debit

b)   The allowance of a period of time before payment is required.

See also Credit sales

Credit customer

A person or body to whom a business has sold goods or services on *credit*.

See also Customer, Credit sales and Sales ledger

Credit note

When goods are sold on *credit* an *invoice* is issued. If the sale is later cancelled for some reason, for example if the goods are returned as being faulty, a credit note will be issued. This may cancel a whole invoice or part of an invoice. Sales credit notes arise where a sale to a customer is being cancelled, purchase credit notes arise where a supplier has sent a credit note for the cancellation of a purchase invoice.

Credit sales

When a business makes a credit sale, *the customer* is not required to pay immediately. An *invoice* is issued requesting payment in perhaps 30 days (the customer is given 30 days *credit*). Once the invoice is issued the customer becomes a debtor of the business.

See also Cash sales and Debtors

Credit supplier

A person or body from whom the business has bought goods or services on *credit*.

See also Purchase ledger

Creditors

Persons or bodies to whom the business owes money.

The main creditors of a business will usually be the suppliers from whom the business has received goods or services on *credit*. These are sometimes termed the trade creditors.

See also Current liabilities and Purchase ledger

Cross-add

Where columns of figures consist of a total column and other columns analysing that total, the figures produced on summing the columns should cross-add that is, the total of the Total column should equal the sum of the totals of the analysis columns. Checking this cross-add checks that columns have been summed correctly and that individual lines have been analysed correctly. This applies to analysed *Sales daybooks, Purchase daybooks and Cash books.*

Current assets

Assets held in the form of cash or with a view to converting them into cash. These include *stock* of goods for resale, *debtors* and money at the *bank* or in cash.

See also Assets, Fixed assets and Balance sheet

Current liabilities

Amounts owed by the business and due to be paid over within one year. These will include trade *creditors* and *bank overdrafts.*

See also Liabilities, Long-term liabilities and Balance sheet

Customer

A customer is a person or body to whom the business sells goods or for whom it provides services.

See also Cash sales and Credit sales

Debentures

A formal loan to a company at a stated rate of *interest.* Debentures may be redeemable, in which case the money will be repaid, or irredeemable, in which case they are only repaid on liquidation of the company (if there are funds available). They may be secured over the assets of the company. A fixed charge gives security over specific *assets* while a floating charge gives security over the assets in general. If the business founders, or if it cannot redeem the debentures at the specified time, the debenture holders have the right to recover the amounts due out of the sale proceeds of the secured assets.

Debit

The left hand side of the *double entry* system. Often denoted as Dr.

See also Credit

Debtors

Debtors are persons or entities who owe money to a business.

The main debtors of a business will be customers to whom the business has sold on *credit.* These are sometimes termed the trade debtors.

See also Credit sales and Sales ledger

Depreciation

The cost of a *fixed asset,* (less any estimated *residual value*) is spread over the expected useful life of the asset by the process of depreciation. Each year's depreciation is charged in the *profit and loss account.* The total depreciation charged to date is recorded in the Accumulated (or Aggregate) Depreciation account.

409

Disaggregation concept

See Accounting concepts

Directors

The owners of a *company*, the *shareholders,* elect a board of directors to run the company on their behalf. The directors may work full time in the company, executive directors, or they may be outsiders (non-executive directors).

Dividend

The *shareholders* of a *company* receive a share of the profits in the form of a dividend. The rate of dividend is usually expressed as an amount per *share* or as a percentage (of the nominal value). The rate of preference dividend is fixed, the rate of ordinary dividend is decided on by the *directors*, to be confirmed by the shareholders. An ordinary dividend paid during the year is an interim dividend, the dividend based on the profits for the year proposed by the directors is a final proposed dividend. Dividends can only be paid if there are profits available to pay them.

See also Share capital, Ordinary shares and Preference shares

Double entry

A system of recording transactions by increasing the amount on the debit (left) side of some account(s) and increasing the amount on the credit (right) side of some other account(s) by exactly the same amount.

Debit entries	Increase *assets, expenses,*	Decrease *liabilities, capital, income*
Credit entries	Decrease *assets, expenses*	Increase *liabilities, capital, income*

Dr

or Dr: Abbreviation for *debit*.

Drawings

For a *sole-trader or partnership*, the amounts taken out of the business by its owner(s). Drawings could be in the form of cash, goods taken for own use or private bills paid by the business. Drawing go to reduce the owner's *capital.*

Earnings per share

A figure required by FRS14 to be disclosed for *quoted companies* =

$$\frac{\text{Profit after tax and preference dividend}}{\text{Number of ordinary shares}}$$

See also Financial Reporting Standards

Expenses

The ongoing costs of running a business. One of the main expenses of a business will usually be the wages and salaries costs. Others will include such things as telephone costs, rent, electricity charges, motor costs, advertising.

See also Profit and loss account

Finance charges

When an *asset* is purchased with payment being made over a long period under an arrangement such as *hire purchase* or a *finance lease*, there will usually be extra charges levied for this extended credit. These are the finance charges or *interest* charges. Such charges are an *expense* of the business making the purchase.

Finance lease

Under this type of lease the leasee effectively pays for the *asset* over the period of the lease. In this case the asset being leased is recorded as an asset of the business and the *capital* amount outstanding is recorded as a *long-term liability*. Lease payments are split into the capital repayment and the *finance charges*. Only the finance charges appear as an *expense in* the *profit and loss account*.

Financial accounts

The annual *profit and loss account* and *balance sheet* prepared for use outside the business.

See also Management accounts and Published accounts

Financial Reporting Standards (FRS's)

Statements produced by the Accounting Standards Board (ASB) giving requirements for the production of published accounts.

See also Statements of Standard Accounting Practice

Fixed assets

Assets held by a business for use in the business rather than for resale. They are usually held for a number of years. Examples are property, machinery, fixtures and fittings, motor vehicles.

See also Assets, Current assets and Balance sheet

Fixed charge

See Debentures

Floating charge

See Debentures

FRS's

See Financial Reporting Standards

General ledger

Another name for the *Nominal ledger*.

Going concern concept

See Accounting concepts

Gross profit

The profit on trading - Sales less Cost of Sales

See also Gross profit percentage and Net profit

Gross profit percentage

Gross Profit expressed as a percentage *of Sales*

$$\frac{\text{Gross profit}}{\text{Sales}} \times 100\%$$

Different businesses of the same type will generally have similar gross profit percentages.

Hire purchase

A hire purchase contract is a contract for the hire of an *asset* with legal ownership of the asset being transferred with the last payment. This however is accounted for as the acquisition of the asset at the start of the agreement with a corresponding *long-term liability* of the *capital* amount on hire purchase. Subsequent payments are split into the *charges* (an *expense*) and repayment of the capital outstanding.

Historical cost (convention)

The usual basis for the statement of figures in the records and *accounts*. The main common exception is the revaluation of property, where the property is stated in the *balance sheet* at its current valuation rather than its historic cost.

See also Revaluation reserve

Holding company

A company which controls another company, its *subsidiary*.

Imprest system

A system of keeping *petty cash* where the cash float is set up at a certain specified level. Periodically the level of cash is made up to that same level again - this is the level of the imprest. At any point, the cash balance + the cash spent since the last reimbursement of the float should equal the value of the imprest.

Income

The monies earned by a business. These will usually be in the form of *sales* income, but there may also be sundry other receipts such as rents or interest received.

See also Profit and loss account

Income tax

Income tax is charged to individuals on their earnings. Where people are employed in a business income tax is deducted from their pay under the *PAYE* system. A person running his own business, either as a *sole trader* or as a partner in a *partnership,* is charged income tax on the profits of the business. This is a private responsibility of the individual, it is not a liability of the business.

See also Corporation tax

Incomplete records

In some businesses a complete *double-entry* set of records is not kept. In addition, there may or may not be some missing figures, for example an unknown figure of cash sales paid out as wages. The set of records in this situation is known as incomplete records.

Input VAT

See Value Added Tax

Integration

Integration is the automatic transfer of information from one module of a *computerised accounting system* to another. Thus an *invoice* entered in a *supplier* account in a *purchase ledger* would, on integration with the *nominal ledger*, update automatically the *Purchase ledger control account*, the *VAT* account and the appropriate *expense* account(s).

See also Modular computer system

Interest

Where money is lent by one body to another it is usual for the borrower to pay to the lender monetary compensation for the use of the money. This is interest payable by the borrower (an **expense**), interest receivable by the lender *(income)*.

Internal accounts

A *limited company* must prepare its annual *accounts* is a specified format for issuing to the shareholders. The accounts to be used within the company, the internal accounts, can be produced in whatever format the company wishes.

See also Published accounts

Invoice

When a business sells goods or provides services on *credit* an invoice is issued detailing the amount being charged. The net amount of the invoice is the amount being charged by the business, to this is added *VAT* to give the gross amount. The invoice will usually specify when payment is due.

See also Sales invoice and Purchase invoice

Issued share capital

The amount of *share capital* that a *company* has issued. This is the amount that will appear in the *balance sheet*.

Journal

The journal is a book used for the original recording of transactions for which there is no other suitable *book of original entry*. This could be for the correction of a previous entry or the recording of adjustments such as *depreciation*.

Lease

A contract, usually long-term, which allows for the use of an *asset* in return for a periodic leasing payment. The contract does not give ownership, but may contain terms for the acquisition of the asset at the end of the period of the lease.

There are two main types of leases - *Operating leases and Finance leases*

Leasee

The person or body to whom *as asset* is leased.

See also Lease

Ledger

A book containing accounts to record the transactions of a business. Ledgers may be in manual form or may be computerised.

See also Manual records, Computerised records, Nominal ledger, Sales ledger and Purchase ledger

Ledger accounts

The individual sub-divisions of *ledger*, for example the Sales account or the *Debtors* account in the *nominal ledger* or accounts for each individual *credit customer* in the *sales ledger*

See also T Accounts

Liabilities

Amounts that are owed by the business. These will include loans that have been made to the business, amounts owed to trade *creditors* and *bank overdrafts*.

See also Current liabilities, Long-term liabilities and Balance sheet

Limited company

A formal business entity set up under the rules of the Companies Acts. The entity has a separate legal existence to that of the owners (the shareholders). The liability of the owners for the debts of the company is limited to the amount of their share capital.

See also Sole-trader and Partnership

Listed company

A company whose *shares* are traded in on the Stock Exchange.

Lodgement

Money deposited in the *bank*.

See also Outstanding lodgement

Long-term liabilities

Amounts owed by the business, but not due to be paid over within one year. These will usually be loans of some kind or could be the *capital* amount outstanding under some deferred purchase agreement such as *hire purchase*.

See also Liabilities, Current liabilities and Balance sheet

Management accounts

Statements prepared to help those running a business, for use within the business. They take whatever form is felt useful, but will often consist of a monthly *profit and loss account* and *balance sheet*.

See also Financial accounts

Manual records

The process of recording the transactions of a business in written (manual) records.

See also Accounting records and Computerised records

Matching concept

See Accounting concepts

Modular computer system

Most *computerised accounting systems* come as different modules where the user can purchase whatever combination of modules is required. Modules will usually include *nominal ledger, sales ledger, purchase ledger, cash book*, invoicing, *stock* control and many others.

National insurance

When wages and salaries are paid, a deduction is made from the employees' pay for National insurance. In addition, the employer must also pay a contribution to National insurance. Both employees' and employer's contributions are calculated as a percentage of pay. National insurance applies where the pay is over a certain threshold. Contributions are paid over the following month with *PAYE*.

Net assets

Net Assets = Total assets less Total liabilities.

Where a *balance sheet* is drawn up with *long-term liabilities* deducted from the Assets section this will be the total of the Assets section of the balance sheet.

Where a balance sheet is drawn up with long-term liabilities being added to the Capital section, the total of the Assets section is :

Total assets less Current liabilities

This can also sometimes be referred to as the net assets.

Net book value

The net book value of *a fixed asset* or class of assets = Cost - *Accumulated depreciation*

Net current assets

Current Assets - Current Liabilities

This figure gives some indication of the liquidity of the business. If negative, it become net current liabilities.

Net profit

The figure left after deducting all *expenses* from total *income* - the figure (I - E) in the *accounting equation*

C + (I - E) = A - L

This is the figure calculated in the profit and loss account - it is found by subtracting all *expenses*, other than *cost of sales* from the gross profit

See also Net Profit Percentage

Net profit percentage

Net profit expressed as a percentage of *sales*

$$\frac{\text{Net profit}}{\text{Sales}} \times 100\%$$

Nominal ledger

The book containing accounts for each sub-division of *assets, liabilities, capital, income* and *expenses,* for example there will be accounts for property, *creditors, sales* (or for several different types of sales) and *accounts* for whatever sub-division of expenses is required.

See also Ledger, Sales ledger, Purchase ledger and Control accounts

Nominal value

See Share capital

Notes to the accounts

In a set of *published accounts* there will be several pages of notes to the accounts. These notes contain information as required by the *Companies Act*.

Open item

When a clear-down of transactions is run in a computerised *Sales ledger* or *Purchase ledger*, details of *invoices* that are now paid, and the payments settling those invoices are often dropped from the system. In an open-item system all unmatched transactions (unpaid invoices and any unallocated payments) are carried forward. In a balance forward system only the balance, with possibly an ageing of the balance, is carried forward.

Operating lease

This type of lease is effectively the rental of an *asset*. Ownership of the asset does not pass to the leasee. Lease costs are charged as an *expense* in the *profit and loss account*.

Ordinary shares

The ordinary shares are the main class of shares of a company. The ordinary shareholders are the owners or members of the company and have the right to vote at general meetings. Their return on their investment, the ordinary *dividend*, is at the discretion of the *directors* and will only be possible as long as preference dividends have been met in full.

See also Share capital and Preference shares

Output VAT

See Value Added Tax

Outstanding cheques

It is often the case that there will be some time between the issue of a cheque and the date on which it actually comes out of the payer's account at the bank. At any point, cheques that have been issued and recorded in the *cash book* but have not yet reached the account at the bank are said to be outstanding or unpresented. Outstanding cheques will usually be the major reconciling item in the *bank reconciliation*.

See also Outstanding lodgements

Outstanding lodgements

Where a *lodgement* is made at business's own branch of the *bank* it will appear on the *bank statement* on the same date. Where however it is paid in through a different branch it will take a few days to reach the business's own branch. Thus at any time there may be lodgements recorded in the *cash book* that are not on the bank statement - these are outstanding lodgements and will form part of the *bank reconciliation*.

See also Outstanding cheques

Partnership

An association of between 2 and 20 persons (or possibly more in the case of certain professional partnerships) carrying on business together. The business is owned by the partners and they will share the profits.

See also Sole-trader, Limited company and Profit sharing ratios

Pay As You Earn (PAYE)

When wages and salaries are paid, a deduction is made from the employees' pay to cover their *income tax* liability. This tax deducted (PAYE) is paid over the following month to the Inland Revenue.

See also National insurance

Payments

Apart from sundry small payments made by *petty cash*, the payments made by a business should go through the *bank* account - by cheque or some kind of direct bank transfer. Such payments will be recorded in the *cash payments book* and will consist of such things as the payment of *creditors*, for previously received *purchase invoices*, wages and salaries, *drawings*, etc.

See also Receipts

Period-end

Computer systems are often run on a monthly basis, with a monthly *profit and loss account* and *balance sheet* being produced. In such systems there will usually be a period-end routine to be run. The effect of this will vary from one system to another, but it may indicate to the system that a new month is being entered and it may clear down some of the transaction listings.

See also Open item and Balance forward

Petty cash

It is often the case that a business will want to have some cash available for making small payments such as the purchase of stamps or milk. Cash kept for such purposes is known as petty cash. The payments will be recorded in the petty cash book which is often kept in an analysed format.

Petty cash book

See Petty cash

Posting

The process of transferring figures into *ledger accounts*.

Preference shares

A company may or may not have preference shares. The rate of *dividend* on preference shares is fixed and must be paid as long as there are profits available to do so.

See also Share capital and Ordinary shares

Prepayments

The *expenses* in the *profit and loss account* should exclude any that relate to the following year. Often items such as rent and insurance are billed in advance. The portion included in the expense accounts relating to the next year (the amount prepaid) should be removed by crediting the expense account. The *debit* is to the Prepayments account (a *current asset*). The adjustment will be reversed in the following year - this effectively carries the expense forward to the year to which it relates.

Private limited company (Ltd)

A company where there are restrictions on the transfer of *shares* - they cannot be made freely available for sale to the public.

See also Public limited company

Profit and loss account

A statement in which the expenses of a business are deducted from the income of the business. An excess of income over expenses gives a profit while an excess of expenses over income gives a loss.

See also Financial accounts and Management accounts

Profit sharing ratios

In *a partnership* the profits (or losses) must be split amongst the partners. They may have various allocations such as salaries and interest on capital. It is usual to apportion any profits remaining after such allocations in an agreed ratio - the profit sharing ratios. As this also applies to the allocation of losses the ratios are sometimes referred to as the profit/loss sharing ratios.

Proprietor

The owner of the business.

See also Capital

Provision

An amount set aside from profits for some expected future loss or expense.

See also Provision for doubtful debts

Provision for doubtful debts

Where it is thought that the full amount outstanding by *credit customers* will not be paid, but there are no definite *bad debts* to be *written off*, a *provision* should be made for doubtful debtors. This provision is set against the balance in the *Debtors* account to reduce the value to the amount expected to be recoverable from debtors.

Prudence concept

See Accounting concepts

Public limited company (plc)

A company, set up as being a public company, where the *shares* can be freely transferred from one person to any other.

See also Private limited company

Published accounts

A *limited company* is required to send to its *shareholders, debenture* holders and the Registrar of Companies a set of accounts each year. The content of these accounts is laid down in the *Companies Act* and consists of much more than the *profit and loss account* and *balance sheet*. These accounts are referred to as the Published Accounts.

See also Notes to the accounts

Purchase daybook

The book in which *purchase invoices* are recorded. The book will usually be analysed with columns for Gross Amount, *VAT* and columns for all the common categories of expenses.

See also Purchase ledger and Cross-add

Purchase invoice

When a business buys goods or receives services on *credit*, it will receive a purchase invoice from the supplier. Note that the term applies to all items purchased on credit not just the purchase of goods for resale.

See also Purchase ledger

Purchase ledger

The book containing *accounts* for each different *credit supplier* (the suppliers of both goods and services). *Invoices* received will increase the amount due to the supplier (*credit*) and *payments* will decrease the balance due (*debit*). The total of all the balances from the purchase ledger should equal the balance in the *Purchase ledger control account* in the *nominal ledger*.

Purchase ledger control account

This account is used where a subsidiary *purchase ledger* is being kept. Individual *invoices* and *payments* are posted to the individual *supplier* accounts in the purchase ledger. This is purely memorandum information. The *double entry* takes place in the Purchase ledger control account in the *nominal ledger*, usually by the posting of totals of invoices and payments. The *balance* in the Purchase ledger control account should equal the total of the balances in the individual supplier accounts in the purchase ledger.

See also Control accounts and Sales ledger control account

Quoted company

Same as *Listed company*

Receipts

The monies received by the business. These will be recorded in the *cash receipts book* and will consist mainly of money received from *cash sales* and from *debtors*, for previous *credit sales*. There may also be some other sundry receipts such as rents or *interest* received.

See also Payments

Reducing balance depreciation

The *depreciation* charge is calculated by applying a percentage to the *net book value* of the asset, for example 25% reducing balance will apply depreciation each year of 25% of the current net book value. Thus the depreciation charge decreases each year.

See also Straight line depreciation

Relevance

Financial information is relevant if it has the ability to influence the economic decisions of users and is provided in time to influence those decisions.

Reliability

Financial information is reliable if:

a) it can be depended upon by users to represent faithfully what it either purports to represent or could reasonably be expected to represent, and therefore reflects the substance of the transactions and other events that have taken place;

b) it is free from deliberate or systematic bias;

c) it is free from material error;

d) it is complete within the bounds of materiality;

e) under conditions of uncertainty, it has been prudently prepared.

Remittance advice

When a *payment* is being made to a *credit supplier* it is useful to send with the payment a statement detailing the invoice numbers and amounts that are being paid. This may be done in the form of a note or a more official statement may be drawn up - a remittance advice.

Reserves

A category of accounts in a *company*, of a capital nature, but separate from the *share capital*. Reserves are of two types -

> Distributable, having been created out of profits
>
> > - principally the profit and loss account balance
>
> Non-distributable, not having been created out of profits, for example
>
> > - *Share premium account*
> >
> > - *Revaluation reserve*

Residual value

The residual value of an asset is its value at the end of the its useful life.

Revaluation

See Historical cost

Revenue

Another term for *Income*.

Reversal

Some adjustments that are made in the preparation of a set of accounts must be reversed in the next year. The reversal will be the exact opposite of the original adjustment.

For example, to include an *accrual*, the adjustment is Debit : Expense   Credit : Accruals

the reversal is Debit : Accruals   Credit : Expense

Reversing journal

Often *computer systems* have the ability to record journal entries as reversing. When the period-end is run these entries will reverse automatically. This is useful for entries like monthly *accruals*.

Revaluation reserve

When property is revalued in a company the gain is credited to Revaluation reserve. This is not a realised gain and so cannot be distributed as *dividends*.

See also Reserves

Sales

A business will usually operate by either buying goods and selling them on at a higher figure or by providing services. The Sales of the business are the amounts charged for the goods sold or for the services provided.

See also Cash sales, Credit sales and Customer

Sales daybook

The book in which *sales invoices* are recorded. The book will often be analysed - the total amount of the invoice will recorded together with the breakdown into *VAT* and an analysis into the type of sale.

See also Sales ledger and Cross-add

Sales invoice

A sales invoice is issued by a business when it provides services or sells goods on *credit*.

See also Sales daybook

Sales ledger

The book containing accounts for each different *credit customer*. Invoices issued will increase the amount due by the customer *(debit)* and *receipts* will decrease the balance due *(credit)*. The total of all the balances from the sales ledger should equal the balance in the *Sales ledger control account in* the *nominal ledger*.

Sales ledger control account

This account is used where a subsidiary *sales ledger* is being kept. Individual *invoices* and *receipts* are posted to the individual *customer* accounts in the sales ledger. This is purely memorandum information. The *double entry* takes place in the Sales ledger control account in the *nominal ledger*, usually by the posting of totals of invoices and receipts. The *balance* in the Sales ledger control account should equal the total of the balances in the individual customer accounts in the sales ledger.

See also Control accounts and Purchase ledger control account

Share capital

A company's capital is split into a number of shares of a certain specified denomination - the nominal value, for example shares of 25p or £1 nominal value. The main types of shares are *ordinary shares* and *preference shares*.

Shareholders

The persons or bodies owning the *shares* of a company.

Shareholders' funds

Share capital and *reserves* of a *company*.

Shareholders' equity

Same as *Shareholders' funds*

Share premium

When *shares* are issued at some point later than the start of the company, they will usually be issued at a price greater than their *nominal value*. The difference between the issue price and the nominal value is the premium on the shares. The nominal value of such shares is credited to the share capital account while the premium is credited to the share premium account.

See also Reserves

Sole trader

A person carrying on a business on his own account. He may have people working for him but he owns the business solely himself.

See also Partnership and Limited company

SSAPs

See Statements of Standard Accounting Practice

Statements of Standard Accounting Practice (SSAPs)

Statements produced by the now disbanded Accounting Standards Committee (ASC) giving some standardisation of matters which could be treated in different ways in the accounts. The ASC has now been superseded by the Accounting Standards Board.

See also Financial Reporting Standards

Statutory regulations

There are various obligations placed on a business by law. This applies particularly to a *limited company* whose dealings will be governed by the Companies Acts.

Stock

Goods for resale, or raw materials and goods in the process of manufacture, being held and not yet sold. They will be valued at cost, unless their expected resale value is lower, in which case this figure will be used.

See also Current assets

Straight line depreciation

The *depreciation* charge is calculated by spreading the cost of the asset (less any estimated *residual value*) evenly over the expected useful life of the asset. The rate is usually expressed as a percentage, for example 25% cost spreads the cost of the asset over 4 years.

See also Reducing balance depreciation

Subsidiary

A company controlled by another company, its *holding company*.

Supplier

A person or body who has sold goods or provided services to the business.

Suspense account

A suspense account is a *nominal ledger* account that should be used on a temporary basis. A figure is posted to the Suspense account if, at the time of posting, it cannot be established which account the figure should in fact be posted to. At the earliest opportunity the correct posting should be established and the figure should be transferred there from the Suspense account.

T accounts

The symbolic representation of ledger *accounts* in the form of a T with *debits* showing on the left hand side of the T, and *credits* on the right.

See also Double entry